LEGAL SPECTATORSHIP

LEGAL

SPECTATORSHIP

SLAVERY AND THE
VISUAL CULTURE OF
DOMESTIC VIOLENCE

KELLI MOORE

DUKE UNIVERSITY PRESS   Durham and London   2022

Designed by Aimee C. Harrison
Typeset in Caslon by Westchester Publishing Services

Library of Congress Cataloging-in-Publication Data
Names: Moore, Kelli, [date] author.
Title: Legal spectatorship : slavery and the visual culture of
domestic violence / Kelli Moore.
Description: Durham : Duke University Press, 2022. | Includes
bibliographical references and index.
Identifiers: LCCN 2021037516 (print) | LCCN 2021037517 (ebook)
ISBN 9781478015703 (hardcover)
ISBN 9781478018346 (paperback)
ISBN 9781478022947 (ebook)
Subjects: LCSH: Family violence—Law and legislation—United States. |
Victims of family violence—Legal status, laws, etc.—United States. |
Slavery—Social aspects—United States. | African Americans—Social
conditions—19th century. | Discrimination in justice administration—
United States—History—19th century. | Photography—Social aspects—
United States. | Legal photography—United States. | BISAC: SOCIAL
SCIENCE / Ethnic Studies / American / African American & Black Studies |
SOCIAL SCIENCE / Media Studies
Classification: LCC HV6626 .M668 2022 (print) | LCC HV6626 (ebook) |
DDC 362.82/92—dc23/eng/20211228
LC record available at https://lccn.loc.gov/2021037516
LC ebook record available at https://lccn.loc.gov/2021037517

Publication of this book is supported by Duke University
Press's Scholars of Color First Book Fund.

Cover art: gamblingwithsouls, *Polaroid 01*, 2005. Source: deviantArt.

CONTENTS

ACKNOWLEDGMENTS

I have been very fortunate to have had the guidance of several teachers and mentors in the writing of this book. At the University of California San Diego Department of Communication I would like to thank Patrick Anderson, Boatema Boateng, Lisa Cartwright, Michael Cole, Zeinabu irene Davis, Kelly Gates, Valerie Hartouni, Robert Horwitz, Roshanak Khesthi, Chandra Mukerji, and Elana Zilberg for the multiple forms in which their generosity appeared in my life as this project took shape. I also want to remember Marcel Henaff, whose beautiful teaching remains an inspiration. A number of San Diego classmates who became excellent friends created the conditions for laughter to emerge while researching the history that hurts. To Benjamin Balthasar, Lauren Berliner, Long Bui, Jason Eliaser, Dayo Gore, Monica Hoffman, Emma Johnson, Nadine Kozak, Olga Kuchinskaya, Robert Lecusay, Erin Malone, Antonietta Mercado-Anaya, Arianne Miller, Reece Peck, Orly Shevi, Pawan Singh, Sabrina Strings, and Alvin Wong, I thank you for your humor and kindness, which are as strong as your political commitments.

A number of folks participating in the President's Postdoctoral Fellowship contributed to the refinement of the arguments of this book. At Berkeley Rhetoric Marianne Constable provided an invaluable introduction to critical legal studies communities and early manuscript feedback. I appreciate the generosity of Michael Mascuch and Linda Williams for allowing me to audit their courses and writing groups on visual culture. I am grateful to Kate Chandler and Anjali Nath for the opportunity to engage with their work during the "Military Optics and Bodies of Difference" colloquium at Berkeley's Center for Race and Gender. Thank you to Michael Dalebout for the productive discussions and generally making postdoctoral life fun.

This book has benefited from transnational women of color feminist reading practices of the Dark Room Collective, a gift given by the amazing Kimberly Juanita Brown. Thank you for providing the critical space that fosters such beautiful expressions of collegiality, comradeship, and intellectual rigor. At New York University, Lily Chumley, Erica Robles-Anderson, and Caitlin Zaloom, conveners of the Oikos Working Group on economy, kinship, gender, and ethics, have my gratitude for funding a colloquium where ideas from the manuscript were further developed with Riley Snorton, whom I also thank. My sincere thanks to Lily Chumley, Lisa Gitelman, and Marita Sturken for reading drafts of the manuscript. Your hospitality, encouragement, and suggestions have been invaluable. Much appreciation to Mara Mills for her keen professional advice, encouragement, and general excitement about what academic scholarship can do. Many thanks to Arjun Appadurai, for extending such a gracious invitation and funding to present a chapter at the "Transubstantiating Transmission: Walls Become Ports Become Channels" conference at NYU's Berlin campus. Likewise, thanks to Ann Pelligrini for inviting me to present a chapter at NYU's Center for the Study of Gender and Sexuality. During this event Jocelyn Simonson, a wonderful legal scholar and friend, asked crucial questions that sharpened many aspects of this book and that I am enormously grateful for. When I first arrived at NYU I found an instant friend and mentor in Allen Feldman, who co-convened a colloquium series on "Unworking Dark Matter: Afro-Pessimism, Black Feminist Theory, Post-Structuralism" through the Center for the Humanities. Thank you so very much for your depth as a person and belief in my scholarship. Many thanks to Ulrich Baer for your words of encouragement.

Many arguments in this book were fleshed out in conferences, workshops, and colloquia, where I had the chance to meet kindred spirits working in the critical intersections in legal studies and media studies. Special thanks to Elizabeth Losh for her support at UCSD all the way to Omohundro Institute of Early American History and Culture, College of William & Mary. Thank you to Esra Demir, Joseph Slaughter, and Leti Volpp, whom I met at the University of Osnabruck Summer Institute for Research in the Cultural Study of Law. At the Society for Social Studies of Science, thank you to co-panelists Joseph Dumit, Natasha Dow Schüll, Rachel Prentice, and Hélène

Mialet, co-presenters of "A Sense of Balance: Techniques and Technologies of Self-Regulation." At the 2015 American Studies Association panel "How Does It Feel? Aesthetics, Minoritarian Politics, and the Political Sensorium," thank you to co-panelists Zakiyyah Iman Jackson, Uri McMillan, and Kyla Tompkins and to attendees Ebony Coletu and Jessica Marie Johnson.

My book was written with the support of care, friendship, and hospitality offered time and again by Charlotte Dereppe, Boris Goesl, Patricia Naftali, Armelle Philippe, Sara Smolik, Anne Sterman, and Julien Wolsey. I am also grateful for the friendship, laughter, and intellectual gifts of Alain Loute. Merci pour les durums mais surtout la conversation philosophique. Thank you, Kirkland Vaughn, for your care and conversation. To my waaay back friends Akilah Watkins Butler, Dirk Butler, Dia Felix, Jane F. Hwang, Ben Kafka, Arianne Miller, Amy Motlagh, Colleen Richards Powell, Adam Clayton Powell, and Anna Smeby, I am so impressed by who you have become, and I'm very fortunate to call you my chosen family. My NYU writing crew, Isolde Brielmaier, Matthew Morrison, and Hentyle Yapp, read chapter drafts with such care. Your company is a real source of joy on and off campus. Many thanks to Craig Wilse for helpful manuscript comments.

Sora Han has been a remarkable source of friendship and encouragement throughout the writing of this book. Dialogues with her allowed me to figure out what I wanted to say about law and/as communication in the book. Other colleagues have also modeled how to give critical feedback, and I continue to learn from them: Rodney Benson, Paula Chakravartty, Radha Hegde, David Marriott, Charlton McIlwain, Nicholas Mirzoeff, Fred Moten, Martin Scherzinger, and Nicole Starosielski.

This research would not have been possible without cooperation from attorneys and court officers working at the San Diego County Public Defender Office, the San Diego District Attorney Office, and the Family Justice Center. Special thanks to Susan Clemens, Abram Genser, Candace Elmore, Casey Gwinn, Charles Millioen, and Sherry Smethurst.

Joe Mistachkin is a wonderful dragon who deserves so much gratitude for knowing just what to say and which episodes of *Star Trek* to watch as my chapters came together, fell apart, and came together again. I uplift the memory of Mary Thompson, whose life inspired me to take the journey of writing this book. To my aunts and dear family friends, Bill, Rita, Sadie, Dorothy, Joyce, Adriane, and Kindahl, thank you for your loving kindness. To my parents, Lenaire McQueen and S. L. Moore, I could not have finished this book without your support.

INTRODUCTION

The United States shall guarantee to every State in this Union a Republican Form of Government, and shall protect each of them against Invasion; and on Application of the Legislature, or of the Executive (when the Legislature cannot be convened) against domestic Violence.—ARTICLE IV, Section 4 United States Constitution

A special notation, "DV" (capital D, capital V), identifies domestic violence cases in US criminal courts. On paper and electronic files, "DV" codes a separate level of concern beyond dozens of possible sorts of criminal charges. As a court officer once informed me, "Next to drug cases, domestic violence is our bread and butter." Domestic violence is a special kind of crime that demands federal forms of increased scrutiny, which result in the production of income and livelihood for criminal courts and personnel. The increased level of scrutiny signified by the "DV" notation includes increased monitoring of legal instruments such as protection orders, warrants, gun registration, media instruments such as recorded 911 calls, and social service instruments such as educational curricula for victims and abusers. While the "DV" mark is meant to increase the efficiency of case processing by prominently labeling criminal charges, case docket numbers, court appearance schedules, and so on, these cases precede with great difficulty.

A common view from a variety of courtroom professionals and service advocates is that victims and their abusers are not easy to work with. This is because these intimate partners frequently have great emotional, cultural, and financial difficulty terminating their relationships and the households they make together. Domestic violence is a conundrum and a set of contradictions that challenge the legal system, because, for many reasons, victims of domestic abuse often refuse to cooperate and enable the law to function. As a result, a variety of legal instruments beyond those mentioned above have developed to mediate how victims and batterers access law to end the violence. Yet, legal instruments, including forensic evidence, are not cure-alls. Domestic violence is a volatile issue not simply in terms of the violent intimacies that demand legal intervention but also because of the way legal instruments historically exacerbate the adjudication of these matters. Numerous studies have examined how forensic documentation instruments and the courtroom testimonial scene retraumatize victims, violating them again through the very instruments that are supposed to help prosecute their assaults.[1] This is especially true in cases of rape and sexual assault and the instruments used to collect evidence of these crimes. The rehearsal of a violent attack before police, forensic nurses, social workers, judges, lawyers, courtroom audiences, and family can violate victims all over again. Moreover, it is not always clear how the rehearsal of one's narrative of abuse before law serves the interests of victims, whose pathways to healing are first directed by forensic instruments that are at best secondarily therapeutic. In fact, the question of victim interest remains unclear when the complications of the legal system intersect with race, class, gender, and sexuality.[2] Photography of domestic abuse is one of these forensic instruments and the subject of this book.

Legal Spectatorship tells the story of the DV photograph, examining its evidentiary function in the courtroom and its relationship to psychological discourse about the flow of feelings that motivate violence and anti–DV activist practices in the era of social media. I trace the origins of this body of photography to the peculiar form of witnessing that slaves embodied in their entanglement in white domestic arrangements and disputes. This book pays particular attention to the visual culture of photographic evidence of domestic abuse, giving it an origin story that positions testimony in contemporary DV prosecution within the archive of slavery. Evidence of DV is managed through techniques of the courtroom that are part of the slave's peculiar capacity to witness events but never testify to them in court in ways that would implicate the brutalities of the master class. Historically, slaves were witnesses to discord between white couples because they were usually the matter over which couples were fighting. Black witnessing could not perform as legal testimony detailing upheaval in white domestic intimacies, to say nothing of the body politic as a whole. The enslaved could not offer court testimony unless both parties were slaves. The quiet and vestibular character with which slaves could witness, I argue, is an antecedent of contemporary forensic instruments in domestic disputes. The entire problematic wherein DV cases are the "bread and butter" of the court system while the majority of victims refuse to cooperate with the state and testify is linked to the ways in which enslaved people were entangled witnesses to white domestic arrangements and marital discord. This book is an attempt to tease out what happened to these complicated relationships between masters and slaves as they were mediated by new technologies of representation and, equally, to offer ideas toward a visual literacy of reading photographic evidence of DV.

Legal Spectatorship attempts to join writing on the image and visual culture more closely with constitutional law. The appearance and reappearance of the slave's condition across multiple cultural domains is captured by legal theorist Sora Han, who argues that "the only way to think ourselves out of the dead end of both liberal and conservative legal development is to insist, as did DuBois, on the claim of the slave that is always there, even in the most unlikely places."[3] This intervention relocates questions about visual culture and slavery's memory to the legal context and the "unlikely places" of courtroom architecture, forensic evidence, and oral testimony in domestic abuse cases. Specifically, *Legal Spectatorship* argues that we cannot understand the spectatorship of evidentiary photographs that document domestic abuse without referring to the archival void in which enslaved people testified about their experience of white households. The racialized lives of enslaved people provided evidence of the instability of white domestic arrangements, including at the levels of neighborhood, state, and national territory. The very nature of Black embodiment from which testimonial utterances issued from enslaved people disrupts the Constitution's dominant understanding of the terms "domestic" and "violence."

The epigraph that opens this chapter pinpoints an earlier domestic violence notation in Article IV, Section 4 of the US Constitution. Known as the "Domestic Violence Clause," this moment of constitutional law outlines federal protections against invasion and other conflicts between states in the union. I draw attention to the visual appearance of the term as it is used in Article IV: "domestic Violence" (lowercase d, uppercase V). Before criminal court papers noted "DV," "dV" was written on the paper of the Constitution. Though written in the Constitution "domestic Violence" does not appear to refer to the violence between intimate partners. Rather, the clause is about the prevention of any state from imposing alternate forms of rule such as aristocracy, dictatorship, military rule, or monarchy. Latent in the clause is a question about whether or not states could deny rights based on race, gender, sexuality, and wealth. Following the interventions made in critical studies of race and law, I argue that the Constitution be read for its latencies such that the Framers are never understood as merely struggling over what type of government we can have, but psychically foreclosing the question of slavery and its role in the structure of white kinship systems in the United States specifically and the modern world more broadly. As Han, puts it: "Democratic political life governed by law is conditional to law's language that in every instance of its written investment in its most prized values—interpretation, judgment, national history, reason, due process, individual autonomy, and so forth—uses words, phrases, images, and affects that are cathected signs of the unmemorializable events of slavery and black freedom struggle."[4] The instance of the philological convention of capitalizing proper nouns is used throughout *Legal Spectatorship* to reorient "domestic Violence" toward the expansive category of violent intimacy structuring white kinship that an uncritical reading of the clause obscures. I bring what appear to be two separate meanings of domestic violence into closer conceptual alignment. In this book the term refers to person-to-person intimacies between racialized individuals and groups that make households, live among each other in neighborhoods, and exchange between each other feelings, affects, fluids, and contracts. The visual appearance of the term written by the Framers signals a theory of media and visual culture in which Black freedom claims can emerge at the very moment when the Constitution guarantees what type of government we can have. The "dV" notation, I argue, is a mark of struggle between the Framers of the Constitution wherein the state and federal dichotomy must be read in opposition to the history of slavery and management of Black populations in the interest of white sovereignty.

RECONSTRUCTING DV IN TWO ACTS

At the end of the twentieth century, violence against women emerged as a prosecution area demanding its own court docket and administrative tools. Embedded within a larger project of law and order crime legislation, violence against women is managed through strategic programs shaping the organization of domestic space, communication protocols among citizens and the state, bureaucratic agencies, and men and women.[5] Two acts of government—one legislative, the other judicial—set the legal course for shifts in the criminal code, in particular the adjudication of violence against women and a revolution in courtroom communicative interaction. First, the 1994 authorization of the Violence Against Women Act (VAWA) intensified the investigation and management of domestic abuse. Introduced into congressional debate in 1990 by then-Senator Joseph Biden (D-DE), VAWA was part of the Violent Crime Control and Law Enforcement Act. Attached to this major law and order criminal justice reform bill, VAWA increased coordination between criminal justice agencies across state boundaries, funded research and prevention initiatives on the nature of DV as a criminal offense, and established communication protocols between medical and social services for victimized women and children. The act passed in 1994 with overwhelming bipartisan support, authorizing $1.6 billion in federal grants for law enforcement and prosecution as well as anti–child abuse enforcement and new shelters for battered women. Funding also supported the establishment of the National Domestic Violence Hotline, which created new hotlines and increased resources and staffing capabilities for extant hotlines.[6]

Second, in 2004, *Crawford v. Washington* intervened in the portions of the Violent Crime Control and Law Enforcement legislation addressing violence against women.[7] The Supreme Court decision in *Crawford* involved the Confrontation Clause of the Sixth Amendment and altered standards for admitting hearsay evidence in trials. Evidence-based criminal prosecution generally relies on the hearsay statements of crime victims to reproduce the effect of live testimony. Early domestic abuse cases presented an ideal circumstance in which such hearsay statements were helpful because abused women are typically uninterested in seeking redress in court against their batterer. There are many reasons abused women do not want to participate in legal processes, including time, cost, their relationship status, and their community status, among others. *Crawford* ruled that, under the Confrontation Clause of the Sixth Amendment, all defendants have a constitutional right to confront their accusers; therefore, testimony admitted under hearsay exceptions are inadmissible without cross-examination of the witness issuing the hearsay statements. As per the Supreme Court case, women (overwhelmingly) were legally ordered to testify in court against their (overwhelmingly) male batterers. When battered women refuse to participate in state proceedings against their accused batterers, they became exposed to criminal charges.[8] Abused women thus became heavily subject to forms of state surveillance.

The *Crawford v. Washington* decision required domestic abuse claimants to present themselves in court to be confronted by their alleged abusers.

Crawford returns and inverts the right-to-confront doctrine, producing female abuse claimants in addition to the partner arrested under suspicion of assault. Before *Crawford*, prosecutors would pass and project photographic evidence without the courtroom presence of female claimants because they were frequently unavailable to testify. *Legal Spectatorship* examines this brief and radical window of prosecution when the photograph appeared in court without the live presence of female complainants. I add new meaning to the concepts of "overseeing" and "authenticated testimony" in the age of digital media projection.

Legal Spectatorship demonstrates how VAWA authorizes the rehearsal of colonial practices of surveillance, defined by David Lyon as the "focused, systematic and routine attention to personal details for purposes of influence, management, protection or direction" by funding aggressive evidence-based prosecution measures.[9] Evidence-based prosecution reforms written in VAWA and the *Crawford* decision fulfill colonial desires to order and control bodies in space while also establishing exceptional zones where sovereign power grows within what seems to be the absence of law, authority, and order in administrative processes. While the reforms routinized and professionalized police investigation techniques, including mandatory arrest and no-drop prosecution policies, they did so in ways that criminalize battered women and their families.

The Supreme Court's decision in *Crawford*, occurring just over a decade after the 1994 VAWA authorization, increased the prosecution of DV and intervened to bring battered women into the courtroom milieu, into direct physical contact with police photographs of their injuries, and into greater contact with their accused batterers. In doing so, both *Crawford* and VAWA foster the conditions under which photographs of battered women are produced and circulated as crucial objects of police epistemology, or "professional vision," without marking them as such in law. *Legal Spectatorship* describes the visual culture that results from the legislative and judicial mechanisms used to modernize the adjudication of DV in the United States and thereby expands the vocabulary that shapes traditional spectatorship discourse to include constitutional law and the arrangement of courtroom space.

With these two acts, American law must fall back on itself, which is to say, fall back on its founding narrative of enslavement, which Han and others argue, is never memorialized. The work of this book is to read the archive of slavery into the legal mechanisms of these respective legislative and judicial acts and the scientific inquiries and media forms they enact. The Violence Against Women Act and *Crawford* bring about forms of scientific inquiry, forensic instruments such as documentary photographs, and experts who are tasked with producing and interpreting them in the courtroom milieu. The ratification of VAWA and the Supreme Court decision in *Crawford* are productive forms of media-making that interact with the performance of testimony. My emphasis in this project concerns the image of the battered woman that facilitates testimony and how this media form binds live courtroom presence to visual evidence of abuse in order to mediate legal fact-finding among courtroom audiences. Here *Legal Spectatorship* is inspired by the irony of Han's crucial discussion of colorblind fantasy through which American law operates and the inaugural moment VAWA and *Crawford* instantiate, when American law commits the courtroom audience to regard and evaluate colorful photographs of injury projected to them during testimony. To be clear, I am not being metaphorical. Fantasy is a real event generated through, of, and upon the real. Fantasy is no less situated in the real than photographs projected across the courtroom for public view are complex acts of physics.[10] The enactment of courtroom fantasies of color-blindness entail the production and circulation of DV photography. These fantasies must be positioned within constitutional law, congressional legislation, and Supreme Court decisions—powerful discursive forms where this body of photography and its fantastical production would appear not to be.[11]

NEW LEGAL PHOTOGRAPHIES

The Violence Against Women Act is the first legislation whose language codifies domestic abuse as a crime through federal action. Its language offers a program for the investigation and prosecution of DV in which photographic evidence becomes central. Two legal lacunae are instantiated by the law and give rise to two corresponding bodies of photography. The two photographies appear to challenge and undo each other, yet their ostensible undoing not only makes the visual culture of DV legible as a communication system, but also alters the qualia of testimonial oaths and corroboration previously mentioned. Let me describe the two lacunae and the emergence of the two bodies of photography.

LACUNA I: *VAWA* AND POLICE PROTOCOL

Since the introduction of VAWA during the 1990s, US DV trials have relied heavily on visual proof. Visual evidence is a crucial element of the claimant's spoken testimony and mediates the investigatory work of police and the rhetorical argumentation made by attorneys. Photographic evidence is a creative act of the police. Herein lies a legal lacuna of VAWA: though visual evidence organizes routines of communication in criminal assault cases, its acquisition, production, and circulation remain an unmarked and unofficial protocol of the police. Why *unofficial?*

It is within this lacuna in VAWA that police discover the best way to capture victims of abuse practice by internally recording their imaging techniques in police manuals that guide their own professional vision.[12] The lacuna extends to victims. Victims of domestic abuse are not legally obligated to be examined, photographed, or counseled by medical or law professionals. Though police regulate techniques of evidence collection, there are no laws regulating the production of photographic evidence of wounding. Protocols advise police how to photograph the body in pain, yet there is a dearth of information instructing the evaluation of these images inside or outside the courtroom. During the nineteenth century, when police invented photographic techniques for representing criminals, such images appeared both official and scientific. While contemporary police photography of DV victims appears official because it similarly traffics in the scientific with its detailed protocols for evidence collection using digital cameras and lighting practices, I argue protocols of police evidence collection are unofficial because they are discretionary practices; they do not follow any "law on the books." Nonetheless, the absence of visual evidence of wounding would make for a highly irregular criminal case file. Without visual evidence, the speech of testifying witnesses, police, and attorneys would be unmoored, unable to orient testimonial declarations through protocols for relating to courtroom audiences. Visual evidence of abuse becomes a currency orienting the rhetoric of law professionals and speculative practices of courtroom spectators.[13]

LACUNA II: *VAWA* AND VICTIM'S SERVICES

The Violence Against Women Act funds the expansion of victims' services hotlines. In doing so, the legislation lays the marketing infrastructure for communicating VAWA policy initiatives to battered women. Thus, a second lacuna resides in how the letter of law authorizes funding streams that result in critical media practices that never appear in law's writing. For example, in telephone service marketing, visual representation of the product remains the gold standard of communication. Crisis hotlines frequently produce promotional materials that employ white female models wearing cosmetically simulated wounds on their faces and bodies. Early DV imagery thus encodes a particular "look" of racial and gender masquerade. Here, advertising campaign imagery offers not a copy of the kinds of visual evidence that circulates in court trials but rather an imitation. The Violence Against Women Act neither anticipates nor regulates the kinds of communication media it inscribes into law. Instead, extralegal deployments of visual evidence of DV regulate how we see and evaluate this inherently theatrical imagery, thereby creating a circuit among law, material culture, and the courtroom stage.

My focus on the ways enslaved people were entangled in white kinship arrangements is in part a rejoinder against the ways that white women in the context of "the couple" are figured as the primary victims of DV.[14] While efforts have been made to demonstrate that this kind of violence knows no boundaries of race, (sex)uality, gender, or wealth, white women are frequently used as models of victimhood in anti–DV communications.[15] Further, as Black insurgent movements such as Black Lives Matter have addressed the relationship between police violence and white domestic terrorism that founded the nation, the movement has struggled from within to recognize (1) the frequency with which police violence targets Black women and (2) the fact that most Black women are killed by Black male partners.[16] It would seem, following Shatema Threadcraft's analysis of Black women's bodies in politics, that political life in the United States is staged through the fantastical and systematic unrepresentability of violence against Black women.[17] Representing DV remains attached to colorblind fantasy in political life, one that is made manifest in conceptions of domestic abuse victims that use white standards of femininity and vulnerability. This occurs even as cultural studies has begun to extend concepts of representation beyond the visual. Here, law, media, and communications continue to work through what Han calls "colorblind fantasy," a "psychic foreclosure imposed on the legal text" and, as I hope to demonstrate, art and science communication as well.[18] The attachment to figuring domestic abuse victims through white femininity structures all aspects of domestic abuse prosecution: the scene of police evidence collection, the scene of courtroom testimony, the public sphere where abuse support services are communicated, and social science research on the dynamics of abuse. Here, what is foreclosed through colorblind fantasy is the history of slavery, the attention to which would infuse the above-mentioned spaces and scenes with quite different logics of redress and reparation. My project in this book is to explain this turn of events by focusing more closely on the development and circulation of this body of photography.

In order to say something about the historical social conditions of Black life in the diaspora, Hortense Spillers turns to flesh for the way its mutilation imposes race upon the body of the victim and perpetrator. Spillers's "hieroglyphics of the flesh," a four-word phrase, contains within it a suggestive theory of enslavement that I use to examine the relationship between photographs, skin, and flesh. Likewise, I rely upon Frantz Fanon's concept of epidermalization, usually described as the psychological internalization of the process of colonialization. According to poet and critic David Marriott, "Epidermalization [transfers inferiority] *inside* the body *qua* introjection and imposition" (85).[19] *Legal Spectatorship* studies epidermalization as a projection of photographic forms to witnesses. The analysis adds specificity to how epidermalization operates through spatialized rituals of human movement involving photographs. From time to time I refer to ritualized acts of movement as "strategies of the flesh." My choice in phrasing is an attempt at two things: (1) to further divest the notion of the moving image from its claim to objectivity and (2) to further invest the moving image within a process of epidermalization that includes Spillers's flesh-body distinction as a mediating factor. Spillers famously hyphenates "flesh-body" to describe how the slave is made through ritualized acts of violence, where violence creates something in excess of flesh and body. I read the hyphenation as a way to understand how violence installs pliability in the slave, which makes her reproductive labor fungible. Yet, the hyphenation also inspires a reading of the photographic image as part of the excess of flesh and body. The examples discussed in *Legal Spectatorship* demonstrate how the courtroom space comes to hyphenate something like "photography-skin." The DV courtroom is a space where the boundary between skin and photograph is made pliable; this, too, is part of slavery's afterlife. The process of courtroom projection of photography-skin is thus an instance of epidermalization. The evaluation regime of visual evidence of DV is "part of the process of *epidermal* or *sociogenic* memorization by which the colony repeats the traumatic after-the-eventness-of-colonization."[20]

This book's reading of the courtroom image is indebted to Fanon's and Spillers's respective theories of the flesh and body. I make a critique of the ahistorical character of legal positivism using their work. The flesh is an analytic that this book deploys and that is in excess of law and its claims to truth. Epidermalization and the flesh-body distinction are layered genealogical concepts that defamiliarize the Foucauldian approach to the body.

The victim of DV, as written in constitutional law and presented in the DV courtroom, must be approached as an epidermalized incarnation.[21]

There is an iconic relationship between Blackness and pain that Nicole Fleetwood argues plays a role in Black liberation. In her study of racial iconicity Fleetwood introduces the Black icon, a public figure whose visual depiction and circulation in visual culture "make us want to *do* something."[22] Black icons are part of a process of "cultural fixation" through which value accrues to the individual's public persona because it is used in the negotiation of meaning of "nation, representation, and race in the context of the history of US slavery and the present of enduring racial inequality."[23] The images discussed in *Legal Spectatorship* are equally entwined in the struggle over what the United States tells itself about itself on matters of race. However, the images I discuss and the conditions of their viewing suggest a different, but no less engaged, way to think about the icon and iconicity from those examined by Fleetwood. Her concept of the racial icon is a crucial intervention for the current study precisely because her examples intend to express the Black individual's personhood and personality in a way that photographic evidence of domestic abuse victims does not.

The images I examine are either taken by police or staged by artists and media activists. The photographs are not taken for the purpose of recognizing the cultural significance of a particular Black individual's identity, deeds, misfortunes, or accomplishments relative to national racial politics. The intent behind the images is not Black liberation. They are not produced to contribute to centuries-long efforts toward Black freedom. When compared with Fleetwood's analysis of the political work performed by the Black icon, photographic evidence of DV depicts an altogether different one—victims who are overwhelmingly white. The racial icon of DV photography is a white woman. *Legal Spectatorship* investigates how this came to be by theorizing the visual culture of DV through the colorblind psychic foreclosure of constitutional law.

Along these lines Courtney Baker homes in on specific encounters where the gaze is brought to bear on photographs documenting Black pain and suffering experienced as a direct outcome from the history of enslavement. Baker points out a difference in sensorial experience when pain and Blackness collide. On the one hand, pain is "resolutely private," "locked in tight within the borders of the individual's fleshly body."[24] On the other hand, "blackness and racial difference" together suggest a being who does not feel pain as "normal" humans do.[25] The accumulation and fungibility of slaves are integral to contemporary narratives in which Black people are denied the capacity to feel pain. Examples of ignored Black pain and suffering may be found in circumstances ranging from hospital narratives where Black women's communication about their physical pain during childbirth are ignored or disavowed by medical professionals to street interactions with police in which the response to requests for air and space is the increased evacuation of air and contraction of space. Baker's examination of the photographic encounter with Black pain and suffering guides my analyses of the DV courtroom scene in which audiences apprehend the look of abuse and are obligated to use spectatorship of visual evidence to decide matters of law.

Encounters with photographic evidence entail performances of citizenship that are made possible through the interlocking First and Sixth Amendments that guarantee free assembly and court trial by one's peers. The arguments set forth in this project also suggest the public encounter with DV photography calls up the moment "domestic Violence" (lower case *d*, capital *V*) is inscribed in the Constitution to guarantee a republican form of government. The 1787 Domestic Violence Clause guarantees a republican form of rule in which the significance of race, gender, class, and sexuality is latent. *Legal Spectatorship* reads the encounter with photographic evidence of DV and its historical development in the United States in such a way that the analysis of race, gender, and sexuality is not latent but manifest. I make such an argument in order to bind the Constitution to the everyday practices of staying with the trouble of DV, which ostensibly refers to both the violence between intimate partners and the violence of internal insurrection or foreign invasion. Citizens engaged in the courtroom audience assume part of the burden of guaranteeing a republican federal government through their courtroom looking practices. To regard images of pain and suffering is to bear witness to domestic violence in both of its meanings.

Kimberly Juanita Brown reads the appearance of Black women in contemporary art installation, documentary photography, book cover art imagery, and ceramic material culture as a way of performing an "attune[ment] to the visual properties of slavery's memory."[26] She draws attention to how slavery's rituals, rites, mores, and ways of living keep coming back in contemporary visual culture. Like Han's argument in the field of critical studies of law, Brown's work points to the phantasmic ways slavery returns through visual culture as a "repeating body." Slavery has an afterlife that haunts the practice of making images and material culture, including the scenes and settings of their display. Brown also offers careful and sustained readings of Black visual art work, evoking Selwyn Cudjoe's consideration of "literary resistance" in Caribbean literature as a way of conceptualizing Black visual artists' use of reference and citation to create resistant images.[27] The link made between literary and visual resistance is one I also employ to consider domestic abuse photography that is created outside the confines of police customs and protocols. Following Brown's titular claim that slavery's visual resonance in the contemporary is a function of the Black body repeating, *Legal Spectatorship* explores the extralegal encounter with domestic abuse imagery as a space where such iconography may take flight as visual resistance.

The activity of witnessing by enslaved people and their descendants is historically discredited or altogether left out of discourse about the domestic sphere and violence. Given the historical disavowal of Black claims to truth and freedom, another reading of the debates that plagued photography in law soon after its inception emerges. In law, photographic evidence operates as a "silent witness." This evidence owes this status to an ongoing struggle between institutions of science and law about the capacity of evidentiary forms to speak for themselves, unmediated by expert verifying witnesses. For example, Sameena Mulla's analysis of the activities of forensic nurses who administer sexual assault forensic exams to rape victims is situated within the legal-scientific problematic of silent witness.[28] Her explication of the simultaneous enactment of care and violence in forensic nursing in the sexual assault investigation context guides *Legal Spectatorship* in its pursuit of one of many possible origin stories of forensic tools used to help victims of abuse. I situate the experiences of enslaved people in the conceptualization of forensic tools that are silent witnesses. Doing so requires reading enslaved people into DV, forensic photography, and courtroom activity—contemporary places and situations where they ostensibly appear not to be.

HISTORIES OF SLAVES AS WITNESSES

According to Karine Schaefer, "A witness is a spectator whose morality or system of judgment has been pricked by a performance."[29] The distinction between spectator and witness is crucial for theorizing the visual culture of DV and the position of the slave within it. *Legal Spectatorship* situates the distinction between the two terms, "domestic" and "violence," in the history of slavery. Specifically, histories of Southern slave-owning households offer valuable details of the role of enslaved Black people as witnesses to white kinship structures in which they were held captive. Loren Schweninger's *Families in Crisis in the Old South: Divorce, Slavery and the Law* examines how slaves were entangled in white marital discord. From courtship to marriage contract to daily life in the home, the health of white marital relations and the tone of the household were balanced on the backs of enslaved people.[30] Moments of marital discord in white households were particularly violent times for slaves. Anger toward a spouse was often displaced onto them. Masters and mistresses would use slaves to mediate communication between each other, frequently with violent results for the slave. Enslaved people were deeply entangled in separation and divorce proceedings of white married couples. In slave-owning families the consequences of divorce between master and mistress could be the same as the death of one or both of the owners—namely, financial trouble and owner capriciousness. Splitting up white households and assets could necessitate selling slaves to raise liquid funds. Slaves could be sold or otherwise distributed among heirs, resulting in a catastrophic rupture of the precarious bonds between family members enslaved together. As Schweninger notes, the very "prelude to divorce could be even worse for slaves who found themselves caught in the middle of a disagreement and forced to choose sides."[31] The divorce petition testimony suggests that "slaves suffered more often from the consequences of being caught in the middle than they did from punishment inflicted because they disobeyed orders, slacked off their work," or from otherwise being troublesome.[32] I quote this part of Schweninger's history to highlight the ways that white people used slaves to displace and thereby resolve their own frustrations with each other.

As they bore witness to every aspect of marriage between white masters and mistresses, slaves were peculiar informants whose testimony about "what they saw and heard," though accumulated in legal records, was fungible. In court documents enslaved witnesses to white marital trouble often appear anonymously. Court papers refer to slaves as "negroe girl," "negroe woman," "Negroe wench," "Negro boy," "house servant," "Negro fellow," "negro paramour," "negro mistress," "grown negroes," "young negroes."[33] The appellations suggest the slave's deeply vexed capacity to appear and perform as a witness made known to the court. When white people interacted with slaves, many did so through surveillance and spectatorship and the absence of moral and ethical judgment these terms entail. In court divorce documents the testimonial utterances of enslaved witnesses emerged not from slaves themselves but indirectly through owners, white plantation employees, or neighbors who spoke on their "behalf."

As they are mentioned in court documents, slaves appear simultaneously anonymous and identifiable as playing particular roles in household relations. Though the generic terms sound innocuous, they would carry within them catastrophic feelings of dread. In the midst of white domestic discord, enslaved people were forced into a diabolical arithmetic. How should they manage their responses to anyone regarding "what they know," given that the wrong answer would surely result in violence that could not be calculated with any exactitude? Enslaved children were also forced to reckon with calculating possible violence as they were frequently used as go-betweens in the master's family exchanges, and with punishing results. Spillers's oft-cited phrase "hieroglyphics of the flesh" names the semiotic system of violence that makes the slave and fundamentally calls attention to how white domestic arrangements and flows become structured around the captured body. The vague mentioning of enslaved people in white couple's divorce documents can be read as a stylized way of incorporating their entanglement in domestic disputes. The incomprehensible mutilation Spillers designates as "hieroglyph" is also referenced in the accounting of "negroe girl," "negroe woman," "Negroe wench," "Negro boy," "Negro fellow."

The slave's anonymous mention in divorce documents is a site of Black accumulation and fungibility as well as a sign system of violent touch and other forms of punishment. Saidiya Hartman's emphasis on the structures of performance on the slave plantation confirms how the slave's capacity for communicative expression was not open to clear legibility. Even the appearance of pleasure and joy in the slave's daily life are manifestations of white sovereign power, the threat of the master and mistress's violence structure the appearance of affect. The capacity of the enslaved to perform witnessing poses a cognitive challenge that *Legal Spectatorship* examines through the use of photographic evidence in the contemporary visual culture of DV.

In *They Were Her Property: White Women as Slave Owners in the American South* Stephanie Jones-Rogers examines the archival evidence of the central role Black men and women occupied in the negotiation of white marriage. Slaves were written into white women's marriage contracts, often by their fathers, in order to ensure that white women had a perpetual source of income-producing property. White women's ownership and command over their own slaves protected them from the profligacy of their spouses, who often participated in a variety of unstable economic schemes, including slavery. Jones-Rogers elaborates on the pedagogical roles of print and material culture in training white mistresses how best to handle their slaves. Children from slave-owning families learned that any household or field object could be wielded upon the bodies of slaves. Knitting needles, shovels, dishes, rope, shoes, rakes, knives, dowels, and furniture could become projectile objects to be hurled, driven, or struck, and paddles could be deployed against slaves until maiming or death. Beyond everyday material objects, a variety of print media forms contributed to a science of disciplining and punishing slaves with calm and controlled measure. These media forms were more than caricatures of Black people common to graphic prints that lampooned abolition as slavery increased in debate. Advertisements selling enslaved wet nurses, for example, can be read for clues about how white families might displace the effects of dV onto the enslaved women forced to nurse their children. Also common were agriculture and planters' magazines that advised Southern farmers how to cultivate their fields. An important component of these communications included suggestions for how to handle slaves.

THE CYBERNETIC SCIENCE OF SLAVE MANAGEMENT

As spectators of enslaved people, white men and women practiced a science at the center of which was the slave's flesh. The decision to beat a slave was both systematic and capricious. The overuse of force could waste a form of living property that would be detrimental to income streams. For this reason, the slave was an object of management. But, so too was the owner. In managing slaves, the slave owner—the sovereign—also had to manage the self. Slaves were learning tools for white family members, women in particular, who quickly found out that violence directed toward them from their husbands mimicked the techniques of violence reserved for slaves. As Jones-Rogers makes clear, white women's "status as slave owners granted them access to a community that was predicated upon the ownership of human beings and afforded them rights they did not possess in other realms of their lives."[34] A line of thought in *Legal Spectatorship* is that for many white women, learning how to handle the people they legally owned through techniques of violence could have been a practice of personal sovereignty that protected them from what in current epidemiological parlance is known as "abuse risk factors."[35]

The Black radical tradition has made important clarifications to Marxist analyses of production by complicating the experience of the worker and her experience of alienation with the concepts of accumulation and fungibility that are central to the slave's experience.[36] In a slave economy agricultural production involves acts of brutal and repetitive violence to integrated systems of the slave's body: nervous, respiratory, reproductive, muscular, integumentary, endocrine, and skeletal. The violence of slave owners affected all of these systems. In this sense slave owners and white people as a class discovered their body politic in the degradation of the slave's flesh. At a more personal level white owners discovered aspects of the self by finding their way into and around enslaved people.

Jones-Rogers demonstrates how and where white slave owners reflected on such matters in print media, including youth-directed weeklies such as *The Southern Rose/Rose Bud* and agricultural journals.[37] The advice in these publications was preoccupied with the planter's ability to control his passions before and during the administration of discipline. Punishment decreased a slave's value. As Jones-Rogers illustrates, agricultural journals recommended "never inflict[ing] punishment on slaves in anger" and "allow[ing] 24 hours to elapse between the discovery of the offence and the punishment."[38] State legislatures were also involved in managing slaves and owners, imposing fines upon owners for *not* punishing a slave's offensive conduct. While brutality would be seen as a deterrent to slaves hoping to escape, "punishments also served to compel slave *owners* to comply with state law."[39]

It is worth noting that in Jones-Rogers's history of slave ownership the object of complaint among non-owning overseers, public officials, and patrollers was *not about wages, but the more provocative question "Who is in charge?"* "Who is in charge?" is a question of the sovereign's ego, and this book shows its projection into behavioral science, psychology, and cybernetics. These scientific fields share a research question about the nature of power, control, and motivation held and exchanged between peoples and machines at the core of the study of sovereignty and its pertinence to DV support services and prosecution. The management of slaves in American law and culture informed social, behavioral, and cybernetic science. Slave owners and state legislatures were thinking in terms of cycles of power, control, and the use of force in ways that would later inform theories of domestic abuse and prosecution strategies.

Cybernetics and the histories by Schweninger and Jones-Rogers are a crucial backdrop for the claims *Legal Spectatorship* makes about how enslaved people functioned as forensic technologies that document and authenticate DV. As witnesses, slaves were the recorders of domestic abuse incidents; their vestibular position within white kinship endowed them with a kind of distance enabled by "objective" technologies of vision while disavowing any claims their witnessing could support. By tracing the production of the DV photograph to the vestibular positioning of enslaved people in white households and surrounding environs, I demonstrate that the slave embodied a form of silent witnessing that characterizes contemporary forensic evidence. Long before the invention of photography, enslaved people witnessed the regular and ritualized events that sustained white kinship systems, systems that include the machinations of law. Enslaved people were expert witnesses of the rhythms and patterns of DV. The obscured and negligible status of their testimony at the time of its creation haunts the contemporary operation of forensic photography in DV cases. *Legal Spectatorship* makes the case that the visual culture in which forensic evidence circulates is rooted in the lives of enslaved Black people ensnared in the broadest conception of white domestic conflicts.

OUTLINE OF THE BOOK

The image of Harriet Jacobs's loophole of retreat and the *carte de visite* of the slave Gordon, known as "The Scourged Back," are frequently discussed in Black studies, literature, and visual culture studies. Chapter 1 returns to these important images, one literary and the other photographic, to explore how their contemporary treatment by scholars and artists criticizes the humanitarian aesthetics of white abolitionism even as they try to authenticate the images. In contrast to these art and historical treatments, I examine how Jacobs's memoir and "The Scourged Back" spatialize the fugitive freedom of the escaped slave. By "spatialize," I mean how both images organize the psycho-physical spaces where the testimony of former slaves is seen through new media forms. Adding to the critique of white sentimentalism framing abolitionist media, I further speculate that sulking and vestibular imbalance characterize the psycho-physical condition of the slave. This reorients the discourse of sulking away from the discourse of child psychology to the history of US slavery while also counter-narrating the sentimental and upright-ness with the sulks and vertigo.[40]

Jacobs's slave narrative and other examples of abolitionist media circulated in a changing media-scape, one in which concepts of authority, authorship, and authenticity were in peculiar tension with ideals of proof and evidence previously set forth by the camera obscura. I introduce a reading of Jacobs's and Gordon's famous images in relation to Article IV, Section 4 of the US Constitution (the Domestic Violence and Republican Guarantee Clauses). This first chapter brings constitutional law and theories of affect and motivation to bear on the visual culture of abolitionist media in order to extricate a model of DV photography that is the subject of this book.

Legal Spectatorship's frequent transitions between narrative and visual technology allow "something on the other side of either the freedom to perform or not to perform (or even to be or not to be), which might open up the possibility of another kind of examination of the metaphysics of 'behavior' and 'decision,'" in critic and poet Fred Moten's phrasing.[41] As part of the legal, technical, scientific, and textual apparatus of DV, Blackness operates as a technological witness while also subverting what we mean by the term "domestic violence." Thus, chapter 1 moves fluidly between literary and visual technologies, between slave narrative and photographic evidence. The transitions are informed not only by the ways slave narratives of the big house and the swamp as sites of liberation and capture drew upon the *sensory images* constitutive of the genre of Victorian gothic literature—with its decaying mansions, wild and threatening forests, and moors—but also the metaphysical disturbance posed by Blackness itself. This book moves between narrative and photography and, gestures toward the digital because, I argue, they are metaphysically intertwined.

The first chapter develops three strands of inquiry that organize the remainder of the book: (1) reading constitutional law into abolitionist media, (2) reading affect and feeling in the former slave's experience of brutality, and (3) examining conventions for authenticating evidence of DV. The second and third chapters continue the arguments made in the first, with different emphases on the space of DV testimony and the tools and choreography through which courtroom testimony is brought forward. For this reason, readers may want to first delve into the third chapter and then the second. If you are immediately gripped by how Jacobs's loophole of retreat informs the experience of the contemporary witness stand in the DV courtroom, you might skip to chapter 3. Should you first be intrigued by how the reproduction of Gordon's slave daguerreotype in abolitionist media informs the circular, microcosmic design of visual tools used to explain DV and condition the photographs circulated therein, continue with chapter 2.

The second chapter follows the migration of "the sulks" into the psychology laboratory. I read the slave and her descendants as social identities that animate the experimental designs of psychologists Martin Seligman, Sylvan Tomkins, and Lenore Walker. From the 1960s through the 1980s these social scientists studied human affect and motivation in a political context that spanned civil rights and the Cold War. Control, helplessness, and power were at the center of these scientific studies, and I show how the lives of Black people were integral to the theoretical development of the experiments. Black subjectivity, even when excluded from experimentation, is at the core of research on the psychology of battered women's syndrome (in Walker), the object of affective distress (in Tomkins), and learned helplessness (in Seligman). What unites these feelings is the condition of being unfree to leave yet unfree to remain in a place of violence. Black feminist and Afro-pessimist (the two are not mutually exclusive, obviously) critiques of the human are germane here because they shift how we read scientific research on human behavior and motivation. So too is the civil rights context upon how we read the experimental designs of Seligman, Tomkins, and Walker. The reading practice of this chapter opens scientific research and experimentation to the political and social purposes of an abolitionist science, even as the researchers examined failed to cite Black authors writing from within or outside other disciplines in the context of the Second Reconstruction.

Readers might question why I read the experiments of Seligman, Tomkins, and Walker—white social scientists—when there is pertinent scholarship from Black social scientists and legal scholars ranging from the 1860s through the 1980s.[42] I do so because it is precisely through white incorporation and erasure of Black experience in social science theories of power, control, and motivation that DV begins to acquire its legal life centered on the intimate couple in the DV courtroom. A feature of this chapter is its contribution to the genealogy of cybernetics and infrastructure. Both topics concern the control and background architecture of media and communication systems and need to pass through the slave narrative to realize their more ardent claims about the spatialization of technology.

I position battered woman syndrome (BWS) within Cold War cybernetics research on the experimentation, theorization, and visualization of control in abusive relationships in the 1970s and 1980s. Martin Seligman and Sylvan Tomkins are two psychologists whose influential experiments inspired Walker, including the Cycle and the Wheel visual aid tools, whose BWS theory they embody. Unlike Walker, who developed her understanding of BWS to offer a feminist analysis of women's experiences in abusive relationships, Seligman and Tomkins were inspired by the tumultuous context of US civil rights struggles, specifically the freedom struggles of Black people. By attending to the experiments and curricular objects developed by Seligman, Tomkins, and Walker, I demonstrate that battered women's subjectivity and their advocacy needs emerged from cybernetics research that based its experimental procedure, instruments, and scientific rhetoric in the experiences of Black folks in the United States. The itinerary of legal and scientific knowledge production of battered women merged Cold War cybernetics research and civil rights claims in which the problem of Black freedom is central to, yet obscured from, the study of how women gradually lose freedom through particular forms of violent interaction.[43] In this chapter, the struggles of Black folks are revealed to have inspired experiments that helped constitute DV as violence between romantic couples through cybernetic theories of control. Blackness as an abject social position is vestibular to the development of BWS, and the Cycle and the Wheel are necessary propaedeutics to conceptualizing the work of power and control in domestic abuse relationships. I reveal how both Walker and the Black subject recede into the background of contemporary cybernetics research.

Chapter 3 moves into the DV criminal courtroom to explore the production and circulation of visual evidence of DV. Here I consider courtroom movement outside the dominant example of video-recording and focus instead on the projection of the still image. Since the Rodney King police brutality trials, the visual culture of the courtroom has focused heavily on the rhetorical use of video evidence. This continues to be the case in the context of nationwide adoption of dashboard cameras by law enforcement. The use of video to surveil the police is a criminal justice reform that has yet to result in meaningful change to the structure of police power.[44] Policing involves the creation and control of communicative interactions in which civilians are exposed to death, rape, and maiming. Moving images capturing nefarious police activities actually strengthen the law's ability to read and sustain police deadly use of force. The third chapter moves away from this recent line of research to return to the historical creation of still image photography by police and its projection of criminality as power-knowledge. The chapter deconstructs the architecture and formal routines of evidence display. I draw on Sianne Ngai's theory of the "ugly feelings" and its link to spatial projection to understand the moment of testimony, when witnesses authenticate visual evidence of their injuries sustained during DV.[45] This chapter demonstrates how the state controls strategies of the flesh through the authentication of visual evidence in DV cases. I present ethnographic observations of the failure of images of wounding that are thrown into courtroom space. A key intervention of the chapter is the inclusion of victims of DV into the strategies of population management that sociologist Issa Kohler Hausmann calls "misdemeanorland."[46] The chapter describes an exemplary DV trial that confirms that victims of misdemeanor-level DV are subject to increased state management schemes as are misdemeanor offenders.

The failures of testimony described in chapter 3 give way to anti–DV activism, examined in chapter 4. Advocates and activists employ numerous strategies in the fight against DV. The fourth chapter performs a reading of a tactical media example in which DV injuries are simulated using cosmetics. "Legal camp" is a strategy of the flesh introduced to explain how the cosmetic simulation of DV wounds establishes a visual literacy for reading courtroom images of battered women. The interaction between skin-photography, color cosmetics, and the physics of the camera help establish a limit in which white and Black skin are naturalized as the possibility and impossibility of vision, respectively.

I argue that legal camp imports the signifying practices of queer camp into the state-corporate space. I compare media deploying legal camp against media examples that center the DV escape narratives of queer women of color. Comparatively, DV media featuring queer women of color may appear dry and informational, yet they offer stronger critiques of the criminal justice system that subjects them to racism and heteropatriarchy than do examples of legal camp. As a strategy of the flesh, legal camp encompasses earlier theorizations of how colonial violence is internalized in the subject—epidermalization and the hieroglyphics of the flesh. The concept internalizes the look of violence between intimate partners at the same time that it aligns the state's desire for visual proof with battered women's psychology. Ultimately, legal camp operates in legal and extralegal settings to establish a baseline for interpreting visual evidence of DV, something queer of color media-makers resist.

Legal Spectatorship concludes with a discussion of the book's claims and strategies. I then briefly explore the future of testimonial performance in the context of digital applications and algorithmic cultures. In media studies of the long nineteenth century the proliferation of communication technologies and systems is a major thematic. *Legal Spectatorship* reorients the development of new media toward the managed emancipation of Black people. While I find antiblackness in the techno-physical affordances of photography, I am more interested in showing how the transition out of slavery informs one of the largest but also most confounding areas of criminal court processing and social organizing: DV cases. Black feminist concerns with representation identify several controlling images that stereotype and dishonor Black women's character. These images rob Black people of membership in the citizenry while naturalizing the failure to belong as the result of dangerous character flaws rather than the outcome of structural violence associated with antiblackness. In this context I position a new controlling image, visual evidence of DV, as one effect of law and media that conditions the contemporary experience of witnessing and claims to vulnerability. These images, whose origins are also linked to governance feminism's hard-won but nonetheless thorny deployments of state power, encompass the visual and textual culture of slavery's repeating bodies.[47] *Legal Spectatorship* amends governance feminism by focusing on embodiment, the epidermalized incarnation of the slave's repetition across time-space and media forms.

Ultimately, this book is a study of the many ways a person might see and read, and be seen and read, in the courtroom space, a space whose activities are historical and always in dialogue with those outside courthouse architecture. It is a book that scrutinizes scrutiny through the case example of DV prosecution, its evidentiary material, and its role in the unfinished project of abolition.

1 AUTHENTICATING DOMESTIC VIOLENCE

Image and Feeling in Abolitionist Media

The Reader probably knows that no promise or writing given to a slave is legally binding; for, according to Southern laws, a slave, *being property*, can *hold* no property.—HARRIET JACOBS/LINDA BRENT, *Incidents in the Life of a Slave Girl, Written by Herself*

IN *Incidents in the Life of a Slave Girl, Written by Herself* Harriet Jacobs describes a "loophole of retreat," a peculiar form of freedom she experienced while hidden inside a garret for seven years. There, Jacobs discovered a refuge from the violent intimacies of racial capitalism, in particular its underwriting laws of slavery. Inside the confined space hidden beneath the roof of an uninsulated shed on her grandmother's land in South Carolina, Jacobs shifted between statuses whose binary theoretical formulation are central to Western aesthetics and philosophy: mind versus body, free versus unfree, maternal presence versus maternal absence, slave versus master, human versus nonhuman, Black versus white, male versus female, movement versus confinement. These binaries have generated much discussion of the prolonged period of time Jacobs lived in the space, with various interpretations of the psychodynamics between Jacobs, her grandmother, children, the Flints, and

Mr. Sands, and they include the psychogeography of the landscape and her transition from captive to runaway to freedwoman.[1]

The loophole of retreat is arguably the major incident of *Incidents in the Life of a Slave Girl*. It has become a form within a text, often read as a model of what freedom can mean for Black gendered subjects of racial capital conditioned by spatial enclosure and capture. Black freedom is lived as struggle; freedom and resistance are one within the confines of the garret. The garret has become a singular Black feminist political inquiry, an evidentiary object pulled out of a larger literary form—slave narrative. I use the term "literary form" here, rather than "genre," to position Jacobs's slave narrative and the garret in particular within the dramatic long nineteenth-century proliferation of technologies of representation. Slave narratives are more than a genre of writing. As I hope to demonstrate in this chapter, the variety of incidents Jacobs describes in *Incidents in the Life of a Slave Girl* function as extralegal testimony that can be mined for an early theory of domestic violence. Prior to its transformation into a theory of violence centered on the intimate couple, the captive Black woman implicated constitutional law, slavery, and psychophysical sensation in theories of domestic violence.

Harriet Jacobs's book and its description of the loophole of retreat are a point of departure into an examination of the authentication of Black women's complaints against slavery in the decades before and after the Civil War. "Authentication" means to "prove or show . . . something [especially a claim or artistic work] to be true, genuine or valid."[2] Prior to the war, abolitionist media sources such as Jacobs's slave narrative and illustrated newspapers disclosed extralegal proof of Black women's experience. After the war, proof of Black women's victimization can be found in legal affidavits. I read these media sources for how the authentication of Black women's suffering is spatialized visually and textually. My reading practice is intentional, with an eye toward locating a theory of feeling and motivation that operates within visual and literary images of suffering. Specifically, I read abolitionist media for evidence of sulking and speculate how "the sulks" characterize the slave's condition as one of being unable to remain yet unable to leave the situation of slavery.[3] White masters used the term "the sulks" to refer to a kind of madness caused by the slave's grief. Rather than center the master's perspective and acts of naming, I want to emphasize that the master's use of the term meant to signal a desire to avoid disruption in the slave's availability for reproductive labor exploitation. The sulks suggest periods of time in which the slave's grief was recognized as fugitive and economically costly.

The condition of being unfree to remain yet unfree to leave is a form of suspended agency I identify with resistance to slavery. By locating agency in sulking behavior in the plantation context, we can read abolitionist media for the ways it authenticates suffering and insurrection simultaneously. Sulking is the experience of withdrawal that tracks fugitive freedom, and my tracing of its literary and visual imagery has the added intention of following its itinerary in contemporary psychological studies of battered women's behavior used in the DV court. To this end, I first read the meaning of domestic violence as it appears in constitutional law. For here, too, exists proof of Black insurrection. The complicated work of this chapter is to read abolitionist media for its dual reflection on federalism and suspended forms of agency that demand federal response.

A rich body of scholarship conceptualizes Black women's experience in terms of carceral rather than domestic violence and begs the question: What does domestic violence do for theories of state and individual power that carceral violence does not?[4] And with good reason. The process of enslavement that conditions Black kinship networks and lifeways involved forms of capture and imprisonment using carceral tools and environments. Many have shown how the rehearsal of these processes is key to modernizing institutions of the liberal state, including the apparatuses of jail, prison, and public housing that accumulate Black lives.[5] Carceral violence is a major aspect of the biopolitical management of the US population. Sarah Haley's *No Mercy Here: Gender, Punishment and the Making of Jim Crow Modernity* considers Black women's bodily experience in terms of carceral environments and logics, arguing that "black women were made juridical inverts: perverse, primitive, and pathological, and therefore unentitled to protection or freedom" as a result of "policing, legislation, and judicial enforcement."[6] Further, "carceral institutions and concomitant ideologies evacuated the black female subject of her claims to the body, much less bodily protection, and in so doing produced a codified white female body subject defined by bodily sanctity."[7] Likewise, Savannah Shange's *Progressive Dystopia: Abolition, Antiblackness, and Schooling in San Francisco* examines contemporary public schooling and demonstrates how liberal progressive reform maps a carceral geography onto the lives of young Black women, which pushes underserved students into a low-paying labor force and futures marked by carceral violence. Historical, anthropological, and sociological studies such as Haley's and Shange's have been crucial to theorizing the racialized and gendered intersection of state policing because they examine the distinction between what slave law legislates for itself and what managerial powers it abdicates to the master class, including what these forms of power suggest about the concept of freedom and the performance of resistance.[8] In this chapter however, a different concept of violence, that of *domestic violence*, is the focus of inquiry into Black claims of victimization and resistant acts. Black women's communication about violence is modified by the word "domestic" rather than "carceral" to explore a more encompassing violence, one that refers to a scalar notion of "the house" and the management of its affairs.

I am drawn to the phrase "domestic violence" because of its singular occurrence in Article IV, Section 4 of the US Constitution, on the one hand, and the high frequency of its occurrence in contemporary feminist jurisprudence and social science knowledge production on the other. In its constitutional appearance, domestic violence is inaugurated as the subject of federal protections. In the contemporary jurisprudence, domestic violence encompasses a violence that systematically recurs among intimate partners where the white heterosexual couple is the primary cultural and legal image and the object of study among countless social scientists. The visual presence of the term in contemporary legal documents and reports about violence between "the couple" is subsequent to its brief appearance in the Constitution. In the Constitution the "Domestic Violence Clause" exhibits a broader concept of violence than the contemporary pattern of violence occurring between sexual intimates. In US legal history domestic violence (dV) is first a theory of unseen, unanticipated upheaval, a catastrophic violence threatening to permanently install itself in all conceptions of the house. In this sense, dV poses a systemic threat that is distinct from policing the other that carceral violence implies. Guided as I am by the language of US constitutional law and policy, I see domestic violence as *any* violence to the security of the states. Whereas carceral violence is implicated in the spatial organization and policing of populations through social valuations of land and people, "domestic violence" is first a rhetoric that is later associated with a particular visual appearance across historical debates and textual formats from the rhetoric of federal protection. Domestic violence is not conceived here as an antagonism of carceral violence. Far from it. From the US Constitution to contemporary courtroom cases, the genealogy of the phrase implicates the many analyses of Black freedom struggles that make carceral violence knowable.

Domestic violence has a dual meaning: the term indicates a long history of Black freedom struggles while simultaneously referring to a broad and unknown category of violence that could befall the nation. A detour through the Constitution's Domestic Violence Clause examines its drafting history for the ways Black women's insurrectionary claims to freedom from slave relations were imagined by pro-slavery southern states. During the 1787 Convention, southern states resisted the conceptualization of the term "domestic violence" in hopes of further shaping the federal arena around the perpetuation of slave relations. The struggle over the insertion of "domestic violence" in the Constitution is significant to DV jurisprudence and the history of evidence used to adjudicate this crime. As I hope to reveal in this chapter and throughout the book, the stakes of tracing the textual appearance of "domestic violence" are nothing less than detailing the erasure of Black women's fugitive acts of freedom from the evidentiary history of domestic violence claims and the significance of their historical claims to the contemporary material culture of police investigation and courtroom communication. This chapter, then, lays the groundwork for how the phrase "domestic violence" comes to illustrate the significance of testimonial paperwork and its format in the genealogy of evidence of other phrases such as "intimate partner violence," "violence against women," "dating violence," and so on. In doing so, my argument does the media historical work of establishing Black women's experience of and rebellion against slave relations as the absent presence within contemporary DV prosecution. What I am tracing is the translation of domestic violence, dV, from an article of the Constitution to a theory of violent intimacy, DV.

Black women theorized dV as a violent intimacy enacted across manifold spatial arrangements. Their writing is generative of the transformation of dV from constitutional article to social science object to formatted criminal court documents, DV. Jacobs's discussion of the interval in the garret situates the Black female captive as a model of the dilemma of testimonial speech facing the contemporary domestic abuse victim. Prior to the Civil War the ability to give legal testimony about experience in the arrangements of white domesticity in which they were held captive was largely unknown to Black women. The slave narrative, with its disclosures about the workings of racial capitalism, is thus a testimonial account of the peculiar institution. I take Jacobs's emphasis on Dr. Flint's obsessive desires for access and control over her body's reproductive capacities as a point of departure into nineteenth-century communication systems and modes of utterance during slavery and Reconstruction. This intervention complicates the geography of theories of labor centered in the workshop and factory floor and moves them toward affective and physical labor in slave-owning households and neighborhoods in which ex-slaves forged homesteads post-Emancipation. Both were domestic settings structured by racial violence. In these domestic contexts, enslaved and newly freed Black people created communicative forms and modes of utterance about a profound violence whose definition would later narrow into "domestic violence" and, alternately, "intimate partner violence."

As ideologies of race and gender transformed during the nineteenth century, so too did notions of observation, reading, and writing. The mid-nineteenth century saw radically shifting ideas of what it meant to be an observer, reader, and writer. Subjects were reordered by the proliferation of new media formats—photography, phonography, typography, and other technologies. Automatic functioning was the distinctive attribute of media forms emerging during the buildup to the Civil War. The problem of slavery is vital to this moment. Forcing slaves into giving their labor freely and without benefit of kinship entailed multiple burdens of risk, obligation, and discipline that the character of the master class could not sustain. Imagining new machines whose operations were defined by automation was a way for the master class to rid itself of the slave by incorporating freely extractable labor untroubled by social relations. In the process, the fantasy of self-operating machines created new experiences of media forms that raised new questions about the authentication of experience, labor, and the body moving in space.

Photography and slave narrative are two media forms emerging in this context; both are endowed with authorial speaking powers, including the ability to authenticate evidence in legal and extralegal settings. During the decades leading up to the Civil War and through Reconstruction, audiences made new claims to experience through new media practices. As forms, photographs and slave narrative proffered knowledge of "what happened" in an increasingly authoritative way. Jacobs's "loophole of retreat" is evocative of these forms. In the context of shifting media practice, we may also think of Jacobs's refuge specifically and the slave more broadly in terms of format. Format concerns the manner in which something is arranged or set out. In the case of DV format reflects how its complaint must appear in order to be true. For example, the description of Jacobs's body hidden inside a crawl space has attained the status of format. But it is no less legible as a format, a way of arranging or laying out components of a complaint. The image of Jacobs and her story appear within a slave memoir and a set of authentication strategies that give her narrative some of the official status of a formal complaint.

The image of Jacobs inside the garret that endured the condition of being unfree to depart and unfree to remain anticipates the visual evidence of the DV courtroom to come. A few years shy of the ratification of the Violence

Against Women Act (VAWA), Ellen Driscoll, a white artist commissioned in 1990 by the Whitney Museum, staged a scene of testimony from the many described in Jacobs's 1861 text. Jacobs's famous description of the "loophole of retreat" would be reproduced in the sculptural work *Loophole of Retreat* (1990–92). The sculpture stood as a museum-based replica of Jacobs's original book chapter of the same name (see figure 1.1). The garret is constructed from wooden planks that form a large sphere. A doorway is cut into the sphere, allowing entry into what, for viewers taking in the entire form, would appear to be a large wooden cone on the museum floor. Above the wooden form are rotating objects suspended from a wheel. The rotating objects cast shadows upon the surrounding museum walls. Thinking through Driscoll's artistic interpretation of the hideaway and the many scholarly accounts of the space suggest that a singular aspect of Jacobs's narrative has been anointed as the most compelling proof of the experience of violent captivity and reproductive exploitation. The garret space and the images it conjured are the most damning evidence. We have no photograph of Jacobs sheltering inside the garret. We have only the literary images she renders in *Incidents* and a daguerreotype used on the cover of her book of her seated in a chair, years after escaping Edenton, North Carolina. Driscoll's sculpture reveals slavery's repeating body through Jacobs's flight from dV and the proliferation of photography in law and culture.

Historian Jennifer Mnookin demonstrates that before the end of the 1850s daguerreotype images were primarily portraits revealing the personhood, status, and bearing of individuals and families. At a time when photographic calling cards (*cartes de visite*) operated as a remnant of the subject's presence at a specific time and place, daguerreotypes slowly contributed to a newly emerging category of freedmen and women on one hand and the legal category of demonstrative evidence on the other. According to Mnookin, daguerreotypes were rarely used in the courtroom.[9] When they were used, it was largely in consideration of matters of document authentication, including questions surrounding forged signatures. In court the images functioned in the same manner as maps, drawings, and diagrams. By the 1870s photographs were frequently used in the courtroom as evidence of a variety of issues: proof of identity of defendants or victims in murder cases and judging visual resemblance in bastardy cases.[10] None of the cases in Mnookin's history point to the use of photographic evidence in the adjudication of the rightful owner of a particular a slave nor the adjudication of the excessive use of punishment by the master. These were uncommon reasons to bring photographic materials into the courtroom milieu. Photographs of

FIGURE 1.1 Ellen Driscoll, *The Loophole of Retreat*, 1990–1991. Wood cone (13′ × 8′) and mixed media on motorized wheel with seven columns suspended reflecting shadow images. Whitney Museum at Philip Morris.

the living, wounded, or dead slave body seldom, if ever, appeared as evidence in court matters where the violation of slave law, the Domestic Violence Clause, or Republican Clause (see the introduction) were at issue.

Nevertheless, slavery's afterlife permeates audiovisual culture. According to Kimberly Juanita Brown, Black women's contemporary appearance in portraiture and poetry has a "visual resonance" through which slavery reveals its haunting afterlife. Brown's is a visual and sonic metaphor that suggests that slave relations reverberate through format. The Black slave is arranged as a fungible "repeating body" in literature, moving images, and audio materials.[11] Jacobs's psychophysical retreat into the garret space occurred during a sociocultural-economic moment when technologies of observation were in flux. Nineteenth-century changes in format—of the reader, of writing, and of the observer—were coincident with expanding the idea of the race represented by the enslaved Black body from optical to aural and literary representational devices.[12] Black enslavement reverberates throughout the design and use of automatic machines. One of these machines, the photographic daguerreotype, supplanted the camera obscura decades prior to the Civil War and would become a format offering troubling assertions about Black subjectivity in the field of vision.[13] Aspects of the garret structure, in particular the aperture Jacobs cut into the wood to see a small portion of the outside world, implicate both photography and the camera obscura in the transformation of the subject of observation. As I hope to show, the loophole of retreat is an embodiment of flux—between the political reordering of slave relations and the transformation of subjectivity through forms of media whose distinctive character was that they operated automatically. Inside the garret, Jacobs's sustained corporeal misalignment is inclusive of the flux between freedom and fugitivity, between the body positioned in one way and then positioned in another. Jacobs's fugitive freedom and Black citizenship as a whole emerged within a media environment whose transformation of the observer, reader, and writer was distinguished by the proliferation of automatic writing machines.[14]

Jacobs demonstrates an early theorization of domestic violence as a pattern of gender and race violence that was inseparable from economic reproduction and manifest through new models of experience and modes of authentication that could lend experience official and evidentiary qualities. Key passages of her text articulate the Black feminist purposes of what is known in contemporary parlance as a "domestic incident report." Thus, I treat the garret as a scene of intellectual as well as testimonial labor about the scourge of domestic violence. As Brittney Cooper argues, "If we want to take black women seriously as thinkers and knowledge producers, we must begin to look for their thinking in unexpected places, to expect its incursions in genres like autobiography, novels, news stories, medical records, organizational histories, public speeches, and diary entries."[15] *Incidents in the Life of a Slave Girl* in particular and slave narratives more broadly may be read as a compilation of domestic incident reports. Jacobs and freedwomen during Reconstruction formulated domestic violence as patterns of white violence against Black folks. In this way they contributed to theories of constitutional interpretation not only as witnesses but also as theorists of violence. As thinkers and knowledge producers, Black women also made incursions into matter, form, and format.

Let me begin with the attribute of slave narrative as a form that performs as evidentiary authentication. Through slave narratives former slaves established conventions for authenticating their testimonies about enslavement.

In doing so, they embedded a double critique of the "peculiar institution" of slavery. By mastering the literary form and inventing ways to authenticate their narratives, former slaves adroitly performed liberal ideas of personhood and thereby indicted the very slave relations that rendered them objects. The critique made by former slaves is discernible through practices of looking at textual elements common to ex-slave memoirs: the portrait of the author, a title page that typically claims the text is "Written by Him/Herself," and turns of phrase that attest to the trustworthiness of the offered testimony. All of these elements, according to Janet Neary, are motivated by the author/narrator's race.[16] Formerly enslaved authors affirmed the authenticity of their painful and triumphant testimonial narratives. They did so through white authoritative forms of writing that they made signify as Black. The moment of critique resides in how former slaves engaged the medium, for "to enter into the slave narrative is to enter a site of racial constraint; the ex-slave narrator must explicitly engage the logic of racial slavery while implicitly critiquing its philosophical presumptions."[17] The visual techniques former slaves used were not merely conventions of publishing; rather, their narratives are distinguished "from other forms of autobiography and are designed to lend an aura of verifiability to the narrative."[18] Neary further argues that "these formal conventions preceded anti-slavery goals of slave narrative and developed in response to the skepticism of white reading public toward black-authored texts and black humanity more generally."[19] Former slaves who were bought and sold as objects published memoirs that challenged the slave economy, law, and culture by self-authenticating their testimonies. They did so during a period in which the idea of the observer and the process of observation were radically transformed.

Historian Hanna Rosen observes that "immediately following emancipation when the promise of federal backing of a new kind of republic was still real," freedwomen "sought, by speaking, to transform their experiences of violence from haunting memories of pain into means of social transformation and thereby to forge a new world."[20] What if the visual conventions deployed in Jacobs's slavery memoir were themselves marked by representational static against slave law and the elements of US constitutional law that underwrite it? The visual culture of the artistic, literary, and administrative renderings of white violence enable a fugitive reading of the US Constitution's Article IV Section 4, known as the "Domestic Violence Clause."[21] The clause reads, "The United States shall guarantee to every State in this Union a Republican Form of Government, and on application of the Legislature, or of the Executive (when the legislature cannot be convened) against domestic Violence."[22] It is a federal power conceived to protect the states. The phrase "domestic Violence" (lower case d and uppercase v) occurs briefly, specifying the kind of violence that the federal government is authorized to counteract.

Let us attend to the visual aspect of the clause. The philological appearance of the Constitution offers visual clues about how the Framer's imagined forms of power conceived within the Constitution's many articles and sections. Lower case d (domestic) and uppercase v (Violence) marks a philological convention used to emphasize important concepts. Recalling Neary's literary and visual approach to the conventions of authentication deployed by former slaves in their narratives, the convention of capitalizing certain nouns is suggestive of a power to make meaning in this federal moment when federal authority emerges within the Constitution. Specifically, in the phrase, "domestic Violence," the combination of lower-case d and uppercase V enshrines a moment when arguments by pro-slavery southern states were undermined. At the Federal Convention of 1787 southern states, which voted as a bloc, attempted to substitute "insurrection" for "domestic violence." The resulting debate highlights the distinction between the original meaning of legal language and its original expected applications.[23] "Original meaning" entails a reading of law guided by the semantic content of legal language. "Original expected applications" suggest a deployment of legal language in excess of its semantic content. The drafting history of the clause demonstrates that, for southern states, slave insurrection was an expected application.[24] The proposed change was narrowly rejected.[25] According to legal theorist Mark Stein, the failure of "insurrection" to replace "domestic violence" "was one of the rare times the slavery interest was defeated at the Convention."[26]

Although the proposed substitution did not come to fruition, the visual appearance of "domestic Violence" is a suggestive remnant of the pro-slavery and anti-slavery debate. The philological convention elevates and broadens the idea of "violence," making it more expansive than the concept of insurrection. Insurrection is a form of violence directed toward an authority or government. It is violence directed toward, and thus circumscribed by, a state institutional power. In contrast, the Framers deployed an alternate strategy for modifying the expansive quality of violence that might endanger the nation. The clause modifies "violence" with "domestic." Where insurrection specifies violence directed at a ruling authority "domestic" modifies violence spacio-temporally. Protection from "domestic Violence" tracks an expansive notion of the house wherein state authority and government are not the assumed objects of violence. Spatially, the modification refers to violence within the US territories rather than foreign lands. Temporally, it refers to a broad set of harms that are inflicted upon the domestic but are as yet unseen.[27] The philological convention through which "domestic Violence" appears in the Constitution entails more than a literary trend. Written this way, "domestic Violence" imposed subversive meaning upon the text. The visual element of the clause marks a brief moment in which pro-slavery interests failed to become the imaginary that guarantees a republican form of government. Rather than instrumentalize the clause to suppress Black rebellion, the Constitution imagines a wide territory of suffering over which to protect. Overall the clause is a device that allowed the Framers to act upon new and novel forms of violence. Black women's testimony about the patterns of white violence they experienced enriches the history of the "domestic Violence" clause and by extension the stakes of a republican government. Their testimony about the spatial and corporeal patterns of white violence recalled the political struggle between pro-slavery and abolitionist blocs over the nature of protection commanded by the Clause versus original expected applications by pro-slavery states.

LOOPHOLE OF RETREAT

Jacobs's confined position gave rise to a feedback mechanism that allowed her to observe the presence of others, in particular her children, who regularly played outside. While confined to the dark, cold, and uninsulated space, Jacobs found a gimlet and used it to bore a one-inch square peephole in the wood. From this vantage point she used the sound of her children to signal her to look outside the peephole. Jacobs writes, "At last I heard the merry laugh of children, and presently two sweet little faces were looking up at me, as though they knew I was there, and were conscious of the joy they imparted. How I long to *tell* them I was there!"[28] Years, later Jacobs comes to learn that her son, Benny, was entirely aware of his mother's hidden location in the garret. In the chapter titled "Preparations for Escape" Benny tells his mother of the day he discovered her presence above the grass where he and his sister, Ellen, played. "I don't know what made me think it was you, but I did think so."[29] Jacobs reports her children purposely played within the line of sight enabled by the peephole. The angle of vision, which Driscoll reproduces as a projection of personal effects rotating as shadows, "concretize[s] and bear[s] witness to Jacobs's anticipated possession of vision and voice" achieved in this interstitial space.[30]

Benny's inability to pinpoint his internal sensation that his mother was nearby in the garret or the external sign that she was there suggests an inversion of the panoptic gaze. Jacobs's fugitive body politics, and their distribution through her children, do not emerge as a spectacle of violence in the same manner described by Foucault. Foucault's famous analysis of Jeremy Bentham's panopticon introduced the institutional vision as a force that turned human subjects into object of observation.[31] Unique to the experience of panopticism is the sense produced in the subject that they are being perpetually watched. The windows of a centralized and darkened guard tower provide a surveilling gaze that is both "invisible and unverifiable."[32] Who is subject to the architectural panopticism of the garret? Who performs the role of the imposing watchtower and for what purpose? Jacobs and/or her children? Jacobs, in her confinement, is partitioned by the interstitial space and, effectively, lives in a cell. The distinction between cell and watchtower entirely collapses when those inside and outside are together fighting for the bonds of kinship. The docility panopticism renders in the subject in order to reduce social and political force is reversed in the garret space. Benny and Ellen are mysteriously drawn to play within physical proximity of the garret. At the same time, Jacobs is called to the peephole by the children's sounds. The actions of mother and children are both controlled by the mutually speculative gazes of the other. Their activity, already circumscribed by legal codes that regulated the movement of slaves, was further spatialized by a gaze as invisible and unverifiable as Bentham's watchtower, yet with the crucial difference of kinship. The garret, then, unsettles the top-down, or center-periphery, relationship constitutive of power-knowledge Foucault imbues in the panopticon. As Joy James contends of Foucault's theory of discipline, his "otherwise impressive critiques of disciplinary regimes missed the depth and dimension" of "the Captive Maternal and Black Matrix."[33] In its critical posture toward Foucault's theories of control, James's invocation of the Captive Black Maternal and Black Matrix suggests Black fugitive purposes and efforts must be brought to bear upon theories of discipline and the carceral state.

In law, a loophole is an ambiguity or lacuna of legal writing. Loopholes may be exploited in order to unsettle laws or sets of rules. In this sense they emphasize change and are oriented toward the future. Because loopholes may be used to unsettle, redirect, or reverse laws and rules, they are also of interest to theories of control. The garret, whose structure is modified by the word "loophole," which allows it to function as a retreat for Jacobs, is an interstitial space similar to the ones architects regularly fabricate to enable specialized forms of labor in a building structure that is out of the way and often unnoticed by regular building traffic. Thus, the "loophole of retreat" hints at both contract law and the practical work of an architect, whose structures are able to conceal or camouflage particular mechanical operations that rarely need accessing.

Assessing Jacobs's inner life of psychophysical sensation is difficult not only because of one's physical and historical distance from Jacobs, but also due to the precarious nature of empathy and the unrepresentability of slavery as an event. Stephen Best has claimed, "There is no visual equivalent of *Incidents in the Life of a Slave Girl*," for "when it comes to the representation of the inner life of the enslaved few of our sources are visual in nature"; that is because "slaves are not the subject of visual imagination, they are its object."[34] The sculptural rendering of the space of confinement that was, in Jacobs's portrayal in *Incidents*, a space "akin to freedom," emerges, then, as a camera obscura.[35]

Driscoll's sculpture replicates the observational techniques of the camera obscura at the same time that it refers back to Jacobs's narrative form. The citation, performed though the gazes of museum spectators, is an example of what Neary calls "representational static," a strategy whereby contemporary artists evoke the narratives of former slavers as a practice in late twentieth-century art-making. Art historian Huey Copeland has suggested that Driscoll's sculpture contributes to the disappearance of the enslaved.[36] In its desire to replicate the interstitial space where Jacobs hid herself, Driscoll's interpretation exemplifies empathy's limitations.[37] Copeland argues that Driscoll's "large-scale installation literally immersed the viewer within an aestheticized update of Jacobs's attic, complete with objects and figures meant to bring out the similarity between the architectural structure or the garret and the camera obscura." By opening up the garret to museum spectacle, Driscoll's artistic rendering creates a distancing effect, one that can diminish the criticality of Jacobs's narrative of fugitive freedom. Accessing and assessing the horrors of slavery entail a "recourse to fantasy" that "reveals an anxiety about making the slave's suffering legible," an anxiety "historically determined by the denial of black sentience, the slave's status as object of property, the predicament of witnessing given the legal status of blacks, and the repression of counter discourses on the 'peculiar institution.'"[38] Indeed, the *Loophole of Retreat* sculpture is a rationalization of Jacob's experience of slave law into spectacle. Yet this is all the more reason to examine the installation and its historical gestures toward racial and feminist jurisprudence more closely. In the attempt to draw out the similarities between the garret space and the camera obscura, the sculpture stages a total testimonial environment for the disclosure of Jacobs's experience, heretofore accessible through slave memoir. In the contemporary moment, Driscoll's sculpture evokes the shifting parameters of observation that occurred in the nineteenth century. When we keep both law and culture in our sights, Driscoll's artwork aligns freedwomen's testimony and the camera as two modes of representation that are endowed with new evidentiary status. Driscoll's *Loophole of Retreat* is not only an example of representational static where Black literary art form historically accords with visual art form. The sculpture also metaphorizes the looking practices constitutive of the scene of legal witnessing and testimony. Installed is a discrete spatial and corporeal fantasy about how and where the slave's experience may be communicated in legal domains through legal protocols. Driscoll's installation would seem to rationalize a specific architectural structure where Jacob's experience may be accessed. In doing so, *Loophole of Retreat* extends the theatricality of testimony to sculpture and the literary. This architecture is that of the courthouse and courtroom where Black people gained the right to legally testify to their experience of slavery and its aftermath amid shifting ideas of the observer, writer, and reader. The camera obscura, slave narratives, photography, and courthouses are forms through which ideas of spectrality and literacy, power and authority, testimony and witnessing transform through Black women's complaint.

TESTIMONIAL SENSATION

Driscoll's evocation of the garret calls forth the technologies of seeing that were transforming during the mid-nineteenth century. The fugitive bonds of kinship Jacobs maintained while stowed away and the architectural form of the camera obscura both unsettle the idea of panopticism as the dominant model of vision in disciplinary society, as conceived by Foucault. Representational static enables Jacobs's hideaway an incursion into the evidentiary power of photography. During the nineteenth century photography emerged as the primary example of mechanical vision. The power of the medium developed not only in culture but in legal procedure as well.

Miranda A. Green-Barteet conceptualizes Jacobs's garret as an interstitial space, a "betwixt and between" state of freedom and captivity.[39] Though uncited by Green-Barteet, Hortense Spillers's use of the vestibule is an earlier architectural metaphor deployed to describe the position of Black people in relation to white sociocultural arrangements. The interstitial space tells us about architectural logics of covering or stowing away certain types of operation from view. In contrast, Spillers's notion of the vestibule emphasizes operations that are off to the side yet crucial to the production of the whole (sociocultural) structure. The distinction between interstitial and vestibular space is made more pronounced in the use of the vestibular (imbalance) to describe vertigo. While many have described the peculiar form of freedom Jacobs discovered in the garret, few speculate on the effect of this interstitial space on her nervous system, specifically her sense of cognitive and bodily orientation in space. In *Incidents* Jacobs variously describes her seven-year sanctuary as "a small shed," "small garret," "a pent roof," "nine feet long and seven feet wide," the highest part "three feet high, and sloped down abruptly," "the darkness total," "without one glean of light."[40] Her restrained movement in the dark is productive of what in psychology is called "vestibular imbalance." Vertigo not only characterizes Jacobs's confinement within the garret; the sensation of vestibular imbalance is also empathetically transferred to many of her readers. Here, Driscoll's conical sculpture, and signaling of rotation, emerges as a reverberation of the awkward and torturous suspension of Jacobs's body in the garret, a form of representational static.

For years Jacobs's body endured misaligned poses, poses where relief is fleeting because it comes by assuming yet another uncomfortable position. Secluded in her awkward contortions, Jacobs produced fugitive performance of economic waste.[41] Her retreat into fugitive confinement reworks the political-economic value of waste as performance. The loophole establishes Jacobs's misaligned limbs and crooked movement as a spurn to the fungible female slave who moves to the master's violent force in captive reproductive labor. Even as she is becoming increasingly and painfully crippled, Jacobs's fugitive body politics are endured and practiced, endured *as* practice. Her fugitive time inside is a refusal to perform labor, both affective and physical, that is a growing fixation of theories of control and feedback in the design of autonomous machines among philosophers, engineers, and inventors such as Charles Babbage and his cohort.[42]

Driscoll's representational static positions Jacobs's experience within a hegemonic optical apparatus that began to collapse in the 1820s and 1830s, "when it was displaced by radically different notions of what an observer was, and of what constituted vision," according to Jonathan Crary.[43] As Crary goes on to say, "If, later in the nineteenth century, cinema or photography seem to invite formal comparisons with the camera obscura, it is within a social, cultural, and scientific milieu where there had already been a profound break with the conditions of vision presupposed by this device."[44] While Crary describes the features of a "new kind of observer" whose subjectivity "was immanent to the elaboration of new empirical knowledge of vision and the techniques of the visible," I want to more emphatically implicate the role of the emancipated slave in unsettling the white supremacist social, cultural, and scientific vision presupposed by the camera obscura.[45]

The interpretation of the loophole of retreat as a camera obscura implicates the garret in emerging projection techniques in the nineteenth century. Driscoll cannot do so without implicating the transition out of slavery. According to Crary, the advent of radically different modes of image-making transitioned observation from the interior/exterior scene of the camera obscura into an "undemarcated terrain on which the distinction between internal sensation and external signs is irrevocably blurred."[46] This transformation, then, was confined not merely to the camera obscura. The liberation of the observer includes the slave, who emerged from captivity imposed through psychic and physical violence. Under the condition of being betwixt and between, unable to leave yet unable to remain, Driscoll's sculpture enacts an inversion of Jacobs's world. Employing the camera obscura, a structure that produces "what can be seen" as an inversion is suggestive of the countless moments of vestibular imbalance that I speculate befell Jacobs in the garret. It is also an antebellum scenario in which to locate the future of extralegal spectatorship of visual evidence of domestic violence. Vertigo entails living orthogonally to the world. In the case of Jacobs, her world is projected upside down. The sensation is betwixt and between passivity and an act of insurrection, "something akin to freedom."[47] Jacobs's "loophole of retreat" is a feedback mechanism that captures the social condition whereby one can neither remain nor leave. Thus, when Crary speaks of the "repositioning of the observer," the observer cannot be assumed to be white and bourgeois, nor white and working class.[48] The intensified stakes of observation include the unfree, former slaves and their emerging literacies, communicative forms, and new contextual spaces and architectures where their forms and conventions are seen and heard. Observation gives way to the legal authentication of new experiences, evidence of ways of life that unsettle white subjectivity and sociocultural and economic arrangements.

I have used Driscoll's *Loophole of Retreat* to examine Harriet Jacobs's garret in relation to the shifting media context in which her narrative emerged. Through representational static, Driscoll's artwork offered a way to position the garret in relation to emerging modes of Black observation and the political need to authenticate Black experience at the time of photography's inception and fast approaching challenge to slavery's regime. Driscoll highlights photography's eclipse of the camera obscura as an authenticating device, a device whose power to stand as evidence rose alongside Black women's emerging capacities to testify to and enact domestic violence. *Loophole of Retreat* renders the crucial scene of Jacobs's fugitive testimony. Though it is marked with the fragility of empathy, the artistic rationalization of the garret space discloses a particular way of reading *Incidents in the Life of a Slave Girl* as testimonial evidence. Jacobs's narrative circulates as a literary portrait at the same time that it performs as a self-authenticated domestic violence incident report (so familiar to the contemporary context of domestic abuse investigations). That such a work, simultaneously an art object and evidentiary material, should appear in the museum constructs a theoretical bridge between the institutions of art and law.

MARGARET, "A TYPICAL NEGRO"

We see other examples of how the slave's body and sensation intersect law and culture in numerous slave daguerreotypes, commissioned by Louis Agassiz and others during the 1850s. "The Scourged Back" is a *carte de visite* of Gordon, a slave who escaped from a Mississippi plantation and joined the Union Army in Louisiana, which demonstrates how the constitutional meaning of domestic violence passed through the slave's fugitive and wounded body.[49] Known also as "Whipped Peter," the image of Gordon is attributed to photographers McPherson and Oliver.[50] Brian Wallis has remarked that slave daguerreotypes strengthened the pseudoscience of race by appearing to confirm racial type at the same time they distinguished themselves from the portrait image that disclosed personhood. "The Scourged Back" derives from the pseudoscientific genre and takes up pornographic meanings that began circulating fervently during the 1850s. Gordon's body assumes a seated contrapposto position from the Classical period. His skin is scarred deeply, welts formed into keloids. As graceful pose and blistered flesh align, the promiscuity of photographic images would suggest "The Scourged Back" as an exemplar of both racial typology and portrait image, a matter further complicated by the formatting of the image in newsprint. In what follows Gordon, too, becomes an example of slavery's repeating body across space-time and media form.

A woodcut reproduction of the daguerreotype appears in the 1863 Independence Day issue of *Harper's Weekly* in a feature on "A Typical Negro" (see figure 1.2). The woodcut version sits among two other images of the escaped

FIGURE I.2 "A Typical Negro," news story published in *Harper's Weekly*, July 4, 1863.

slave that mark his official entry into the Union Army. The page's lower half depicts the reproduction of "The Scourged Back" at the center and is depicted larger than the other two images of Gordon. When read from left to right the images offer a "before" and "after" account of Gordon's transformation from slave to Union solider. The left image reads, "Gordon as he entered our lines," the center, "Gordon under medical inspection," and the right, "Gordon in his uniform as a U.S. soldier." The transformation detailed is not only that of the slave into the Union forces, however. "A Typical Negro" features a news story in which Gordon's escape to the swamps leads into a narrative of intensified patterns of violent punishment devised by Southern whites as the Civil War approached.

Yet, the origins of "The Scourged Back" image and its woodcut version printed in *Harper's Weekly* are the subject of considerable analysis.[51] Previous readings limit themselves to the triptych and highlight the ways that Gordon's transformation suggests slavery is wholly comprehensible through the spectator's visceral experience of the image of torture. The image helps confirm that universalizing the evil of slavery occurred by using the image to conjure the sensations of the master's use of violent force, rather than imagining the psychological or intergenerational effects of slavery on its slave descendants in particular and American society as a whole. Kathleen Collins critiques a quotation, located on the back of the image, from the surgeon who examined Gordon's back for the ways it belies the sentimentalism and respectability politics structuring the abolition movement and its media.[52] The famous image is also known as "Whipped Peter," and Margaret Nicola Abruzzo examines other versions of the scourged back finding that "Gordon from Mississippi was really Peter from a cotton plantation in St. Landry Parish, Louisiana."[53] Historians of photography rightly point out how the uncannily similar images "express the extreme instability of the term *subject*."[54] David Silkenat provides perhaps the most rigorous of investigations into the authenticity of the image and its reprinting in *Harper's Weekly*. He confirms that a number of fabrications of authorship, narrative, and photographed subject pervade not only the original "Scourged Back" photograph but also its reprint in *Harper's*, including the two flanking images that complete the triptych, "Gordon as he entered our lines" and "Gordon in his uniform as a U.S. soldier."[55] Much of what is known of the seminal scourged back image—used to universalize the brutality of slavery through a look—"may be inaccurate."[56]

I do not disagree with previous readings. However, I do pivot away from their preoccupation with authenticating evidence of slavery to dwell instead on the ideology of proof. My interest in all of the many investigations into "The Scourged Back" lies in issues related to the elsewhere and else-when of abolitionist media, ranging from (1) the future ideological significance attributed to authenticating visual evidence of the brutality of slavery for verification by white spectators, (2) to how the whipped male slave achieves investigatory priority by historians, and (3) what might be the contemporary antecedent(s) of "the scourged back." As I show in the following chapters, the contemporary authentication of visual evidence of injuries in the DV courtroom is informed by the "scourged back" image as an abolitionist strategy of the flesh. The choreography of the DV courtroom space has inherited the ideology of authentication, a key function through which whiteness gains its property. In other words, universalizing the pain of slavery (through authentication) assumes a future subjectivity, one that is projected into the DV courtroom.

As scholars examine the translation of "The Scourged Back" across media forms, from the *carte de visite* image to woodcut engraving, they highlight the influence of the nineteenth-century new media context in which visual evidence of slavery and testimony to its experience were produced. However, another interpretation surfaces when the *entire* layout of the page is considered. The reading I offer implicates the triptych in a battle scene above and the extended text that details the experience of female slaves and the strategies of flesh applied to their skin for amusement and punishment.

Closer analysis of the "A Typical Negro" story reveals that prioritizing the analysis of the "scourged back" occludes the experience of enslaved Black women. Located above and effectively framing the *Harper's* triptych is a typed narrative about Margaret, a woman enslaved to Mrs. Gillespie and her plantation. None of the investigations of the authenticity of "The Scourged Back" nor the *Harper's* triptych mentions the story of Margaret featured in "A Typical Negro." At the center of the page is the article, unattributed to any author. It tells a story of power and control by the mistress, one the reader is led to understand as common, not extraordinary or in any way irregular from the title. It is not only control of the slave's milk and its immunity-building properties but an entire system of reproductive labor extraction experienced between master, his wife, and female slaves. Stephanie Jones-Rogers's history of punishment in white domesticity details the master's strategy of impregnating his wife and female slaves in close proximity in the interest of providing extra milk for his legitimate offspring.[57] The magazine feature moves from a representation of Gordon's visual transformation—through images that have little in the way of discernible background, as they are neither inside nor outside an identifiable space—to the article detailing violent events common on the estate of one Mrs. Gillespie (see figure 1.3). The letter tells of Mrs. Gillespie's mutilation of a female slave, Margaret, who continued to nurse her child after being ordered to discontinue. A week after her warning, the mistress finds Margaret's milk still in. Margaret's refusal to discontinue nursing is met with a paddling over her entire body, held down by two other slaves, "Becky" and "Jane." "Mrs. Gillespie then paddled her with a handsaw, sitting composedly in a chair over her victim."[58] Eventually the handsaw is replaced by a leather strap dipped in water. This technique gives way to another in which Mrs. Gillespie called for hot tongs to burn Margaret's nipples.

Reading above and around Gordon's triptych reveals multiple testimonial narratives. The heavy production of the page layout is an attempt to disclose, in tool form, the violence facing different figures held captive in the slave economy. "A Typical Negro" creates a world-in-miniature. The combined and compact quality of the illustrations and text reduce the experience of slavery to what white abolitionists perceived as the most brutal element

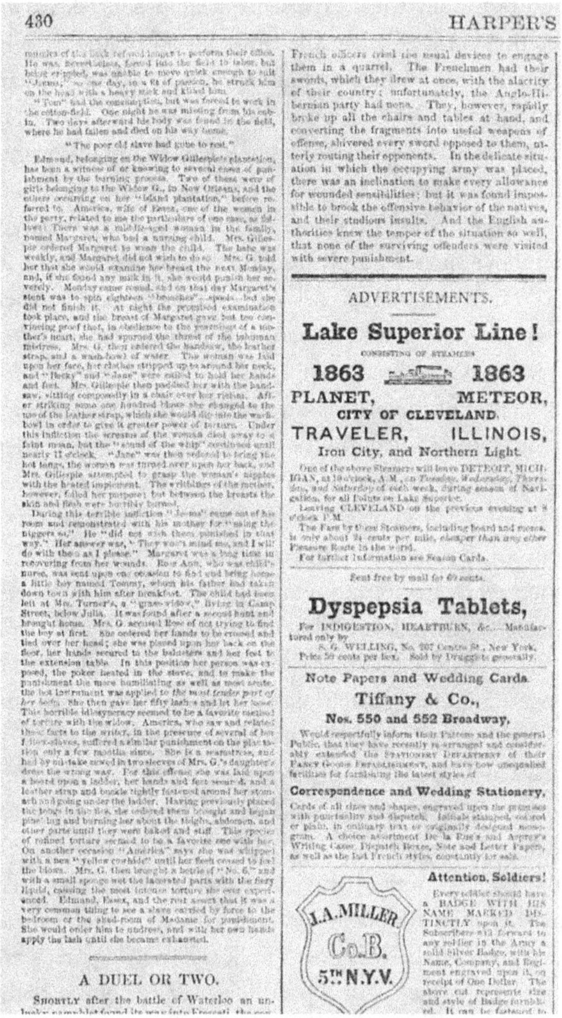

430 HARPER'S

"The poor old slave had gone to rest."

French officers tried the usual devices to engage them in a quarrel. The Frenchmen had their swords, which they drew at once, with the alacrity of their country; unfortunately, the Anglo-Hibernian party had none. They, however, rapidly broke up all the chairs and tables at hand, and converting the fragments into useful weapons of offense, shivered every sword opposed to them, utterly routing their opponents. In the delicate situation in which the occupying army was placed, there was an inclination to make every allowance for wounded sensibilities; but it was found impossible to brook the offensive behavior of the natives, and their studious insults. And the English authorities knew the temper of the situation so well, that none of the surviving offenders were visited with severe punishment.

ADVERTISEMENTS.

Lake Superior Line!

1863 1863

PLANET, METEOR,

CITY OF CLEVELAND.

TRAVELER, ILLINOIS,

Iron City, and Northern Light.

Dyspepsia Tablets,

Note Papers and Wedding Cards.

Tiffany & Co.,

Nos. 550 and 552 Broadway,

Correspondence and Wedding Stationery.

Attention, Soldiers!

J.A. MILLER Co. B. 5TH N.Y.V.

A DUEL OR TWO.

FIGURE I.3 Margaret's narrative on page 430 of the feature "A Typical Negro," *Harper's Weekly*, July 4, 1863 (side left column).

of the slave economy and the most dangerous to the republic. As it describes the mistress's abuse in gruesome detail, "A Typical Negro" also conveys the everyday rebellion of captive people. From the pro-slavery vantage point *all* of the action of the enslaved figures depicted in the woodcut engraving and article are criminal. Federal and abolitionist perspectives powerfully imagine the action as progress narrative.

Above the woodcut images is another scene captioned, "Raid of the Second South Carolina Volunteers among the Rice Plantations on the Comba-

RAID OF SECOND SOUTH CAROLINA VOLUNTEERS (COL. MONTGOMERY) AMONG THE RICE PLANTATIONS ON THE COMBAHEE, S. C.—[SEE PAGE 427.]

FIGURE I.4 "Raid of Second South Carolina Volunteers," image published in the feature story, "A Typical Negro," *Harper's Weekly*, July 4, 1863.

hee" (figure 1.4). The image captures the Union Army destroying the valuable South Carolina rice crop in a strategy of financially crippling the state. To the left riverboats are making their way down stream. To the right many slaves are on land fleeing this way and that, some jumping into the water in hopes of boarding the boat. Nearby a conflagration consumes a granary. Gordon is centered as an example of the violent process of enslavement while the enslaved figures above erupt in insurrection through the act of leaving. As Union soldiers shoot and blow up the barn from the boat, razing the stored rice, a sign of white Southern labor exploitation, the enslaved take to the swamps, in a manner similar to Gordon's story and Harriet Jacobs's narrative. What appears as catastrophe is the very same moment of perilous Black independence.

Published on Independence Day, the page visualizes the Constitution's dual obligation to guarantee a republican form of government and to protect against domestic violence. Its layout makes a series of political arguments about the position of Black people in the theory of domestic violence and republican form that harken back to the drafting history of Article IV, Section 4. As Union soldiers set about destroying the plantation crops they act as federal forces to secure the republic against the threat of domestic violence. Slavery is the threat to the federal guarantee; it is the primary example of domestic violence at the drafting of the Constitution and its present instance of representational static depicted in *Harper's* story. The feature page references the original meaning of domestic violence formulated by anti-slavery states and the original expected meaning of the term anticipated by pro-slavery states. Black people are vestibular to both meanings, on the edge of the constitutional definition of domestic violence and its drafting history yet central to its signification.

Thinking with the drafting history of the domestic violence clause means attending to the distinction between the original meaning and the pro-slavery state's expected application of the term in ways that render the images below and above the page with new criticality. Though the Union forces are crippling the Confederacy's ability to secede from the republic the arrangement of enslaved people on the page cannot confirm or deny access to freedom or hospitality or solidarity from the Union. One might imagine the Black men diving into the waters above to enlist as Union soldiers, exemplified in Gordon's narrative of progress below. Yet, guided by the original meaning of domestic violence to guarantee a unified republican government and protect against domestic violence, one might focus more attention on the boats as they are executing the primary mission of decimating the Confederate crops. This reading cannot assume welcome or help from the Union forces but anticipates rejection, with Union soldiers leaving the men who escape to drown like so much collateral damage. The enslaved remain vestibular to the activity in both instances. From this position, "A Typical Negro" anticipates the vestibularity of so-called Black freedom in US law and culture.

But what of Margaret? I return to her story by way of a problem Silkenat poses to the historian of slavery about "how singular the image of the 'scourged back'" remains among the representations of slavery."[59] Silkenat's observation attests to the persistence of visual proof as the highest form of evidence. But significant erasures are also revealed since the "scourged back" is the province of spectacular Black male pain. Given that the stories printed in pro-slavery and abolitionist publications were often composites, Margaret's story was likely used to represent enslaved Black women emblematically. Rather than authenticate the true existence of Mrs. Gillespie or Margaret, as historians have done with the images of "The Scourged Back" and Gordon/ Peter triptych, I leave the question of her testimony entirely open to the tradition of Black feminist speculative thought. "Venus" is the name Saidiya Hartman gives to unnamed Black women whose experience of colonialism and chattel slavery are accessible largely through the language, desires, and representational technologies of the oppressor.[60] We might understand evidence of Margaret's story as confounded by the same archival troubles Hartman names through "Venus" and therefore open to Black feminist speculative thought.[61] While no such images of Margaret accompany the

Harper's triptych, speculatively, the female rival of the "scourged back" could be daguerreotypes of wet nurses, whose stretched, engorged breasts and sullen faces establish the coordinates of violent intimacy. As I develop in the next chapters, the "scourged back" will come to inform the representational logics of images of battered women. Yet, here in a page from *Harper's* the testimony of Margaret is vestibular to "A Typical Negro" in terms of space and the disclosure of suffering. I pull out Margaret's story, easily passed over by historians of abolitionist media, to locate a Black maternal antecedent to contemporary visual evidence of domestic violence.

The details of her mutilation are located outside "A Typical Negro's" page layout. Readers must find Margaret's story on another page. Though her story is located within "A Typical Negro," its textual appearance outside the main action of the Gordon/Peter triptych and the rice raid suggests a form of vestibularity at the level of illustrated newspapers. Spillers's description of Black folks' vestibular relationship to American culture and techniques of the flesh apply equally, then, to technologies of representation such as print media. The destruction of Margaret's breasts is located inside and outside "A Typical Negro." Her vestibular appearance is the result of production decisions that prioritize the space of storytelling. We will see how the DV courtroom is prioritized in ways that produce witnesses as vestibular to their own images in chapter 3. For now, visual evidence of domestic abuse is one of many futures made possible through the intersection of law and abolitionist media.

Earlier in the chapter I examined how Harriet Jacobs worked to authenticate her experience to white audiences through conventions of self-identification. I speculated on the sensation of vestibular imbalance, vertigo, that she may have experienced in the garret. Taking up sensations of body and flesh is politically challenging. And with ostensibly good reason. For we are warned by historians that the slave daguerreotype and *cartes de visite* images play upon sentimentalism, a gendered and racialized aesthetic in which the victim may only appear in agony, never speaking for the self. Jacobs's slave narrative "written by herself" charts an alternate future from that of Venus. It is a future whose potential we also find in Margaret's vestibular position to "A Typical Negro."

Margaret's testimony is not her own. Rather, it is given to us through the enslaved Edmund, who also implicates "Becky" and "Jane" as the enslaved accomplices to Mrs. Gillespie's brutality. Margaret's participation in the political tactics of insurrection are obscured by the vestibular positioning of her story outside the main page layout, which itself is structured by the gendered aesthetics of the "scourged back" as the universal image of slavery's brutality.

Positioned offsite, a page away from the Gordon/Peter triptych, Margaret's story hints at a way of being in rebellion on the plantation through feeling.

Feelings of sickness wretchedness, humiliation, desolation, and loneliness pervade slave narratives and other abolitionist media. They are the sentiments Jacobs uses to account for herself in the stifling heat of the garret and for other slaves. Margaret's story conjures the same complex of negative feelings. Whites often referred to the display of negative emotions in slaves as "the sulks." The sulks point toward the slave's affective state read and used by masters to devise their own punishing response. It should be no surprise that the sulks are associated with children, given that masters understood their relation to slaves as absolute and parental. Sulking is an appraisal of powerlessness in the face of hurt feelings. Individuals may argue aggressively or retreat defensively; they may withdraw or express feelings by crying or pouting. The sulks were productive of hiding places and techniques of the flesh belonging to the slave and their descendants. To sulk was to make a hiding place within the self—to locate within the self an empowering affective display that threatened the master's exploitative designs to perpetually extract energy from the enslaved, such as Margaret. The sulks are feelings that oscillate within and between passivity and aggression, sullenness and empowerment, fungibility and fugitivity. In their negative in-betweenness the sulks are, above all, a testament to how domestic violence erupts as a movement of feelings within the self and among enslaved people. Jones-Rogers observes that "the sulks" is a name whites used to describe the aggrieved mood of Black women they forced to nurse and otherwise care for the children of their masters to the detriment of their own, who were always under threat of being sold off or killed.[62] We might speculate on the manifestation of the sulks in Margaret after being told to stop nursing: a tightening of her face, a pout, silencing communication until an injustice (within a litany of injustices) is repaired. Margaret's withdrawal from Mrs. Gillespie's sight would be physical and emotional. Hiding herself away to nurse her child in secret would constitute a break in her attunement to her mistress's desires and orders. In the context of master-slave relations the sulks evince both hurt feelings and the rebellious desire to be free of the relation or at least—and this is crucial—continue the relation under less disturbing parameters.

If the sulks are manifestations of negative feeling in the domestic violence context, then taking to the swamp is one possible result. More recently, Riley Snorton has examined the presence of the "Snaky Swamp" in Jacobs's work for how the wetland ecology allegorizes the slave's fungible status in combination with fugitivity to produce hiding places for those "in no situation to choose."[63] "A Typical Negro" also references the swamp visually and textually: the article details Gordon's application of onion skins upon his body to evade bloodhounds; the image of the Union troops burning the rice fields features slaves escaping into nearby waters. Taking to the swamp, however, is not Margaret's fate. Her decision to keep her milk is an insurrection orchestrated inside the household. If we think of the sulks as inseparable from whatever interstitial space on the plantation Margaret found to stage a withdrawal, then something like the "loophole of retreat" is implicated in resetting the routines of violence in master-slave relations. Margaret's sulks are met with the master's terror. By mutilating Margaret, Mrs. Gillespie escalated the assertion of power and control—ownership—over Margaret's body, the capacities of Margaret's flesh to provide milk.

In its emblematic and singular function, Margaret's story positions the history of the breast as vestibular to the scourged back's ideal representation of the brutality of slavery. The mutilated breast is established here as an evidentiary look at slavery, a repeating body that allows us to see law: the Domestic Violence Clause and *partus sequitur ventrem* (offspring follows belly).[64] *Partus* and the Domestic Violence Clause index the persistence and surveillance of Black women's insurrection. Within the libidinal economy of the plantation, sulking would be one of many ways feeling and affect were mobilized as rebellion. Though buried in the depths of *Harper's Weekly*, Constitutional law and slave law converge as Margaret's milk defiantly remains.

The look of the breast, whether in a slave daguerreotype or a literary description, offers a window into the sulks as a way of accounting for Black women's psycho-physical experience of enslavement. In other words, the image of the body stands in for a complaint, a complex negotiation of negative feeling in situations where one has little power and control. In theorizing the sulks, my intention is to explain how physical violence erupts between master and slave. Sulking highlights the minor affects that could be installed within the enslaved to appraise everyday brutalities of plantation economy that left no mark upon the skin. The chapters to follow suggest that the sulks have contemporary afterlives, first in scientific studies of human motivation, and second in the appearance of courtroom images of battered women.

THE MEMPHIS RIOTS

Patterns of domestic violence can be seen in two other sketches completed for *Harper's Weekly* completed by different artists. In "Scenes in Memphis, Tennessee, during the Riot," artist Alfred R. Waud visualizes a deadly episode at a Tennessee homestead in the aftermath of Emancipation (see figure 1.5).[65] Published in 1866, the sketch depicts a small hilly development of six log cabins. Wooden fences separate each homestead. White men are in the act of shooting freedmen and freedwomen in open daylight. Freedmen lie in the dirt slumped over dead or contorted in agony from gunshot wounds. In the foreground freedwomen and children are taking flight, some running away holding hands while others run with their hands outstretched, gesturing fear at the catastrophe. They run in the direction of a small creek in the lower half quadrant in an attempt to flee across the water.

The space is organized such that smaller action scenes create one composite scene of terror. The rendering is tight, with a dirt path leading into a creek whose opening is abruptly blended into a hillside of unmatched proportion. Perspectives are blended together not in the interest of realism but to capture the commonality of the white gunmen violently resisting the new encounters among free Black citizens. While the sketch appears to depict the specifics of the Memphis Riot of 1866, its composite form, which

FIGURE 1.5 "Scenes in Memphis, Tennessee, during the Riot." *Harper's Weekly*, May, 26, 1866.

blends together different perspectives, suggests "this is the general pattern of white violence," "it happened in this way on May 2, 1866." Equally striking in the drawing, which I suggest is composed of multiple scenes of violence, is the dress of the white men. They are all figured wearing hats, long sleeves, and white pants in the act of firing or reloading a shotgun. As Rosen notes, scholars have rejected understandings of riots as discrete and spontaneous eruptions among lower classes; instead they demonstrate that such events were "planned in advance and even at times were led or sponsored by local elites."[66]

A variation on the theme occurs in Frank Bellew's 1872 sketch, "Visit of the Ku-Klux," also published in *Harper's Weekly* (see figure 1.6).[67] An intimate homestead scene by the fire is violently interrupted. A family of freedmen and women is seated by the fire and candles. One figure in a white mask looks into a window. Two others similarly cloaked are at the open door. One points a shotgun at those seated in front of the hearth. Six years after Waud's image, the magazine published another, which offers a more intimate scene of violence. The white men in Bellew's sketch are now formally organized into the Ku Klux Klan, seen in the white masks worn by all three men and the ritualistic garb worn by the shooter.[68] In Waud's image white men are drawn with their hats and backs facing the viewer. Their shared pose emphasizes the acts of violence to which they are committed. Bellew's differs in that the white men who are committing violence together are explicitly projecting a second commitment, that of the Klan's anonymity. Across the two sketches, published six years apart, is the suggestion of the organizational and strategic development of the Ku Klux Klan. Bellew's drawing depicts the nascent Black home and hearth breached by a more culturally solidified entity, with specific political objectives linked to the performance of customs and rituals. It is a picture of white men who have assumed a new costume, neither the Confederate uniform nor their everyday clothing, to respond to the former slave's new legal body.

In the illustrations lining the pages of *Harper's* and other publications the pattern of white violence is staged in the interstitial spaces of the homestead and inside Black dwellings. Print media contested "outrages of frequent occurrence" against free Black citizens at the end of the Civil War by acknowledging how events seen in the culture were connected to political interventions.[69] The script accompanying Bellew's sketch concludes, "It is to be hoped that under a rigorous administration of the laws these deeds of violence will soon cease forever."[70]

FIGURE I.6 "Visit of the Ku Klux," depicting the moment before a massacre. *Harper's Weekly*, February, 24, 1872.

RAPE AFFIDAVITS

Two months before the Civil War's end the Bureau of Refugees, Freedmen, and Abandoned Land was created to provide food, shelter, and legal assistance to former Black slaves—now freedmen—and local poor whites—now "refugees." It was to the bureau that former slaves testified to numerous accounts of violence experienced in their homes and surrounding areas. In *Terror in the Heart of Freedom: Citizenship, Sexual Violence and the Meaning of Race in the Post-Emancipation South*, historian Hannah Rosen argues that "the period of Reconstruction was an exceptional moment in U.S. history when African-American women's stories of sexual violence counted in official public arenas as 'truth' and, temporarily, reshaped the meaning of rape, of black womanhood, and of citizenship."[71] The making of Black women's complaints about white violence—to their individual persons, private property, and livelihood—occurred as a moment of compromised political and social freedom.

The visual cultures of slave narrative texts and optical techniques are not the only ways the observer is reimagined in the mid-nineteenth century.[72] Post-Emancipation legal testimonies, like those reported to the Freedmen's Bureau, indicate a notion of the observer who is operating in new legal contexts. Specifically, the Black observer of violence is operating in the new context of rightful legal citizenship guaranteed throughout the United States. Within the national transition from creating and managing slaves through punishment to creating and managing the legal complaints of former slaves about the violence that marked their lives exists a minor media history of the space and affective resonance of domestic violence testimony.

During Reconstruction the complaint affidavit and the spaces of their collection emerged as new social media environments where law and culture were destabilized and resettled. Black women were eager to seek federal assistance to secure and infuse greater meaning into their newly won freedom, particularly on matters pertaining to the integrity of their feminine virtue. Their desire to testify and protest against systematic victimization by whites was equaled by the state's investment in the documentation of white resistance to Black freedom.[73] Black women and officials of the Freedmen's Bureau thus converged over complaints of rape and other forms of white violence. Together they generated affidavits attesting to patterns of violence that were symbolically directed at the homes of Black people and the interstitial spaces where Black people traveled from one location to another, such as yards, city streets, and pathways.

Affidavits containing the testimonial statements of freedwomen and freedmen constituted a new form of record-keeping in the post-Emancipation era. Though its work was brief, the bureau collected testimonial evidence about patterns of violence dispensed upon Black households and dwelling spaces. Recalling Neary's scrutiny of the visual culture of text and the conventions of authentication featured in slave narratives, "affidavits relating to outrages" were literal forms of victim authentication. They are what historian Lisa Gitelman might call "textual devices" for the inscription of complaints about dV into federal law.[74]

Framing bureau affidavits as "new" highlights the emerging federal infrastructure through which the violence of slave relations was transformed and archived post-Emancipation. As systems of slavery were being dismantled, the Freedmen's Bureau built an infrastructure of complaint that shaped Black citizenship. In this brief historical moment, the federal government authenticated and preserved the experience of Black citizenship, a form of freedom marked by terror and fugitivity, through complaint affidavits. According to Gitelman, "Inventing new ways to write or new kinds of writing presupposes a model of what writing and reading can be."[75] Reports of white outrages were new forms of reading and writing; they were textual devices that materialized Black women's legal claims to victimization. More importantly, they were new records used by the bureau to amass power, albeit for a short time. Cornelia Vismann's explication of the difference between records and documents is pertinent here. She argues that documents employ distinctly representative forms of writing that make them different from records. Documents "are not designed for any particular administrative use; rather, they are made to impress. Their letters are signs of power; their very appearance represents the authority of the issuer. The layout of a document is a 'gesture of power.'"[76] Unlike typeset narratives published by former slaves, Black women's bureau affidavits were handwritten by officials. As a new model of writing and reading, Black women's complaint affidavits to the bureau officers reconfigured the processes of observation and authentication. They did so in ways that draw attention to Black people in the scene of the production and circulation bureaucratic paperwork. As a scene of legal spectatorship, the creation of complaint affidavits with formerly enslaved people entered the state into new practices of observation, reading, and writing. The affidavits mark a sociopolitical moment in which the slave and her descendants are accounted for in a set of records that differ from the "ship's ledger in the tally of tidbits; or in an overseer's journal."[77] Black women are the authors of testimony about their lives. They are eager to file their complaints against the patterns of white violence in the domestic sphere. Vismann prioritizes how documents operate through a distributive mode in which power is conferred to the recipient; in the bureau's case, formerly enslaved Black people were integral to the establishment of new legal structures for dealing with violent intimacies. Their newfound and tenuous freedom was expressed and distributed through the complaint affidavit.

In congressional hearings on violence in the aftermath of Emancipation, freedmen and women testified before the bureau. The pattern of talk during the hearing was frequently to ask, "Have you been a slave?" Congressman Elihu Washburne posed this question at congressional hearings held at the Gayoso House hotel in Memphis, Tennessee. Washington was a Republican from Illinois and close associate of Abraham Lincoln. Though Rosen describes Washburne as someone who opposed slavery throughout his political career, she notes that his intention behind the question "Have you been a slave?" is "unclear."[78] She suggests that Washburne's question meant to "highlight for the record that it was former slaves who had been brutalized by white southerners" in order to demonstrate the need for federal intervention. Rosen is of the view that the question created a dangerous distinction among citizens who had been slaves versus those who had been free before the Civil War. Engaging the media histories of Crary and Gitelman on the radically shifting notions of observation, reading, and writing, I want to suggest that Washburne's question also constituted a new mode of authenticating documents, in this case complaint affidavits. The question seems to establish freedmen as new data subjects of a particular kind of testimony about particular sorts (and sources) of complaint. As such "Have you been a slave?" assists in overlaying a new body who could make testimonial authentication atop an earlier position that the enslaved body could not occupy. Vismann (recalling Weber) might understand Washburne's inquiry as contributing to the "bureaucratic principle of filing things" meant to track new patterns of slave relations.[79]

Black women's appeals to both the state and neighboring white individuals were new forms of testimonial utterance and entailed novel rhetorical proofs and spaces of enunciation that captured emerging patterns of slave relations in the post-Emancipation context. They engaged in frank speech about their routine experiences of rape by white men. In their testimony to congressional committees, white neighbors, newspaper reporters, and more, Black women "claimed identities as honorable women, but not within the confines of conventional definitions of [white] women's virtue."[80] Black women testified to observing patterns of white violence that both emphasized the domestic settings where violence occurred and linked their current experiences to those during the antebellum regime in which they had no citizenship. Changes to the idea of the observer equally entailed changes in the notion of the reader and writer. Amid these transformations of representational techniques were also shifts in the characteristics and patterns of violence. The new modes of Black enunciation were disrupted by new modes of white male refutation of Black testimonial utterances. One of the ways white men refuted Black women's testimony about the violence they experienced was to physically penetrate Black homes and communities.

Night-riders, gangs of white men, frequently invaded Black domestic spaces and converted their private homes into bawdy spaces, brothels, and saloons with their rapacious behavior.[81] Rosen argues that in these staged invasions white men were "[re]constructing black homes and communities as spaces for white [male] pleasure" and "possibly mimicking common practices in brothels."[82] These actions spoiled the chance of free Black people to organize their own spaces. They constructed domestic life, the architecture of a home, as the province of white manhood and the protection of white femininity. In the process, the spatial arrangements of the plantation, including slave laws that buttressed its architecture, could be restored.

Important for my purpose here is not only the rehearsal of plantation captivity but also *how* the performances of white violence attempted to reconstruct domestic spaces according to plantation logics. The violence of the night riders conformed to a script. Before stripping Black women in their home, out in front of their yards, or on the side of the road and out in the woods, men would discuss the quality of the impending stripping of clothes, whipping, beating, and rape they were about to perform. They would enter into conversations about what they were about to do, inviting and encouraging each other into action. The night-rider script also included victims being told "more and more often that they were being punished for political activities and were ordered to cease voting or organizing for Republicans."[83] Rosen's history describes how violent attacks to Black settlements suggested "the reenactment of a scene of the disciplining and domination of a slave" where "white men's physical coercion and violence were open and part of the scene being staged."[84] Thus, patterns of DV were ignited in the immediacy with which free Black citizens constituted a new body of legal speakers post-Emancipation. The emancipation of Black people is integral to nineteenth-century shifts in observation, reading, and listening. From the camera obscura to photography, illustrated newspapers, and legal affidavits, freedmen and women emerged as speakers with new voices who authenticated their experiences in the cultural and legal domain. As a new rights-holding body in law and culture Black citizens could authenticate much more than prior captivity allowed. And they had to. Their authenticated testimonies, buttressed by assaults on their perilous and brief ownership of their own lands, homes, and kinship bonds, would take hold in abolitionist media.

Yet, political commitments to the reparative work of the Bureau of Refugees, Freedmen and Abandoned Lands did not last. Its activities on behalf of freedpeople ceased by 1868. A remainder did emerge nonetheless in the form of an image that disclosed not only the look and scene of DV, but also a theory of the psycho-physical interaction between perpetrator and victim, master and slave. In taking up the visual appearance of domestic violence in the Constitution, this chapter explored what dV and its demand for federal response could mean across literature, photography, and legal language. Slave narrative, abolitionist news stories, and legal affidavits elaborated modes for authenticating Black experience of fugitive freedom. The drafting history of the Domestic Violence Clause conceptualized a federally guaranteed response to unseen threats to the republic. Included in this history was a struggle to associate its concerns with slave insurrection. Preventing the unexpected violence to US domestic territories encompasses the trace of the slaves' fugitive actions, their ceaseless desire to be delivered from the condition of being unable to leave and unable to remain.

Jacobs's authenticating acts mark her description of the garret as a peculiar space of autonomy where she both escaped yet remained within conditions of violence. Guided by Jacobs's work, this chapter has explored other extralegal media examples where the testimony of former slaves is disclosed. "A Typical Negro," a feature story from *Harper's Weekly*, reveals how the problem of authenticating evidence of the brutality of slavery was negotiated differently from the way that Jacobs demonstrates: contemporary historians of "the scourged back" are as invested in authenticating the visual evidence they study as they are in unsettling the racialized gendered humanitarian project of abolition aesthetics. By offering a critique of abolition aesthetics even as it is preoccupied with authenticating its visual evidence, historians would appear to serve two masters. Where former slaves deployed conventions of authentication that performed a critique of the culture, laws, and media systems that ostensibly proved their humanity, historians' obsession with the true origins of the *Harper's* triptych, Gordon/Peter's *carte de visite*, dominates the interest in the visual evidence of slavery to the detriment of Margaret and the unnamed, unauthenticated Black women whose insurgent strategies for coping with the condition of being unfree to leave or remain Margaret represents emblematically. The historiographical preoccupation with visually authenticating the brutality of slavery has left a theory of fugitive freedom I associate both with Black women's vestibular placement in abolitionist media and with the sulks underdeveloped.

This chapter shows that dV was used by the Framers to conceptualize slavery and its unraveling long before its use to describe violent intimacies between couples. This has significance for how we read abolitionist media. The conventions used by Jacobs and other freedmen and women to authenticate experiences that would be published within the extralegal domain of culture are informed by the constitutional conception of domestic violence and federal guarantees to protect the nation from its scourge. Thus, in the contemporary United States, the legislative and judicial acts of VAWA and the *Crawford* Supreme Court decision must locate their antecedents in legal and extralegal media forms.

Abolitionist media are complex forms in which legal concepts of domestic violence and the republic are apparent. But more than legal language can be indexed therein. Theories of feeling and motivation of the enslaved and masters may also be read for the ways they connect to major obstacles to amending the US Constitution by invoking Black insurrection. By closely analyzing the format and layout of abolitionist media textual and visual arguments, we can see that there were different ways to "take to the swamp." The sulks were also a means to gain power and control over the circumstances of a brutal captivity.

It is to the ugly feeling of the sulks and their spatialization that I explore in greater depth in the next two chapters. There I locate a speculative itinerary of the sulks in contemporary psychological research on affect and motivation and the authentication of visual evidence in DV courtroom trials. In the next chapters sulking assumes new names and mediatized expressions about intimate relationships and their adjudication in court.

2 BATTERED WOMEN IN A CYBERNETIC MILIEU

I want depression, too, to be considered part of the "afterlife of slavery," but it can be hard to trace the connections between contemporary everyday feelings (especially those of white middle-class people) and the traumatic violence of the past and present—they might emerge as ghosts, or feelings of hopelessness, rather than as scientific evidence or existing bodies of research material or forms of deprivation.—ANN CVETKOVICH, *Depression: A Public Feeling*

The wheel makes the pattern, intent, and impact of violence visible.—DOMESTIC ABUSE INTERVENTION PROGRAMS, 1984 description of the Power and Control Wheel

THE PREVIOUS CHAPTER read the Domestic Violence Clause and sulking behavior into abolitionist media. It also demonstrated how the disclosures of the abolitionist media, in memoir and illustrated newspapers, are preoccupied, in different ways with the authentication of evidence of slavery's brutality. This chapter takes up the behavioral and affective strand from chapter 1 in order to speculate on how the sulks and the memory of the enslaved reappear in psychological research on domestic violence. Here a different concept of DV surfaces, one that describes violence between intimate romantic couples. What I describe in the previous chapter as the sulks is transformed into a complex of behaviors characteristic of DV between intimate romantic partners and battered women's experience in particular. Thinking about how the sulks inform battered women's psychosis is one way to read depression into (and out of) the archive of slavery that Cvetkovich argues, in the epigraph, can be difficult to trace.

So, too, does an alternate concept of media surface, one that extends the project of abolition toward clemency for battered women and the development of teaching tools to understand psychological responses to DV. Despite the conceptual reevaluation of DV and its visual culture, the remnant of slavery persists.

Psychologists' cultural awareness of the experience of the slave and her descendants organized Cold War—and civil rights–era science through psychic projection. In psychological research on motivation, spanning the 1960s through the 1980s, the slave's claims are remembered yet forgotten, brought to the forefront in experimental research on human behavior and motivation and then disappeared. Scientists working in this area contributed to the scene of legal spectatorship through acts of fantasy in which Black people's experience of racism was projected into scientific experiments and instruments. Examining how, when, and if psychologists thought about Black people in relation to their research protocols is an invocation of legal spectatorship that guides this chapter. This mode of looking for law in scientific spaces allows one to comprehend legal spectatorship as a site of control, the history of which in DV prosecution must be told through scientific knowledge production. By detailing the production of scientific knowledge about human motivation in the face of violence, I suggest how the figure of the slave endures in the scene of legal spectatorship.

In the first half of the chapter, the vestibular position of Black people to advocacy tools developed for DV surfaces through reading the prefaces written by Lenore Walker and psychologist Sylvan Tomkins for their respective books, *The Battered Woman Syndrome* and *Affect, Imagery, Consciousness*. I also read Martin Seligman's reflections in *Learned Helplessness: A Theory for the Age of Personal Control* about his research and the way it inspired Walker's study. In keeping with Spillers's theory of the vestibular position of Black people in white culture, I peruse prefaces and short comments in books, because, architecturally speaking, they are vestibular components of a monograph's overall content. As a book's circulation grows, an author may use the preface to further qualify, correct, or contextualize the stakes of the argument. While a preface affords the author with opportunities to revisit the original themes of a book, it is a portion that is often overlooked by readers and researchers, including those of Walker and Tomkins. In this chapter they are tracked for how Black people's experience of white violence are briefly alluded to as the inspiration for scientific work on human motivation and the experience of helplessness that ultimately informs the design of the Cycle and the Wheel, visual instruments used to explain the dynamics of power in DV. Together, readings of book prefaces and experimental instruments offer clues into institutional relationships between Walker, Seligman, and Tomkins. But more importantly, these relationships reveal how white psychologists projected Black experience of white violence into their experimental work on emotional response and motivation in a way that fed into the power and control script depicted in the Cycle and the Wheel. I track how Black freedom struggles are at the margins of a cybernetic theory that would inform clinical and legal pedagogical approaches to managing battered women's claims in and beyond the DV courtroom.

The second half of the chapter considers how battered woman syndrome (BWS) was incorporated into legal arguments in DV cases during the 1980s. A review of DV case law illustrates that judges reacted negatively to the scientific claims of BWS. I then return to the Cycle and the Wheel, reading them anew for how they resolve the scientific problems befalling Walker's BWS theory in the DV courtroom. Here, Paul Gilroy's idea of the "Black Atlantic" enables an overseas crossing to examine clinical studies of the psychological effects of colonialism in Africa during the 1950s.[1] I discuss Frantz Fanon's use of the Thematic Apperception Test (TAT) in ethno-psychiatric studies of the colonial mind. The TAT drawings are used in socio-therapeutic psychological encounters to test emotional responses to ambiguous situations. As Gieser and Stein remark, "The TAT had all that the Rorschach had and more. Whereas the clinician used the Rorschach data to infer personality dynamics from perception, the TAT could be used to infer personality dynamics from apperception. The Rorschach inferred psychodynamics from how the person understood and made meaningful people's motives, intentions, and expectation, in social situations."[2] Fanon's experimentation with the TAT in the contexts of decolonial African struggle and Jim Crow in the United States provides insight into how colonial subjects unsettle yet establish the techniques of Euro-Western social science.[3] Ethno-psychiatric experimentation with the TAT is helpful for thinking about how social scientific methods were brought to bear on those most affected by radical freedom struggles and the difficulty of interpreting the psychology and actions of the oppressed. In this way, the chapter charts not only the vestibularity of Black subjectivity in cybernetic research on control but also how legal spectatorship of the DV courtroom is conditioned by the absent presence of US slavery and colonial imperialism, an absent presence that manifests in the projection of colorblind fantasy in the visual culture of DV.

Battered woman syndrome has not been associated with the study of the control of autonomous systems among animals and machines. Yet, decades before visual evidence came to organize looking in the electronically networked DV courtroom, Walker's theory was an important though ignored example of feminist cybernetic theorizing. To insist on Walker's contribution to cybernetic thought amid the bevy of male techno-scientific pioneers is to stage Eve Sedgwick's concept of triangulation, where male desire (in this case for scientific knowledge) is transmitted through a woman in the development of techno-scientific theory, tools, and experimentation.[4] Her work was informed by male psychologists within the field of cybernetics research who were positing models of violence and affective response as a form of communication that operates through systematic internal and external controls.

Reading the experimental research of these psychologists should give one pause about the role of the unthought in contemporary cybernetics scholarship. Not only is Lenore Walker's BWS theory not understood as part of the cybernetics canon, but the management of abject populations has only recently been connected to the writing of computational algorithms and protocols. The cybernetics literature is replete with histories of pioneering white male scientists, philosophers, computers, and games. It is a literature whose connections to the Cold War context are often explored at the expense of drawing out earlier relationships between cybernetics, enslavement, and civil rights politics. While cybernetics has emerged as a deservedly important theory of learning and motivation in manmade machines, as Seb Franklin argues, "It is necessary to look not only at but through the specific technical objects, economic practices, industrial formations, political ideals, and organizational diagrams" to trace how the logic of control animates courtroom spectatorship.[5] Thus, my task in this chapter and throughout the remainder of the book is to center the role of enslavement as a learning event, as a digital logic of control and communication that is crucial to delimiting the structure and operations of photographic evidence of domestic abuse and the visual culture of the DV courtroom. The scientists explored in the chapter attempt to unlock the key to individual action, agency, and resilience in order to explain our collective sociopolitical condition. This milieu of social scientists responded to Jim Crow *de jure* racial segregation and subsequent civil rights struggles. From the 1960s through the 1980s scientists developed

cybernetic theories to explain how the subject learns to be helpless and enslaved. The Cycle and the Wheel embody a set of psychological conclusions
about the development of helplessness. The autonomous and discrete system
of control and communication they represent frames a new question around
the scientific findings: Why don't abused women leave?

It is difficult to imagine the legal history of DV prosecution without the
psychological research of Lenore Walker, who theorized intimate partner
violence from the perspective of women. Prior to the courtroom circulation of visual evidence of DV, psychological research on battered women
explained violence between intimate partners in systematic terms in which
power and control are exchanged in a dramatic cycle where violence pro-
gresses, appears in a crescendo and recedes, resetting the process again, like
a clock. Walker's scientific research in the field of psychology intervened in
a moment of ongoing civil rights and Cold War science about human motivation and was incorporated into the legal project of feminist jurisprudence
in cases of DV in which women killed their abusers. Walker's concept of
BWS was both a scientific finding and a legal argument about how women
respond to repeated acts of violence.

Two victim advocacy tools, the Cycle of Violence and the Power and
Control Wheel, emerged out of Walker's research on BWS. These circular
scripts are used as teaching tools in victim advocacy. Their modular and
infographic representational form also constitute a node in the emerging
visual culture of DV courtroom spectatorship of witness testimony and photographic evidence. In the Cycle and the Wheel, the intimate world of the
romantic couple is visually represented as an information processing system.
Rebecca Adelman might describe such representations as "figuring," meaning "a process of imaginative construction that dwells on the suffering of its
objects and entertains fantasies of amelioration."[6] Attending to the ways
these two representations figure positive and negative feedback between
couples is meant to focus on the tool's intention "to parse, measure, and
quantify how much particular figures are suffering."[7] These circular tools
explain how intimacy as a social good is transformed in phases into acts of
violence. They are important material culture of DV advocacy and courtroom
activity. It is difficult to imagine the absence of these circular tools from
feminist organizing around DV.

In *The Battered Woman* (1978) and *The Battered Woman Syndrome* (1984),
Walker sought to bring women's perspective into the dynamic proposed by
learned helplessness theory. Learned helplessness, which I discuss in greater
detail shortly, describes behavior exhibited by the subject of repeated adverse

stimuli outside their control. Walker's research, based on a sample of 110 middle-class Anglo-American women, emphasized duration and repetition as structuring elements in relations of domestic abuse. She tried to diagnose psychological and sociological dimensions of battered women's action in DV by collecting their autobiographical narratives in therapeutic settings. Her research and many subsequent investigations by other psychologists and sociologists tried to establish how battered women organized their discourse about their abuse. Based on battered women's discourse, three phases are thought to induce cognitive paralysis in battered women. The first phase is a period of tension building, followed by a violent event in the second phase, which results in the display of loving contrition post-violence. This third phase, commonly understood as the contrition or "honeymoon" period, circulates positive affect that both closes and restarts the cycle of violence. This pattern of tension, violence, and positive affect constitute the interaction in which women learn they have no control over the violence they experience.

Through the concept of learned helplessness Martin Seligman elaborated a theory of the response to torture.[8] In animals, the experience of torture was found to alter several cognitive capacities. Researchers encountered animal subjects whose nature had, in some cases, changed irrevocably; shifts in the cognitive abilities of the animal could be produced from the behaviorist's serial administrations of shock. The theory of learned helplessness thus explained a deeply entrenched personality change at the cognitive level that was generally observable. The formulation of learned helplessness meant to explain crucial alterations of the human condition brought about through the experience of torture. Learned helplessness explained a shift in the animal subject as a result of transfers and intensifications of affect.

The theory of learned helplessness proved to be controversial from the start, with several rebuttals published soon after Seligman's initial results in the field of psychology. None of these rebuttals, however, would be as controversial as Lenore Walker's application of learned helplessness theory to explain the passive behaviors of women who had been repeatedly beaten within marriage, an issue occupying more and more of the public culture in the United States and abroad during the 1970s. Seligman intended the theory to be applied to a variety of human populations and social circumstances. Walker adapted Seligman's research to construct a view of agency, an aspect of human capacity that persists in current debates about human and animal rights, legal culpability, and the experience of trauma and recovery among soldiers and other survivors of violent conflict and catastrophe. Walker's employment of learned helplessness theory would move away from a theory of animal learning into a gendered description of disordered sexuality and desire.

In the 2009 preface to the third edition of *The Battered Woman Syndrome*, Walker reflects on the process through which she adapted Seligman's theory of learned helplessness:

> I also demonstrated that scientific support continued to exist for the theories I proposed earlier. Learned helplessness, despite its politically incorrect name, was one of the outcomes for women who remained in battering relationships. However, subsequently, even *Martin Seligman* who named the phenomenon from his earlier experiments in the laboratory changed its name. First, learned helplessness became reversed or even prevented by learned optimism and then, it became part of the movement toward positive psychology.[9]

Shortly thereafter, in the 2009 introduction, Walker mentions Seligman's work on the theory of learned helplessness:

> In the intervening years since Seligman (1975) first formulated the theory of learned helplessness, his work has moved towards finding ways to prevent it from developing in subjects. He has concentrated his research efforts in the area of positive psychology, teaching children and adults what he has called "learned optimism" (Seligman, 1990). In this area of empirically supported interventions, Seligman and his colleagues have provided new understanding of human resilience and the ability to survive such horrible traumatic experiences as family violence, terrorism and torture, wars, and catastrophic environmental disasters such as hurricanes, floods, tsunamis and earthquakes.[10]

These passages are more provocative samples of prefatory rhetoric than they may at first appear. Seligman initially disagreed with Walker's adoption of his theory to the experiences of abused women. Contra Walker, Seligman argued that learned helplessness applied very well to the predicament of Black folk in the United States. He emphasized the plight of Black people for economic reproductive freedom. His theory addressed the experiences of white America through the experiences of Black folks. The theory of learned helplessness, borne out of the animal laboratory, recalled dreams of Black freedom from white violence that were unsettled during the nineteenth century.

Walker's application of the theory of learned helplessness to battered women was, according to Seligman, a "middling example" of the particular display of "inappropriate passivity" experienced "in the wake of uncontrollable events," which are "mediated by particular cognitions acquired during exposure to uncontrollable events and inappropriately generalized to new situations."[11] At the time, abused women did not demonstrate the kind of learned helplessness exhibited according to the factors isolated in the animals in the laboratory. Seligman imagined Black people to guide his study of passive subjectivity within the social sciences, whereas Walker's initial study of battered women excluded Black participants.

Thirty years later, Walker's introductory comments to the new edition of *The Battered Woman Syndrome* do not recall Seligman's initial dissent thirty years prior. Instead, as she details the "intervening years" comprising Seligman's influential research program in positive psychology, a sanguine tenor is created in which learned helplessness and optimist psychology are ultimately arranged into a holistic spectrum that clarifies helpless victim-resilient and nonvictim positions. Seligman's and Walker's respective research trajectories appear to coincide without debate. Seligman's subsequent work on learned optimism appears as a preventative against learned helplessness. Walker argues that steeling the self against helplessness illustrates the unified goal of learned helplessness and BWS. The Blackness of learned helplessness disappears from the prefatory remarks entirely.

CREATING THE CYCLE OF VIOLENCE AND
THE POWER AND CONTROL WHEEL

In 1984, ten years prior to President Bill Clinton's signing of the Violence Against Women Act (VAWA) into law, the Domestic Abuse Intervention Programs in Duluth, Michigan, created the first visual representation of the theories of Lenore Walker. The Cycle of Violence is a circle divided into three parts with a smaller circle in the center (see figure 2.1). The inner circle is labeled "denial." The outer three sections, "tension building," "acute explosion," and "honeymoon" turn around a core of denial. The Power and Control Wheel (figure 2.2) shares the basic circle-inside-a circle design of the Cycle. However, the Wheel adds layers of complexity to the escalation and eventual reset of violence: an outer circle is labeled "physical and sexual violence." An inner circle is labeled "power and control" and is broken into spokes creating eight sections labeled "using coercion and threats," using intimidation," "using emotional abuse," "using isolation," "minimizing, denying and blaming," "using children," "using male privilege," and "using economic abuse." The sections turn around a core of "power and control." The differences

FIGURE 2.1 The Cycle of Violence (the Duluth model).

between the Cycle and the Wheel reflect the significance of Walker's theory of bws for thinking about the mechanisms of violence. As psychologists and anti–DV advocates progress from the Cycle to the Wheel, increments of time are divided into more and more discrete and subtle behaviors. The emphasis shifts from the Cycle, which focuses on the timed reset of violence, to the Wheel, which homes in on multiple forms of manipulation at play in the operation of violence. Though both graphics employ cybernetic circles to represent violence as a system, they make different arguments about the nature of DV. Both models are used widely in the training of law professionals and advocates for victims and survivors of DV. Neither model competitively supplants the other. Both dominate the visual representations

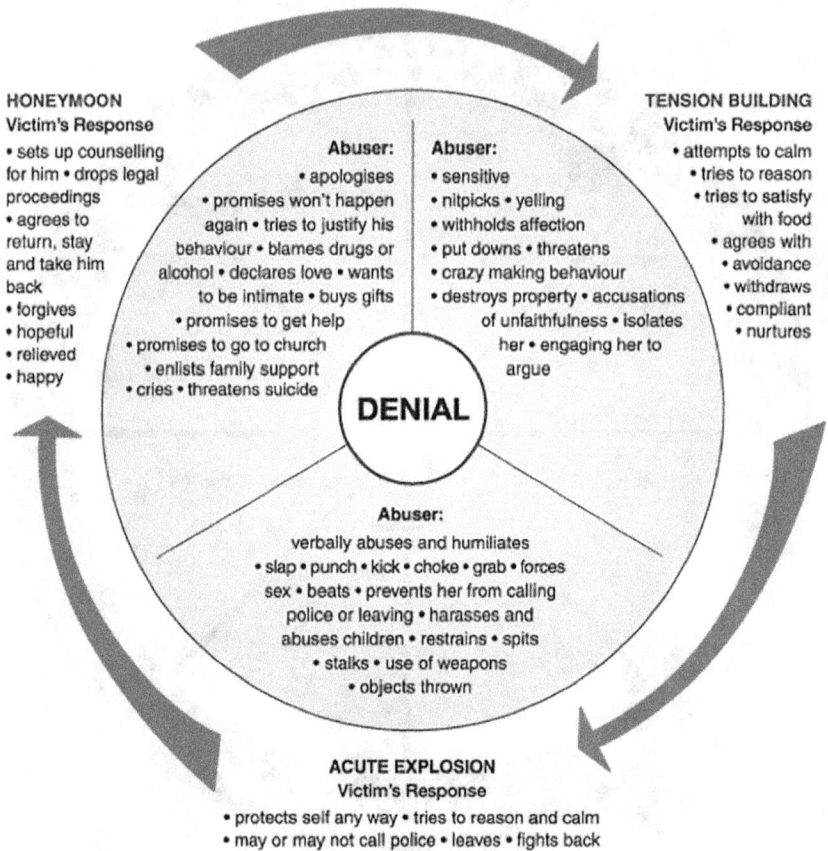

The wheel diagram contains:

HONEYMOON
Victim's Response
• sets up counselling for him • drops legal proceedings • agrees to return, stay and take him back • forgives • hopeful • relieved • happy

TENSION BUILDING
Victim's Response
• attempts to calm • tries to reason • tries to satisfy with food • agrees with • avoidance • withdraws • compliant • nurtures

Abuser:
• apologises • promises won't happen again • tries to justify his behaviour • blames drugs or alcohol • declares love • wants to be intimate • buys gifts • promises to get help • promises to go to church • enlists family support • cries • threatens suicide

Abuser:
• sensitive • nitpicks • yelling • withholds affection • put downs • threatens • crazy making behaviour • destroys property • accusations of unfaithfulness • isolates her • engaging her to argue

DENIAL

Abuser:
verbally abuses and humiliates • slap • punch • kick • choke • grab • forces sex • beats • prevents her from calling police or leaving • harasses and abuses children • restrains • spits • stalks • use of weapons • objects thrown

ACUTE EXPLOSION
Victim's Response
• protects self any way • tries to reason and calm
• may or may not call police • leaves • fights back

FIGURE 2.2 The Power and Control Wheel (the Duluth model).

that bring Walker's theories to life through projection in DV prevention and prosecution training.

SILVAN TOMKINS AND THE MILIEU OF EXPERIMENTAL PSYCHOLOGY

One also has to look to the preface, a vestibular site within Tomkins's larger text, to draw out the Black power and feminist struggles nestled in the cybernetic fold of Tomkins's cybernetic scripts. Tomkins's theory positions affect and feeling as the very substance, the precise content, of human consciousness.[12] The concept of feedback that figures so prominently in Tomkins's presentation of the affect scripts as intersubjective derives in part from nuclear scenes in which Tomkins was a locus between his parents.[13] The rendering of nuclear scenes and scripts is no mere rehearsal of the Freudian Oedipal complex. Rather, scripting affect occurs through repetitive inter-subjective interactions imbued with *degrees of freedom* and are therefore not determined through the un-free Freudian drives. Features of the nuclear script that enable degrees of freedom to emerge as a principle include sets of ordering rules, selectivity, sets of incomplete rules, continual reordering of rules, scripts within scripts, scripts that self-validate more than self-fulfill, auxiliary augmentation of scripts through media, alternative variables, modularity, and partition of scripts.

The emphasis on feedback and degrees of freedom on the writing, or scripting, of affect locates Tomkins's thought within cybernetics. Placing Tomkins's theory and method within the cybernetic fold is a theoretical maneuver embodied in the Cycle and the Wheel. It is a move recalled in a feature of Tomkins's writing: his employment of lists to represent the intersubjective flow of affect. It is worth quoting an example of one of his lists at length:

> If you like to be looked at and I like to look at you, we may achieve an enjoyable interpersonal relationship. If you like to talk and I like to listen to you talk, this can be mutually regarding. If you like to feel enclosed within a claustrum and I like to put my arms around you, we can both enjoy a particular kind of embrace. If you like to be supported and I like to hold you, we can enjoy such an embrace. If you like to be kissed and I like to kiss you, we may enjoy each other. If you like to be sucked or bitten and I like to suck or bite you, we may enjoy each other. If you like to have your skin rubbed and I like to do this to you, we can enjoy each other. If you enjoy being hugged and I like hugging you, it can be mutually enjoyable. If you enjoy being dominated and I enjoy controlling you, we may enjoy each other. If you enjoy communicating your experiences and ideas and aspirations and I enjoy being informed about the experiences, ideas and aspirations of others, we can enjoy each other. If you enjoy telling me about the past and I enjoy hearing about the past, we may enjoy each other. If you enjoy speculating about and predicting the future and I enjoy being so informed, we can enjoy each other. If you wish to be like me and I wish to have you imitate me, we can enjoy each other.[14]

However:

> If you enjoy talking and being listened to and I enjoy talking and being listened to, then we may be incapable of achieving a rewarding interpersonal

relationship. If your social needs require that you be looked at, and for me to enjoy another person I require that he look at me with love and respect, then we may frustrate each other. If you wish to cling, be held and supported, and I wish to cling, be held and supported, it may not be possible to satisfy each other. If you wish to be praised and I wish to be praised, we may not be able to praise each other enough to enjoy each other. If you wish to be instructed and controlled and I wish to be instructed and controlled, we may frustrate each other. If you need a model or identification figure to enjoy personal interaction, we may not be able to satisfy each other and therefore not enjoy each other.[15]

Yet, a turn to Tomkins's prefatory remarks in *Affect, Imagery, Consciousness* would suggest another imaginary being marked by Tomkins's listing technique, one that does not continue to emphasize the computer but rather a different object of the episteme of control:

> To Charles Sellars, Fellow at the Center, I am indebted for the exposure to his volume *The Southerner as American*, which made me aware for the first time of the tragic conflict within the heart of the southern American. Long conversations with Sellars taught me that many of the endopsychic problems encountered in the consulting room were not as different as I supposed when writ large in historical settings. The problems with which the historian is confronted are not as distinct from the problems which confront the personality theorist as historians and psychologists have come to believe.[16]

Here, the psychologist of affect and motivation also links the development of internal mental processes to larger historical situations. He moves from the individual to civil society, suggesting the disciplines of history and psychology confront the same problems in the people and activities they study. *The Southerner as American* is the only title mentioned by name in the preface. Although the acknowledgment is brief, Tomkins suddenly breaks from the traditional rhetorical pattern of thanking colleagues and collaborators to say something more substantive about the history of racial animus in the United States and its connection to endopsychic (unconscious) mental formations.

The Cycle and the Wheel help recall the flow captured by Tomkins's cybernetic lists. Tomkins kept the responses of pairs in view: "*If you like* to be looked at *and I like* to look at you, *we may achieve* an enjoyable interpersonal relationship," and alternatively, "*If you wish* to cling, be held and supported, *and I wish* to cling, be held and supported, *it may not be possible* to satisfy each other." In doing so, he abided by the intersubjective ethos—between humans and nonhuman objects—that advanced the science of cybernetics. Like Tomkins's lists, the Wheel and the Cycle apprehend the circular movement, the round rhythm and rotation of the feedback loop.

Yet, while both DV curricular tools utilize the cybernetic feedback loop, they do not abide by Tomkins's concern with intersubjectivity. Both models visualize the behaviors of abusers, not the abused. Legal scholar Jane Stoever argues, "While these two models might help people understand the abuser's wrongful actions, they fail to describe what the abused individual does in response to the violence. They do not convey the survivor's process for ending the relationship or the violence in the relationship, nor do they illustrate the survivor's needs or the many actions the survivor takes to live through the violence."[17] Stoever's analysis is based in ethnographic work in clinics where law students are trained in DV relationships using curricular tools such as the Cycle and the Wheel. We can see how psychologists and advocates respond to the flaw common to the Cycle and the Wheel in how contemporary versions of the graphic tools now add narrative about victim responses outside and inside the cybernetic circles that previously focused on the actions of abusers. The icon is not enough. Narrative complexity asserts its place.

Unfortunately, the flaw of over-representing abuser behavior is not the only problem to befall the Cycle and the Wheel. Again, I turn to Stoever's ethnographic work with these two important instruments of DV curricula. Stoever writes, "[The Cycle and the Wheel] illustrate the dynamics of DV and purport to explain the battering experience but do not describe the survivor's experience of living in a violent relationship or what he or she does in response to the violence."[18] Even as both the Wheel and the Cycle visualize the control and the expression of violence and its timed reset, they do not account for environment, nor the settler slave regime that constitutes the political history of US economic reproduction. This flaw embedded in the design of these curricular tools is a primary reason the concept of legal spectatorship achieves presence to mark the foreclosure of colorblind fantasy in law and social service advocacy. In chapter 3 I discuss the contemporary courtroom as a space of public abandonment. In an era of decreasing trials, courtroom audiences need more context than ever for the legal decisions with which they are tasked. The archive of slavery and settler colonialism is a crucial aspect of this context that is missing from courtroom cognitive-affective activity through which audiences project themselves into the lives and experiences of others. In other words, it is not only the experiences of victims and law and advocacy professionals that are left out of the reception of curricular instruments, but also those of courtroom audiences. I showed in chapter 1 that the slave in the United States is at the forefront of debates on the meaning of federal power and the capacity to act and contract. The slave's peculiar status—legally refused kinship through *partus sequitur ventrem* and legally restrained from freedom through capture and brutal physical violence—is the actual stuff of DV left unrepresented in the Cycle of Violence and Power and Control Wheel. These curricular instruments that organize the education of law and support services professionals erase the figure of the slave and the idea of freedom from the analysis of the very power and control the instruments are trying to visually represent. The courtroom audience, whose own peculiar status is given by its separation into economically enfranchised juries and disenfranchised members seated in the courtroom pews, is also unacknowledged in the important curricular moment when the Cycle and Wheel tools are presented in DV trials. These tools negate the history of both settler colonialism upon indigenous land and life ways and Black enslavement upon contemporary DV prosecution. In other words, the Cycle and the Wheel "present a drive toward colorblindness" and universalism that beg the question of why Blackness and colonial imperialism must be excised from propaedeutics in DV advocacy.[19]

Returning to Tomkins preface citation, *The Southerner as American* reached back to the history of slavery in the South, offering analyses of the affective life of the Southern type. Published in 1960, the book was an intervention into mounting civil rights struggles during the Cold War. Blackness returns in the volume on negative affects when Tomkins discusses the negotiation of "objects of distress." In the shame-humiliation and contempt-disgust section of *Affect, Imagery, Consciousness*, Tomkins discusses the vicarious experience of affect. Again, the Southern Negro is at the core of a geometric flow of affect:

> Another form is the vicarious shame at the shame of another, which is generated by the other's affect inhibition. *If he is angry towards me or anyone else and must swallow his anger and this generates shame in him, as in the case of a Southern Negro confronted by a Southern White, then I may feel vicarious shame for him.* Similarly, if my child feels forced to inhibit the expression of negative affect toward me, and he further feels shame because of this, I can experience vicarious shame. I can also feel vicarious shame at

affect inhibition whether or not the other feels ashamed of this. Thus, a Southern Negro may suffer severe inhibition of his anger but be relatively unaware of this and feel no shame about it, and yet I may feel vicarious shame just because he is under such restraint that he is relatively unconscious of the degree of his defense against the display of anger.[20]

Further,

> *I may experience vicarious shame if someone controls another individual through the self-conscious use of bi-polar affect.* If a friend of mine is encouraged by someone to become more and more intimate and then is shamed by indifference or withdrawal, and then seduced again and shamed again and this cycle repeated continually, I too may be shamed by my friend's shame or by his vulnerability.[21]

Here, the Southern Negro is again imbricated in Tomkins' cybernetic script. If cybernetics provides historical grounding to the episteme of control, then so, too, do the processes of enslavement and Blackness as global abjection. Tomkins does not, or perhaps cannot, conceive of the interactions that emerge as affect, as consciousness, as imagery without the experiences of Black folks. In this passage, writing the shame of the Southern Negro flows immediately into what could be a model of battered woman's symptomatic behavior. The "bi-polar affect" involves a feedback loop of control that coincides with the cycle of violence developed by Walker. The mechanics of the affective script are explained through Black and white social relations that always already entail violence. Tomkins's affective scripts have political significance; they should not be understood as writerly idiosyncrasy, and they should certainly not be overlooked. The description of the current episteme of control is inseparable from the appearance of the Negro in the preface of *Affect, Imagery, Consciousness* to the affective scripts listed throughout the book.[22]

Walker's evacuation of Black and Native women's experience from the formulation of BWS illustrates how white feminist priorities organized BWS as a universal women's experience. Though Walker's thinking did not incorporate the colonial-imperial history of racial or ethnic difference-making, her theory nonetheless offered a powerful intervention into the emerging caseload of DV prosecution, to say nothing of *inscribing an explicitly feminist purpose for cybernetic theory*. In the next part of the chapter I consider how BWS was incorporated into US courts, including a discussion of its dismissal from the courts as an accepted theory of behavior and trauma theory.

In the 1980s, learned helplessness migrated from the animal behavior laboratory, transforming into BWS in the context of Walker's psychotherapeutic
milieu, and finally moving into the domestic abuse courtroom. The scientific
and jurisprudential itinerary of Walker's theory of control encompasses
three interpenetrating discourses: social science, law, and cybernetics.[23]
Translating BWS across institutional domains of knowledge occasioned significant controversy over the communicative capacities of victims of trauma
in which the claims of BWS were spurned as pseudoscience. A review of case
law of early domestic abuse trials of the period illustrates how the complex
identities of battered women were rendered as scientific claims. While these
early cases affirmed BWS as a theory of trauma, its claims about women's
action in the face of repeated abuse were at odds with jurisprudential standards for incorporating novel scientific innovations.

Each migration of BWS, from animal experiments, to therapeutic settings, to courtrooms, offered a semiosis of the complex agency of abused
women. In clinical and legal settings, researchers found that battered women
displayed complex agency, which in turn led to both feminist and nonfemi-
nist critiques of Walker's research that had read battered women's behavior
as mental illness. The aggressive behaviors of women who killed their batterers, for example, contradicted the theory of battered women's learned
helplessness. Several studies subsequent to Walker's found that battered
women did many things to end or control when and where violence occurred, challenging the cycle of violence and learned helplessness theories.[24]
Resourcefulness demonstrated by many women was found to be inconsis-
tent with the passivity associated with BWS.[25]

As a legal defense, BWS was also found to have racial, class, and heterosexual biases.[26] Arguing against Walker's data, Carrie Baker writes: "The
battered woman syndrome does not 'work' for poor and minority women
because the standard is based on the experiences of white, middle-class
women."[27] Critiques of the BWS model contest it on the basis of the embodied performances of battered women in addition to the durational aspects
of the abuse they endure. These studies pondered the question of what kind
of body could interpret BWS. In doing so, they established that the theory
inventoried its various meanings through therapeutic and legal encounters
with battered women where narratives of race, class, and sexuality circulate. Donavan and Wildman discuss how court testimony on BWS inevita-
bly leads to a distinction between reasonable, "good" and "normal" victims

of abuse and others—a model that has in effect resulted in discrimination against battered women who are lesbian and/or of color, identity groups traditionally excluded from conceptions of which subjects may embody reason.[28] Elizabeth Bochnak analyzes domestic abuse court cases and finds that in predominantly white juries, women of color often do not fit the category of passive victim captured by the BWS model.[29] In response, Sharon Allard calls for more work that considers the intersectionality of race, class, and sexuality in investigating the dynamics of domestic abuse and its constituent diagnoses.[30] Still others, such as Posch and Johann and Osanka, argue that BWS pathologizes women; they advocate that interpretations of battered women's behavior in court focus instead on how the structure of gender inequality informs women's behavior, whether it is apparently passive or aggressive.[31] These studies focus on the role that practices of looking play within networked institutional settings: courtrooms, battered women's shelters, police stations, hospitals, and home. They question the emphasis placed on battered women's psyches relative to the politics shaping their environment.

The discourse organized battered women's court testimony against their batterers. It was also deployed as a legal defense for women who killed their abusers. Thus, the use of the BWS defense has contributed to a deep ambivalence concerning the behaviors and subject positions of battered women. As a descriptive term, BWS captured the psychological paralysis discussed in Seligman's theory and Walker's subsequent application of that theory. However, when deployed as a legal defense for abused women who killed their abusive partners, the discourse collided with a tradition of American law that reads the act of murder as an expression of agency, albeit of the worse kind. As research on the syndrome found that battered women often attempted to direct the course of anticipated violent conflict through a variety of planned acts and ruses, the defense strategy founded on BWS became difficult to support. The large number of women incarcerated for murdering battering husbands and the attendant clemency movement and activism on behalf of these women—a significant number of whom are on death row or serving life sentences without parole—is a testament to the ambivalent efficacy and logic of BWS as a legal defense.[32] As evinced by feminist collectives such as INCITE! and Survived and Punished, contemporary queer woman of color–led activism radically works toward decarceration. A look at their organizing materials emphasizes extralegal testimony about their experience. There are few, if any, Cycles and Wheels explaining the various actions of DV victim in terms of social science. There is a refusal of the very mastery of social science that informed Walker's feminist theorization of BWS that I discuss in the following chapters.

Some legal scholars have nevertheless written against BWS as a legal defense, calling into question the science of the BWS in its entirety. They turn to well-developed case law in which the proper methods and standards for assessing evidentiary admissibility are traced. These legal scholars specifically contested the research methodology behind survivor theory II, an adapted theory combining the inactivity from the victim's learned helplessness with her activity in the face of failure of her partner and of meaningful assistance from society. Scholars argued that the theory's continued use in the courts would lead to the erosion of standards of evidence in self-defense legal strategy.[33] This scholarship also targeted the role of expert testimony in the science informing BWS to support their critique. In 1986, David Faigman addressed the question of the validity of expert testimony on BWS by arguing that the weakness of the scientific methodology behind the disorder endangered the doctrine of self-defense in American courts.[34] Four elements comprise the doctrine of self-defense in the United States: the defendant must believe themselves to be in imminent physical danger; the defendant must use only reasonable counterforce against the threat; the defendant must not be the aggressor of the violence; and the defendant must have experienced circumstances that afforded no opportunity for escape. Faigman cited case law in which American courts struggled over the admissibility of expert testimony.

The legal history of testimony on BWS is currently organized largely by the *Daubert* test and, previously, with respect to the findings in the 1923 case of *Frye v. United States*.[35] *Frye* involved the admissibility of evidence from a systolic blood pressure deception test—a precursor to polygraph technology—given to a defendant standing trial for murder. The court ruled that the deception test was inadmissible because the technology was not "generally accepted" within the scientific community, thus creating the *Frye* rule. Congress adopted the Federal Rules of Evidence in 1975, leading to a question as to whether the Federal Rules invalidated the standard of expert testimony using novel scientific evidence set by *Frye*. In 1993, in *Daubert*, the Supreme Court reached a landmark decision regarding the relationship between science and law. *Daubert v. Merrill Dow Pharmaceuticals* was a case in which the Supreme Court resolved the question about the Federal Rules and testimonial standards. The case involved the role of the drug Bendectin in causing a birth defect in two boys, Jason Daubert and Eric Schuller. The defendant, Merrill Dow, presented published evidence that its drug did not cause birth defects, while Daubert and Schuller presented evidence of their own that suggested it did. Daubert and Schuller's research was based on reanalysis of Merrill Dow's published findings and new in vitro and in vivo research on animals—experiments of destruction. The court concluded that the methodologies used by Daubert and Schuller to produce evidence was not "generally accepted" by the scientific community. Plaintiffs petitioned the court, arguing that the Federal Rules of Evidence took precedence over the *Frye* standard. The Supreme Court agreed but endowed judges, not juries, with the responsibility to ascertain the general acceptability of new scientific evidence. By superseding *Frye*, the *Daubert* standard assigned trial judges to a "gatekeeper" role on decisions about scientific evidence and its proper expression through expert testimony. Judges establish the admissibility of scientific evidence, as communicated through expert testimony, according to their interpretation of the relevance and reliability of the evidence to the case at hand; how well "scientific knowledge" derives from its "scientific methodology"; and the validity of scientific method demonstrated via multiple streams of empirical testing and publication within the relevant scientific community. Judges must themselves be convinced of the scientific evidence before them. "They cannot, as was the practice under Frye, defer to the 'pertinent field.'"[36]

Being convinced of the inadmissibility of such evidence empowers judges to exclude it form the jury's view based on "bad science." By placing the responsibility of excluding invalid science from jury consideration on judges, the *Daubert* court risked burdening judges with the responsibility of becoming expert scientists in addition to their role as legal experts. For this reason, the court established guidelines for judges to use to quickly assess the validity of scientific methodology informing BWS, ultimately finding it did not match any of the standards established in the guidelines: the syndrome has not withstood sufficient empirical testing; the syndrome is not sufficiently falsifiable and therefore is not reflected in acceptable error rates; most research on BWS is published in the popular press and not peer-reviewed journals; only a comparatively small community of clinicians constitute the "pertinent field" of scientific research animating BWS in court.

Four cases challenged the validity of expert testimony on BWS in terms of the scientific soundness of its methodology under the *Frye* rule. Walker's credibility as an expert witness was discredited through these cases. In 1979, *Ibn-Tamas v. United States* introduced BWS as a self-defense strategy; it stated that, with respect to the admissibility criterion regarding scientific methodology, "satisfaction of the criterion begins—and ends—with a determination of whether there is a general acceptance of a particular methodology, not an acceptance, beyond that, of particular study results based on that methodology."[37] Related to *Ibn-Tamas v. United States*, the court in 1983 asserted its authority to judge the scientific research methodology informing the BWS discourse. The court required the methodology to conform to the research standards of the legal community. In a second case, the 1984 *State v. Martin*, Walker intended to provide expert testimony on BWS for a wife, Helen Martin, who had hired someone to murder her husband. Martin was convicted of murder. Martin appealed her conviction on the grounds that the trial court refused to enter evidence that she suffered BWS and that her actions were committed in self-defense. This evidence relied on Walker's theory to retain the significance that the defense intended, even though Walker had not testified in this particular case. Faigman argues that Walker's willingness to testify as an expert witness in a case such as *Martin* discredited her expertise in the science of BWS. Not only was there a preponderance of evidence against Helen Martin—including her confession—but the temporal aspect of the "cycle of violence" component was unspecified by the science of BWS, leaving Walker's method an insufficient one on which to build a defense.[38]

Faigman's criticism of Walker concluded that in *State v. Martin*, the psychologist was too sympathetic to battered women; although Walker never testified in the case, the fact that she intended to suggests that she misjudged her role as an objective expert witness by taking on an advocacy role on behalf of the wife-defendant.[39] Turning to scientific methodological concerns, Faigman discussed the requirements for admitting novel scientific evidence into court, ultimately reading BWS as an example of novel scientific evidence. The 1985 finding in *State v. Hawthorne*, a third case, offered a more rigorous standard of admission of BWS as novel scientific evidence. This case found that methodology *and* the results of the scientific inquiry emerging from said methodology must be validated by the court according to a demonstrable depth of the field of scientific knowledge of BWS.[40]

Faigman's and Wright's work on the collision between BWS–based defense strategies and the *Daubert* standard continues to be instructive on the issue of the current status of the complex agency of battered women.[41] Faigman and Wright argued in 1997 that we should anticipate the waning of BWS in cases where it is employed as a self-defense strategy for battered women who kill. This is because the syndrome was endorsed by the politics that sought to advance the social conditions of battered women and the matter of their agency, rather than the scientific validation of its model or method of analysis. The battered women's movement brought DV into the purview of American courts, drawing attention to how common domestic abuse is to American culture and organizing resources and theory to eradicate the problem. Faigman and Wright acknowledge these facts. At issue in their analysis, however, is the potential threat posed to the *Daubert* precedent of establishing the use of a particular interpretation of what counts as scientific to measure methods of evidence interpretation. By extension, at issue as well is the fate of justice in the balance struck between law and science. Changing the admissibility of the methodological approaches behind BWS hinged on a delinking of women's agency and science. Domestic violence trials have unique discursive patterns and scripts that I discuss in chapter 3. Ethnographic observations of several DV trials do suggest that Faigman's and Wright's predictions that BWS is on the wane are bearing out. Many moments emerge during the DV trial in which attorneys speak in ways that are designed to qualify aspects of witness testimony to juries. Prosecuting attorneys in particular are often motivated to explain to juries why key witnesses to DV—usually the battered woman and her children—recant their testimony while on the witness stand. The pattern of prosecutorial testimony also includes expert witness testimony to the psychological effects of domestic abuse. Ethnographic observations informing this book demonstrate that prosecuting attorneys do not utter the phrase "battered woman syndrome." The pattern of expert witness testimony appears to have similarly evacuated BWS terminology from its testimonial script.

The discursive waning of BWS predicted by Faigman and Wright refers us back to the path taken by Lenore Walker in formulating women's affective responses to abuse. Lisa Cartwright argues that the idea of destruction clarifies a key distinction between experiments and observation.[42] Experiments support their hypotheses through the destruction of or interference in the inner life and being of experimental objects and subjects in ways simple observation does not. This distinction lies at the heart of scientific approaches to the study of affect and motivation in the animal behavior laboratory. Learned helplessness theory emerged from the experiment of destruction in which dogs were repeatedly electrocuted.[43] The loss of instinctual will that defines learned helplessness was produced not through observation of natural phenomena but rather through its disruption and suppression. The laboratory dog emerged as the "source of life" whose traumatic response was grafted onto the battered woman.[44] Walker's application of learned helplessness theory to battered women is thus an important example of a feminist mobilization of the master discourse of science to speak on behalf of women. The result was an equation between science, the experiment, and masculinity on the one hand, and clinical specialization, observation, and femininity on the other. Ultimately for these legal scholars, the danger the scientific discourse of BWS poses to the *Daubert* standard concerns the distinction between "science" and "specialty." Battered woman syndrome is a clinical specialty, and its experts were specialists, not scientists. By Walker's own admission in another case where she gave expert testimony, research on BWS was in its infancy.[45] Thus, Judge Gallagher, in his 1983 decision in *Ibn-Tamas*, pointed out, "*Frye* requires the profferor of the expert on a new scientific theory to show that the evidence is not still in the experimental stage but has gained a scientific acceptance substantial enough to warrant an exercise of judicial discretion in favor of admissibility."[46] The difficulties of empirically testing and falsifying BWS make lowering the evidentiary standard especially tempting considering the hardships faced by battered women as a group. Yet the *Daubert* standard, critics contend, refers to generally accepted and testable *science* and not clinical specialties. Faigman and Wright argue that the narrow field of research and lack of formal training in scientific research methods has destabilized BWS on a micro level and illustrates a problem with the law's incorporation and use of scientific evidence at a macro level. In other words, law may incorporate only scientific findings that are informed by the violent penetration of the experimental object of subject, not the mere observation of the same. Yet, the subtlety Cartwright makes clear is that the scientist's experiment of destruction is indelibly linked to the courtroom observer who may vicariously exert "control over a living being's life and death."[47] We see the degree to which the "arrangement" of the living being who testifies is "regulated and disciplined by the experimental apparatus."[48] So, while law may attach observation to a distance between scientist and scientific objects in a way that assumes a lack of scientific rigor, observation is an activity beset with its own vicarious experience of terror.

As BWS has waned, post-traumatic stress disorder (PTSD) has gained ground. The place of BWS is no more stable within the discourse of mental health disorders—an area of medical science and clinical practice. The vexed incorporation of BWS into the *Diagnostic and Statistical Manual of Mental Disorders* (DSM) demonstrates the contradictory negotiations of battered women's complex agency. Battered woman syndrome continues to inform jury understandings of women who kill their batterers as well as women who exhibit more passive behaviors. As a result, advocates of its inclusion in the DSM have had a difficult time achieving its designation as a mental health disorder. Battered woman syndrome has in fact gained partial inclusion, as a subcategory of the rigidly defined PTSD in the DSM-V:

> Traumatic events that are experienced directly include, but are not limited to, exposure to war as a combatant or civilian, threatened or actual violent personal assault (e.g., sexual violence, physical attack, active combat, mugging, childhood physical and/or sexual violence, being kidnapped, being taken hostage, terrorist attack, torture), natural or humanmade disasters (e.g., earthquake, hurricane, airplane crash), and severe accident (e.g., severe motor vehicle, industrial accident).[49]

Currently, BWS does and does not exist within the PTSD diagnosis. Violent personal assault, including sexual assault and physical attack, do archive DV; however, the diagnostic criterion assumes none of the gendered behavioral specifications proposed by BWS.

We cannot help but notice the stable scientific ground upon which the PTSD diagnosis stands. Where BWS is on the wane as a scientific research program and legal argument, research on PTSD has flourished in the aftermath and ongoing retreat from both Iraq Wars and the war on the Taliban in Afghanistan. Post-traumatic stress disorder has emerged as a much more viable research tool than BWS; interestingly the PTSD model benefits from experimental and observational research approaches. Battered woman syndrome is merely incorporated within the firm and heavily funded experimental research program of PTSD that has centered on the body of the American soldier coming home from war. In this sense, the PTSD diagnosis is a masculine disorder category that ironically entered the public discourse in part through domestic abuse phenomena between traumatized soldiers and their wives. A clear displacement has occurred here from dog electrocution to the US soldier in which battered women have become the absent subject of the PTSD diagnosis. This becomes painfully ironic in light of the prevalence of spousal abuse among veterans.

Arguments against BWS come from advocates for battered women working from a theory of intersectionality of race, class, gender, and sexuality as well as from legal scholars who are more explicitly concerned with law's incorporation and use of science. Battered woman syndrome has proven to be unsatisfactory for both women's advocates and those directly concerned to protect the evidentiary standard established by *Daubert*.[50]

Given the legal and scientific arguments that spurned BWS from the courts, how might one explain the continued cultural presence and relevance of BWS discourse? Domestic violence victim advocates transformed Walker's theory into the Cycle of Violence and the Power and Control Wheel. As cybernetic icons, the Cycle and the Wheel work to control the unreliable science of BWS. They perform the work of control in DV advocacy, the DV courtroom, and extralegal settings where gender and sexual violence are discussed. Both infographics are pictorial representations of a nuclear script. Through words written in and around a circle, the Cycle and the Wheel perform what Tomkins's cybernetic scripts perform through a series of lists. But further Black feminist sense of the Cycle and the Wheel can be made. In "'Theorizing in a Void': Sublimity, Matter, and Physics in Black Feminist Poetics," Zakiyyah Iman Jackson considers how motifs of chaos theory and physics are deployed in Black gender and feminist theory.[51] Jackson seeks to intervene in the problem of representation plaguing Black gender and feminist materialisms. The poetic gesture of Black feminisms often addresses how antiblackness represents Black femininity and maternity as simultaneously hypo- and hyper-positioned: Black women are asexual Mammies or hypersexual Jezebels; we are both subject to under-reproductive, at-risk birth statistics while also maligned for possessing hyper-fertile wombs. Black women are at the center of cybernetic theories of control at the same time that we are erased from its intellectual history. Amid these extremes, Jackson argues that Black feminism's preoccupation with representation is "not due to a naïve fidelity to representationalism but rather to a sense of urgency regarding how representation performs in discursive-material terrains of antiblackness and empire."[52] For Jackson, metaphors of chaos and physics, where Black women are positioned as vestibular,[53] intersectional,[54] absent-present,[55] "thought and unthought,"[56] and "black holes,"[57] associate both Black matter and the Black *mater* with the sublime. Likewise, the Cycle, and the Wheel, and Walker's theory of control to which they give shape, are produced out of a void in which Black femininity functions as an "invisible companion" to the pedagogy of DV.[58]

Both nuclear scripts offer a program for action in abusive relationships in which all actions oscillate around a center. In the Wheel there is power and control. In the Cycle there is denial. While these (w)holes constitute a void to be theorized, nuclear scripts of DV are beyond measurement. The many programmatic actions comprising BWS that victims may exhibit are deemed unreliable by science and law. As the Cycle and the Wheel give shape to, or visually represent, BWS they might appear to inherit the inability to reliably delineate the contours of Walker's theory. They may also inherit the absent-presence of Black women from Walker's theory. Part of how we might make sense of the Cycle and Wheel in the aftermath of the rebuke of BWS by law is through a reading of these icons that is informed by scholarship on the racial icon.

Nicole Fleetwood's account of the racial icon illustrates how Black activists have "used images as a weapon to fight racial oppression," as seen in the circulation of a hoodie-clad Trayvon Martin's selfie in Black Lives Matter activism and the gruesome open casket image of Emmett Till.[59] In both examples images of Black boys murdered in the heat of mythical narratives of Black male criminality are reproduced to "enact a mode of racial belonging and collective mourning."[60] In the case of Trayvon Martin's selfie, its iconic function has materialized into sartorial performances where activists for a variety of associated causes—anti–gun violence, Black Lives Matter, anti–police brutality—don the hoodie to incorporate the dead child into our own narratives of kinship marked by vulnerability and morbidity. If, as Fleetwood avers, racial icons make us want to *do* something, then I pull her concept into discussion of the problem of the Black maternal sublime function that Jackson highlights as a preoccupation of Black feminist theories of visual culture. With Jackson's emphasis on the "burdened sublimity of the black *mater*(nal)," or nonrepresentability in discourse, I expand Fleetwood's notion of the racial icon to theorize the Cycle and Wheel as icons, including the theory of control they embody for Black gender and feminist purposes.[61] Black women's chaotic absent-presence occurs across the cybernetic theories of human motivation and control of Seligman, Walker, and Tomkins.[62] As *mater* and matter, Black women are equally vestibular to the Cycle and Wheel icons. Although in Fleetwood's study the racial icon pertains exclusively to images of Black folks circulating in public discourse, taking seriously the Black maternal sublime function in and as theory would suggest the relevance of such a reading practice for the Cycle and Wheel. Racial violence is DV. Domestic violence is racial. Blackness resides in the iconicity of visual DV advocacy tools.

Fleetwood's study of the iconography of Trayvon Martin ends by pointing out how Martin's murder by George Zimmerman reopened the "stand your ground" legal debate. She briefly considers the hyper-presence of Martin's iconic hooded selfie with the absence of any imagery of Marissa Alexander, a Black woman who fired upon her abusive husband in Florida.

Alexander's case was taken up to critique the disparities between Black and white criminal conviction and sentencing as well as the variety of barriers, legal and social, facing women who, violently and nonviolently. attempt to end their abuse. The difficulty in garnering a robust response to Alexander and women in similar situations raises the question of the sympathetic victim. The sympathetic victim emerges as an object of activism, advocacy, and courtroom justice through curated looks and techniques of the racial icon. The Cycle and the Wheel are formidable tools that function in techniques of control and human motivation. Reading them as racial icons involves Black feminist sense-making of their formal structure and their contribution to communicative interaction.

The Cycle and Wheel eschew facial expression. They spell out dramatic scenarios that cyclically lead to violence rather than representing them using human figures. There is no fleshy matter or *mater* depicted in the Cycle or the Wheel icons. What is achieved by such a representation of control and motivation that reveals no face or affective expression? Recall it was precisely the performance of victim testimony mediated by photographs (chapter 1) and expert witnesses on the science of BWS that were unconvincing to the courts. When projected from the seat of courtroom architecture neither victims nor BWS experts proved stable or reliable. I argue that the Cycle and Wheel icons have similar projective functions as DV victim photography and BWS experts. By declining to use human figures in their design, these projection tools remove the troubled courtroom testimonies of both battered women and the feminist experts on the science that explains both the passivity that prevents their escape and the aggression that can lead to harming their abusive partners. In this sense, the Cycle and Wheel archive the minor affects and vestibular imbalance of women's testimony about personal experience and formal scientific observation. But here I am digressing from how the Cycle and Wheel function as racial icons.

Frantz Fanon's use of the Thematic Apperception Test (TAT) at Blida-Joinville Psychiatric Hospital in Algeria can help situate the Cycle and Wheel within the projective operations of socio-therapeutic instruments and Fleetwood's concept. The test consists of thirty black-and-white cards (fewer cards are used today) illustrated with ambiguous personal and social situations and can be administered to adults and children. During hour-long sessions, individuals are asked to tell a story about the ambiguous images before them; a blank card is also included for individuals to create their own picture. The instrument may reveal insight about worldview, social relationships, self-concept, and coping styles. Fanon's ethno-psychiatric studies of the effects of colonial domination on the psyche included administering the TAT on Muslim women. This particular use of the instrument meant to contest the universalism embedded in the picture theory and storytelling structuring the appearance of human beings depicted in the test. In other words, Fanon used the TAT subversively, deploying it among hospitalized Muslim women to enact a counternarrative to the TAT's universal logic. The original TAT "arose from [bourgeois Western] society whose artistic traditions cultivated numerous genres for representing human bodies and faces."[63] Though designed to be the picture of ambiguity and vagueness, the images are representations that encode white Judeo-Christian values.[64] Muslim women were "failed" readers of the images.[65] In contrast to the reactions of Euro-Western women, the Muslim women offered confused narrations of the pictures shown them. The TAT is a site of minor affects when read by cultural others. The Fanon-Geronimi TAT experiments highlight the imperial dynamics of social science testing design. They are an example, decades prior to the work of Seligman and Walker, of the vestibular role of Black people and colonial subjects to the study of affect and motivation.

Obviously, my claim is not that TAT images are latent depictions of Black women's freedom struggles. Rather, the moments captured by the images and the aspects of personality and group dynamics they evoke are scenarios

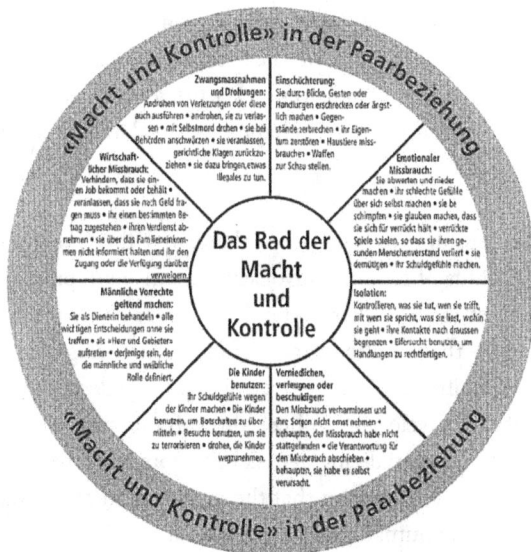

FIGURE 2.3
International Power and Control Wheel (the Duluth model): Germany.

완력과 통제-폭력

1. 위협: 표정, 행동, 몸짓으로 상대방을 두렵게 하기 •물건을 때려 부수기 •상대방의 소유물을 파손하기 •애완 동물을 학대하기 •무기를 소지하고 있음을 상대방에게 과시하기.

2. 정서적인 학대: 상대방을 비하하기 •상대방이 자신에 대해서 부정적인 느낌을 갖도록 하기 •자기 자신이 미친사람 이라고 생각하도록 만들기 •상대방을 심심하므로 조롱하려고 하기 •상대방을 모욕하기 •죄의식을 느끼도록 만들기.

3. 고립: 상대방이 하는 일, 만나서 얘기하는 사람, 읽는 것, 어디로 가는지 등의 모든 것을 통제하기 •질투심에서의 행동을 정당화하기 •자기의 질투란 행동들을 상대방에서 비롯된 것이라고 합리화하기.

4. 자기 행동의 책임회피, 부인, 상대방 비난: 상대방에 대한 학대를 중요하게 여기지 않거나, 상대방이 그에 대해서 우려를 표명할 경우 진지하게 받아들이지 않기 •학대란 책임 있다고 말하기 •상대방의 학대란들을 상대방이 유발시켰다고 말하기.

5. 자녀를 이용하기: 상대방에게 자녀들에 대한 죄의식을 일으켜 하기 •자녀를 이용해서 상대방에게 전하기 •아이를 방문의 기회를 상대방을 괴롭히는 기회로쓰기 •아이들을 데려가 버리겠다고 상대방을 위협하기.

6. 남성 우월주의: 상대방을 몸녀로 부리기 •중요한 가족 상황에 대한 결정을 혼자서 내리기 •집안의 왕처럼 행세 하기 •자기 마음대로 남성역할, 여성역할을 규정하고 이든 상대방에게 그대로 따르도록 강요하기.

7. 경제적인 학대: 상대방이 직업을 찾거나 유지하는 것을 방해하기 •생활비를 항상 읽이 손에 쥐어 구걸하는 느낌을 받게 하기 •생활비를 제한시켜 경제적으로 종속 시키기 •상대방의 돈을 빼앗기 •가계의 수입이 얼마나 되는지, 그것을 어떻게 사용할 수 있는 지를 상대방에게 전혀 알려주지 않기.

8. 강제와 협박: 상대방을 괴롭히거나 폭행하겠다고 위협하여 •떠나겠다거나, 자살할 것이라거나, 사회복지 기관에 보고하겠다고 위협하기 •상대방으로 하여 기소를 철회하게 만들기 •상대방을 불법적인 일을 하도록 하기.

완력과 통제 -폭력

완력과 통제-폭력

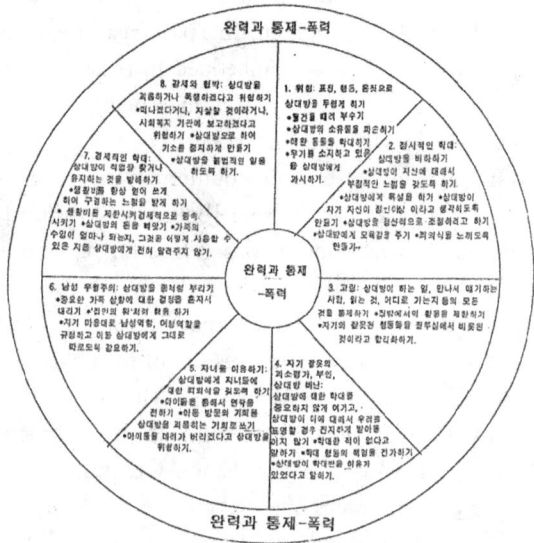

FIGURE 2.4
International Power
and Control Wheel
(the Duluth model):
Korea.

in which the subject, both within and outside the image, is conditioned by degrees of freedom to feel and to act. The projective work of eliciting personality and social dynamics occurs through photographs where meaning is ambivalent but productive of "root fantasy." It is precisely when the subject loses herself in the perplexing images that the TAT summons affect, a power that Fleetwood attributes to the racial icon. In this ethno-psychiatric instance, however, the test performs its work on the spectator-subject through a vague or ambiguous "look." Here I want to bracket the remainder of discussion of the racial icon to the following chapter, where I take it up in greater detail.

In the aftermath of the spurning of BWS from the courts the Cycle and Wheel icons assume the status of feminist advocacy tools through practices of projection in advocacy settings. Walker's cybernetic theory of control has achieved a literary and socio-therapeutic form, migrating to extralegal audiences around the world, in multiple languages (see figures 2.3 and 2.4). These international versions of the Cycle and Wheel also refrain from using a human face, instead listing and spatializing at-risk behaviors with the onset of violence. While I do not make the claim that the signification of colonial imperialism relies on a specific human facial type, I do argue the icons are designed to appear as universal and necessary representations of power, control, and motivation. Walker's theory of control, BWS, has failed to become the organizing term, argument, or precedent of the DV courts and the legal decisions produced in the court's official networked space. Her theory exists culturally, in the public discourse and material culture of anti–DV activism and advocacy. Cycle and Wheel are iconic voids that are the stubborn remainders of BWS theory, still standing in US culture. As both icon and void, they always return to a cybernetic theory of control in which Black subjectivity and the history of slavery in US law and culture are simultaneously absent and present.

Legal spectatorship surfaces here, in the disciplinary void that leaves the continued cultural relevance of BWS and the Cycle and the Wheel unexamined. Without a reading of the enduring, but unmemorializable question of colonial-imperial conquest, chattel slavery, and the management techniques of control enabling their procession in US law and culture, the tools suffuse colorblind fantasy in anti–domestic abuse activism and victim advocacy. Ascertaining the meaning(s) of domestic violence and how it structures economic reproduction then becomes all the more difficult and may explain the masculinist technocratic media theory engagement in a "frenzy of periodization," endlessly theorizing the postindustrial society, the information economy, the third wave, late capitalism, post-Fordism, the network society, neoliberalism, the new spirit of capitalism, empire, and so on with little mention of the intimate relationships that spatialize periods of reproduction.[66] Franklin is again instructive when he writes that not "examining the contingency of conceptual frameworks, spatial diagrams, and metaphors one uses in order to" assert the distinction between past and present "risks obscuring those shifts in the conditions of knowledge that are required for diffuse groups of individuals, institutions, and systems to desire, conceptualize, and enact such differences in the crucible of history."[67] As a framework, BWS conceptualized how violence (re)evolves in terms of power, control, and motivation between the intimate couple. Battered woman syndrome transformed and migrated by judicial force from law to cultural encounter. The Cycle and Wheel become projection tools used to stage performances of apperception where individuals and groups make sense of DV by assimilating the nonfigurative representation of power and control to their experience. Legal spectatorship makes Black feminist sense out of the Cycle and the Wheel by reading the historical techniques of enslavement into their iconic voids.

Ultimately, the curricular fates of battered women syndrome and the Power and Control Wheel would diverge, with BWS taken up as a legal argument and quickly rejected by judges. What BWS theory could not do as a legal argument it performed in spades as a socio-therapeutic tool that is constitutive of anti–DV advocacy. Well after BWS became defunct as a legal argument, the Wheel continued to be used to train law professionals, social workers, and nonprofit leaders working in the areas related to domestic abuse. The symbol of the circle and the management of power and control it represents remain in anti–DV pedagogy. Although the Cycle and Wheel are suffused with colorblind fantasy, their universalist rendering is nevertheless an effective control for or buttress to Walker's theory, now waning in law. Walker's theory of control mediates a robust anti–DV advocacy culture that this chapter explored by tracing the vexed status of BWS in law and how its theory of control transformed into iconic tools of apperception. The tools and the theory they embody implicate the field of cybernetics and its machinic elaboration of power and control.

While the computer is the most explored object of cybernetic theory, psychological theories and research on motivation constitute a "minor literature" in the field. As the itinerary of BWS suggests, cybernetic theories of control also manifest as technologies of representation. The Cycle and the Wheel are tools that render victims of abuse legible within and beyond the courtroom. They mediatize BWS from theory into an icon. In doing so, the tools perform the pedagogical work in legal settings that judges refused in the discourse from expert witnesses, social workers, and victim advocates. These curricular objects, then, are part of what Seb Franklin calls the "materialist concept of control" in cybernetics because the tools are bound up in the networked computer's technical procedures of projection.[68] In courtrooms, classrooms, meeting houses, and online the tools are projected to audiences in the construction of anti–DV activism and advocacy. Through projection, the tools spatialize learning environments where the operation of power and control in DV relationships occurs.

A milieu of minor cybernetic thinkers, scientists from Tomkins to Fanon, and Seligman to Walker conceived theories of psychological projection to understand motivation and control within individuals and groups. They did so in different ways and from different political perspectives. Common to all of them, however, is the enduring (absent) presence of the Black subject and the historical experience of the colony and enslavement. Each scientist engaged in their own acts of projection to theorize the individual's agency and motivation. In doing so, their theories of personality and the experimental procedures and instruments recall the idea of freedom and how the concept is conditioned by the slave and her descendants.

The following chapters continue to explore the relationship between law and culture, power and control through the visual culture of DV. Chapter 3 delves further into the learning environments where power and control in DV is disclosed through witness testimony about visual evidence of DV. Photographs of battered women do not merely contain evidence of wounding. In addition to performing the "hieroglyphics of the flesh" as projected images of skin, photographs also give form to cybernetic theories of control and the confined laboratory settings from which these theories arose.

3 AUTHENTICATING TESTIMONY IN THE DOMESTIC VIOLENCE COURTROOM

A FAMILY COURT CIVIL TRIAL identified by a standard DV (domestic violence) prefix followed by a six-number case docket number was filed in the Superior Court of California in March 2012. A civil trial was heard in family court May 2012.[1] The case involved domestic abuse between a husband and wife residing in San Diego County. Eleven photographs were published, seven of the witness and four depicting the home: an image of the garage, the master bedroom, a front door view of the house, a ransacked living room, and the hallway to the kitchen.

The testifying witness is seated on the witness stand. Her speech emerges from the elevated chair situated between the judicial powers of judge and jury and the visual evidence authenticated. The prosecuting attorney uses both PowerPoint technology to project the images and printed 8.5-inch by 11-inch color photographs, which are displayed on a small separate projector. The prosecuting attorney in this trial—like most of the assistants to the city attorney, a recent law school graduate—uses all of the images collected by the police, including images of furniture and papers strewn about in three different rooms and several images depicting bruises on the witness. Some of the evidentiary exhibits include a set of injuries sustained during an accidental fall that the witness reports unrelated to the trial. The images are introduced to draw a distinction between them and the injuries pertinent to the case.

The prosecutor hands to the jury box an 8.5-inch by 11-inch color image depicting the witness's arm. The courtroom audience cannot yet see these images. The lights are turned off, and the prosecutor then projects the image on screen. It is a close-up of one bruise and includes a ruler for scale, a common feature of many evidentiary photographs in domestic abuse cases. On screen, the bruise is a pale purple line about an inch in length. Another image is passed to the jury and then projected on screen. The photograph is a bird's-eye perspective of the witness lying down wearing a neck brace. Her mouth is closed and her eyebrows are in a strained position. She is wearing a hospital gown. No bruising is present in this image, only the neck brace as the signification of injury. A third image of the witness's arm is passed and projected on screen. The image is dark, and the injuries are difficult to make out. The prosecutor is obligated to clarify that the image is blown up. A forearm image is projected with a faintly perceptible bruise; a ruler is included in this image. A fifth image of the witness's neckline is passed and projected. A slight scratch is present showing a red abrasion at the neck. Finally, the jury is handed what appears on screen as an aerial view of a limb. It is another close-up image taken from the hospital bed. Five bruises are depicted accompanied again by the ruler.

At this final thrown projection, the witness is initially unable to discern whether the image depicts her leg or her arm. She admits she is confused: Are the colorful yet fading bruises depictions of her forearm or leg? The prosecutor projects another image from the hospital bed to help reorient the witness to her body projected on screen diagonally from her where she is seated.

In this misdemeanor courtroom scenario, the witness is beginning to testify about abuse she experienced from her spouse. Photographic evidence of her wounds is projected to the entirety of the courtroom—the audience in the pews, the jury, attorneys, court officers, court clerks, and the judge. This moment is arguably the most important one of the trial because the witness's live engagement with photographic evidence is one of vestibular imbalance where spoken-word testimony, skin, flesh, body, and photograph collide in the courtroom. Describing the encounter with images of vulnerability and suffering, Courtney Baker has argued that "looking at suffering does not entail only looking at its representation"; it is also "conducted 'in the flesh' upon another's flesh, inhabiting the same space as the body being held."[2] The experience of this encounter is an example of legal spectatorship. Testimony, occurring in the traditional architecture and acoustics of the courtroom, is mediated by images, and voices that are thrown, or projected, in space. Multiple subjects comprising the courtroom audience are bombarded with the voice of the testifying witness and documentary photographs.

This chapter argues that photography—remediated flesh—imposes a body on the diverse members of the courtroom audience, especially testifying witnesses. It deconstructs a courtroom audience encounter with live witness testimony and images for what it reveals about spectatorship in DV cases from the vantage point of testifying witnesses and the courtroom audience. As my reading of the trial will illustrate, one may lose a sense of the body in the very moment of flesh-photography's imposition. Anxiety and vestibular imbalance during testimonial observations suggest that "feelings may be formed and even 'shaped' by the means used to project, 'discharge' or 'expel' them."[3] The hand rhetorics of law professionals, the frequency with which talk is interrupted during testimonial playback, and the delicacy of first impressions of courtroom players are often viewed as inconsequential; they can be taken-for-granted aspects of courtroom looking practice. Court-watching domestic abuse trials can reveal how irritation, disconcertion, and confusion—minor affects sutured to thrown projections—contour legal spectatorship and the establishment of legal facts. Legal spectatorship marks the looking practices of the public in matters of law. It acknowledges the paucity of discourse about visual literacy in law communication at the same time as it encourages minor, micro-level analysis of law and photography amid the growing incorporation of digital media interfaces and social media practices into law's environments. Legal spectatorship is established as a looking practice that results in legal decisions that affect the freedoms of others at the same time that it problematizes evidence in the courtroom milieu. This form of spectatorship retains a gravity and delicateness for those involved in the courtroom, in particular the defendant and witness. It also emerges as a site of critique of legal architecture where repressed forms of looking and movement may be (re)discovered.

The potential of legal spectatorship for theories of visual culture follows a question Hortense Spillers had about the processes of US chattel slavery: What or who are the "unacknowledged legislators of our discursive and economic regime," and how is status made?[4] As I demonstrate legal spectatorship suggests a methodological approach to law and the image, one that traces the movement of affect and feeling in the form of thrown flesh–photographic projections within and between court audience members broadly conceived. Axiomatically it views the courtroom as a space that rehearses testimonial practices from slavery to adjudicate domestic abuse in the contemporary moment.

In DV cases legal spectatorship occurs in law's official environments (and extralegal settings, which I discuss in subsequent chapters) and is characterized by the directed influence and mobilization of affect and feeling by attorneys. In order to draw out the fragility and stakes of legal spectatorship, I describe how testimony is projected in the courtroom trial that opens this chapter. I examine how abuse is projected as data to the witness, from the witness, and to the rest of the courtroom audience. These data are transformed into information that is the product not merely of reason but also of feeling. By deconstructing the apprehension of witness testimony, this chapter seeks to read and name the dominant affects that shape participation in the DV courtroom. Doing so helps characterize legal spectatorship as a distinctive form of democratic looking that can be organized against the psychic foreclosures of colorblind fantasy that resist memorializing the structuring aspects of slavery in so many aspects of contemporary US culture. Again, Baker is instructive when she writes that "looking can be understood structurally and, consequently, as substantially disconnected from the racial identification of the onlooker ... such that the body that looks and the environment in which that look takes place are imbricated in and determined by complex discourses of history, region, race, gender and so on."[5] As I hope to show, the history of slavery structures the contemporary DV trial and the encounter with spoken testimony and photographic evidence that it stages.

As chapter 1 demonstrated, in the history of US law the slave occupied a dual position of silent witness and silenced witness in a way that informs the contemporary complainant under the Violence Against Women Act (VAWA). US slavery is part of the history though which ideological state apparatuses acquired the role of making acts of violence transparent, in particular the frangible acts of evidence collection of Black women's rape claims during Reconstruction. Through Hannah Rosen's history of sexual violence and the struggle for citizenship in post-Emancipation United States, we get a sense of how the extreme difficulty of representing the sexual coercion and other forms of violence suffered by Black women under slavery acts as a hidden remainder structuring contemporary representation of the violence of domestic abuse.[6] Slaves were at the center of domestic discord; they were both witness to disputes and the subjects of those disputes. By law their abject status forbade them the ability to testify about the things they experienced or witnessed at the hands of white people.[7] The meanings and interpretations of their words were regularly coopted by white masters. Historically then, the role of the witness, including courtroom experts, is closely associated with whiteness and mastery, while evidentiary materials share the qualities of accumulation and fungibility that marked the slave's life. The development of DV as a set of laws, police, medical and social service advocates, and courtroom activities may be traced to the complex ways enslaved people were entangled as witnesses to domestic disputes in white households and the body politic more broadly. When slavery is made central to the idea of witnessing and testimony, enslaved people emerge as early examples of forensic technology and the knowledge-making practices of silent witness. As Sameena Mulla argues, forensics constitutes a temporality.[8] I demonstrate how forensic time may be historically situated such that the complex relations of enslavement are seen to resonate in the United States.

When we acknowledge how slavery's afterlife continues to resonate in DV work, the dominant affects through which we understand and research slavery are expanded. So too is DV, heretofore a discrete, deracialized, unclassed category of social science. In Black Studies much of the scholarship on captivity and enslavement positions the slave's experience, to borrow from Saidiya Hartman, at "the convergence of terror and pleasure in the libidinal economy of slavery."[9] The spaces in which slaves lived their lives were spaces of destruction and death, and they coincided with the experience of white pleasure and the peculiar experience of the slave's own pleasure. One can understand pleasure and terror as major, or grand, affects that condition the slave's experience of the master's dominion. For its part, DV is understood as a cycle where violence ramps up and is then defused only to ramp up again. Violence between couples swings from love to terror. Most of the research details how domestic abuse, like slavery, is experienced through grand affects. But what if we were to assume that slavery and DV are historically aligned and in dialogue? What if we were to inquire about the affects and feelings that flow in these relations through something other than the grand affects of love, hate, pleasure, and terror? Pleasure and terror are in the same class of affects and feelings as anger, rage, pride, and shame. They are the affects and feelings that preoccupy political discourse about reform, revolution, and the nature of freedom. Put simply, the grand affects dominate how we theorize enslavement and intimate partner violence. We might unravel both a bit further by expanding the affective constellation that invigorates these relationships.

In *Ugly Feelings* Sianne Ngai takes a powerful excursion away from the tradition of examining the grand affects in politics, moral philosophy, and aesthetics toward a consideration of the political significance of the minor affects. Where rage, shame, and fear are the "grand affects" represented in Western political thought, minor affects attach to a vulnerable state of confusion or weakness felt variously as envy, animation, disconcertion, and so on.[10] There has been less interest in exploring the relevance of the "minor affects" in the experiences of enslaved people, perhaps because on the surface minor affects suggest smaller, seemingly low-stakes emotions and feelings. Slavery is a grand historical narrative that can seemingly be comprehended only through grand affects.[11] However, as Ngai implies, it is to the flow of the seemingly innocuous, minor, or as Ngai conceives them, *ugly* feelings, and their organization of space and dwelling where social information is exchanged that serious political thought about the history of slavery and the relationship between law and culture ought to be enjoined. This chapter describes, through a fraught moment of testimony, the minor affects and feelings organizing the DV courtroom.

Prior to Ngai's work on suspended agency, Spillers characterized Black existence in white patriarchal heteronormativity in terms of vertigo, arguing that Black life is lived in a vestibular relation to white domestic arrangements.[12] Neither outside the home nor inside the parlor, vestibular space is the liminal, queer element of Black presence in a white heteropatriarchal domestic community. "Vestibule" also refers to the opening region of the vagina. The vestibular, then, refers to a convergence of architectural space and anatomical systems; here social, cultural, and economic status are produced. Spillers positions Black life as vestibular to American culture, locating "a cultural *vestibularity* and *culture*, whose state apparatus, including judges, attorneys, 'owners,' 'souldrivers,' 'overseers,' and 'men of God,' apparently colludes with a protocol of 'search and destroy.'"[13] In this account, Spillers signals the relationship between techniques of enslavement, the reading of the body's flesh, and its subsequent organization of space. Spillers writes, "If we think of the 'flesh' as a primary narrative, then we mean its seared, divided, ripped-apartness, riveted to the ship's hole, fallen, or 'escaped' overboard."[14] In the DV trial, the image of damaged skin and the specularity of its blood are the primary narrative.

For the legal spectator, the DV image can be a site of minor affects such as irritation and disconcertion. These affects concern not only how to read photographic evidence in these matters but also its inseparability from the haptic customs of law professionals during the publication of photographic evidence of wounds sutured to the architecture of the courtroom. The encounter observed between witness testimony and photographic evidence is one place the history of slavery may reappear as minor affect in the contemporary DV courtroom. For this reason, diagnosing the mood and tonal quality of a destabilizing courtroom audience encounter with witness testimony is the ambition of this chapter on spectatorship of photographic evidence.

Hortense Spillers's use of the vestibular metaphor also suggests a more expansive constellation of human motivation where the vestibular is inter- and intrasubjective. For her, the vestibular describes the cultural positing of Black people with respect to white culture and encapsulates how Black abjection is spatially and globally registered as a *sociohistorical process*. Her sociohistorical formulation draws attention to communicability and the contaminating effects of abjection exemplified in the process of enslavement. Carrying out Spillers's idea of the slave's vestibular position takes seriously the depth of slavery's reach within the subject who becomes disoriented in space. The vestibule is an architectural form that embodies Foucault's "microphysics of power," which offered a guide to the analysis of power from the bottom up rather than top down, or, as Spillers might have it, an extension from the historical figure of the slave to the DV courtroom, to the testifying witness, to the courtroom audience.[15] Vestibular imbalance has an abject social meaning that is transmissible across bodies, technologies of seeing, and reproductive economic regimes in which they occur. The psychological, neurological, and literary preoccupations with the vestibular system and the sensation of suspended agency may be read sociohistorically. Through Spillers's use of the vestibule/vestibular the spatialized cultural and legal positioning of slave critically informs processes of psychic foreclosure in the courtroom that are either unthought, ignored, or undertheorized due to the prevailing fantasy of colorblind racism.

The disorientation and confusion experienced by the testifying witness whose case opens the chapter suggest a failure in the process of photographic projection and the ability to constitute a space of clear testimony. Something subtler than the convergence of pleasure and terror, which Black Studies makes apparent in the figure of the slave, inhabits this fragile moment of testimony. The interaction between the testifying witness and the images of herself projected across the courtroom space is a moment of disorientation from the self in space catalyzed by seeing the parts of the self projected as an image. The witness's loss of self, mediated by the image of self, problematizes not only the existence of photographic evidence but also the form of spectatorship that enables legal decisions in these matters. I also draw upon Ngai's work to conceptualize legal spectatorship because of the synergy between her study of the spatial representation of anxiety in literature and my interest in confusion in the cybernetic courtroom milieu. She proposes two theories, "suspended agency" and "thrown projection." In psychology, projection is a defense mechanism whereby one displaces a shameful quality found in the self onto another. Ngai shifts from an emphasis on projection's timing (i.e., when the subject is motivated to project onto the other) to the matter of *location and means*, suggesting that through projection "affect assumes a particular form," thrown in space.[16] Suspended agency is the "situation of passivity itself, [including] the allegorical significance it transmits to the ugly feelings that both originate from and reflect back upon it."[17] The two concepts are dialogical, such that a suspended agent can be any witness or bystander of a thrown projection, "a passive body hurled into space" such as photographic evidence.[18] In the DV courtroom, the audience apprehends photographic evidence via thrown projections by attorneys, court officers, and projection systems. Suspended agency in this context articulates the audience legally ordered into passive silent viewing under threat of contempt of court.

As the witness in the opening vignette states her confusion, she demonstrates an example of Ngai's theory of suspended agency. It is precisely the emergence of confusion, interest, and the like that indicates the need for conceptual work on the origins of DV photography. Photographic intimacy of these images makes the differentiation between the criminal mug shot and images of vulnerability possible. By photographic intimacy, I mean the ostensibly advocative and objective gaze belonging to documentarians, forensic nurses, and police camera operators. In the courtroom example, the witness's disorientation at the sight of her own wounded skin, flesh, body projected on screen opens a portal to not only the circumstances of the abuse, whose inquiry is before the court, but also the conditions under which the images were made, stored, filed, examined, and arranged by attorneys for courtroom projection. Thus, forensic time may itself be engulfed by the suspended agency and ambiguity characteristic of the minor affects.

Domestic violence prosecution increased nationally in the 1980s–1990s and operates according to a special choreography of legal rhetoric and image display. In cases of domestic abuse, digital evidence proves decisive in criminal conviction rates. Drawing upon literatures in critical legal studies, visual culture, and science and technology studies, I show that the production of images of battered women signals an invitation of battered women into humanity. This body of photography simultaneously discloses itself as a racial project through the historical evacuation of women of color from social science and police investigations of DV. State photography of battered women institutionally emerges in an attempt to normalize the diverse and contradictory language and feelings that battered women display in clinical milieus. Through trial observations conducted at the San Diego County Superior Courthouse, I examine how color, feeling, and display screen animate the psychic transformations constitutive of spectatorship among juries and law professionals.

Though I interviewed public defenders and prosecuting attorneys, I did not seek out interviews with battered women. My decision not to do so was informed first by my theoretical disarticulation of the clinical-scientific discourse on battered women from battered women who testify in court. Second, creating distance between clinical narratives of domestic abuse from court appearances on domestic abuse allowed me to attend more directly to the evidentiary photographs that were co-present with claimants ordered to court. This distance is crucial to my argument about how the image analogizes the body of the live complainant.

Interviews were conducted at the San Diego County Superior Court, San Diego City Attorney's Office—Domestic Violence Unit, Office of the Public Defender, and the San Diego Family Justice Center from autumn 2009 until autumn 2012. All interviewees who identified as practicing attorneys had at least two years' experience handling DV cases in addition to other legal matters. Practicing attorneys and photographers were asked the same questions in addition to follow-up questions that emerged spontaneously during the interview.

The interview texts considered in this section concern attorney descriptions of their practice of domestic abuse prosecution. I home in on interviewee responses to the question: "How would you characterize the early days of domestic violence prosecution?" In what follows, a forensic photographer and former prosecuting attorney affirm something like what Spillers terms "the unacknowledged legislators through which status is made." For both interlocutors the "early days" of DV prosecution initiates talk about the introduction of new technologies of legal fact-finding and emerging photography customs. They regard photography with certainty because it fundamentally improved their professional practice of acquiring visual evidence of DV for prosecution.

THE COURTROOM: ARCHITECTURE, AUDIENCE, AND AUDIOVISUAL TECHNOLOGIES

Courtroom architecture and design organize the courtroom audience. The audience of family, friends, and neighbors who support those involved in making court appearances is a crucial yet neglected aspect of legal looking. Courtroom space is designed to situate bodies, including these visitors, in the performance of the trial. Whereas the jury sits to the side of the judge and witness box, the courtroom audience sits in rows of seats facing the stand frontally, much like a theater or cinema audience. Constitutionally protected through interlocking terms of the Sixth and First Amendments, the courtroom audience is instantiated as a central and permanent crowd of witnesses whose spectatorship, conducted from this optimal classic viewing position in the space of the courtroom, both materially and symbolically fulfills the individual's democratic right to a public trial (per the Fourth Amendment). The spatial situation of the audience also affirms the public's combined rights of free speech, free press, and free assembly (First Amendment). Thus, constitutional law organizes and gives shape to legal looking. For the purposes of this discussion, I focus on free assembly. In this context, US courtroom audiences perform a type of civic witnessing that, through the design of seating and acoustics, is rendered historically subordinate to the work of juries, who observe from the side. Much legal scholarship and activism are dedicated to analyzing the demographic composition of juries and the logic of its legal fact-finding.[19] Less attention has been paid not only to the moral economy of courtroom audiences, but also to the unofficial and unsupported means by which these community witnesses participate in the production of public goods such as mutual recognition, care, and information dissemination about courtroom activity to the public.[20] Central to this prospective area of research would be an understanding of how the spatial architecture and design of the courtroom, in their positioning of courtroom audiences as prime legal spectators, shape and inform these potential roles.

Since the 1910s, audiences have been organized in the space of the courtroom in relationship to technologies of courtroom projection as well as to the stand. Today, algorithmic projection software and hardware, PowerPoint technology, digital cameras, and images—all of these together instantiate forms of spectatorship that inflect and reshape the everyday public and private looking practices of legal spectatorship in US courtrooms. Thus, not only constitutional protocols but also visual and algorithmic protocols condition the practice of legal looking.

In a 2016 themed issue of the *Journal of Visual Culture* devoted to architecture, editors Jae Emerling and Ronna Gardner propose that contemporary architecture has failed to address "the full complex of issues engaged by visual culture studies."[21] Martino Stierli, in his contribution to this issue, considers "how a building serves as an apparatus for the production and display of an image" and places the emergence of architecture as the art of space in the late nineteenth century, a period during which, he notes, "psychology, theories of perception and empathy theory became driving forces in art history."[22] This chapter accords the spaces in which law is enacted the status of architecture in Stierli's sense to examine affective immersion among witnesses and spectators engaging with digital visual material in law's environments. Legal scholar Neil Feigenson has proposed that "each dimension of legal visuality creates tensions in our conceptions of what law and legal knowledge should be."[23] Enactments of law in the field's built environments are precisely one of these dimensions of visuality. Yet, scholarship in visual theories of law has mostly limited itself to interpretation of the image and its technical production. Scholarship about the space where legal interpretation is visually managed through legal protocol is surprisingly sparse. This is especially the case regarding the architectural domain of the courtroom, a place where photographic evidence is routinely circulated by law professionals and consumed by legal spectators.

Until recently, legal theory has seldom accounted for the role of the courthouse and courtroom and the historical shifts in architecture in the discovery of justice. More importantly, legal theory has neglected the question of how the design of the courthouse and courtroom disclose valuable insights about slavery in Anglo-American political history and its structures of feeling. Also infrequently explored are courtroom dynamics after the incorporation of electronic projection, digital media, and digital filing systems into courtroom architecture.[24] The US courthouse is a special architecture in which the problems and conflicts of white domesticity are adjudicated. Throughout the country many courthouses remain virtually unmodified from their colonial construction; courtroom seating from the judge's bench, bar, jury box, witness stand, and courtroom audience retain the same configuration. What has changed in the modern courtroom are the forms of projection of information that traditionally would have been paper files and dioramas. Today, files are objects that are thrown, projected to those in the various seats of the courtroom. In *Files: Law and Media Technology* Cornelia Vismann examines how files control and formalize law. Files are things that cannot be defined because they are "variables in the universe of writing" that "elude any general, context-free determination."[25] Though files have no definition, they do have distinguishing features. According to Vismann, files have two basic actions: transmission and storage. Photography is one kind of file thrown within courtroom architecture. Its movable presence mediates courtroom activity by storing and transmitting data about injury to courtroom spectators. Vismann's focus on the material status of files implies that their transmission and storage work is institutional but also architectural. In the DV courtroom, the material presence of photographic evidence writes the history of VAWA. In contemporary VAWA cases evidentiary photographs are movable components of courtroom architecture. Photographic evidence is material and dematerialized, sitting physically in attorney file folders and projected electronically to screens. Photographs are not only the crucial elements of DV case files; they are also part of courtroom architecture because they are projected within the room to each audience member.

The discussion of the encounter with photographic evidence that circulates within courtroom architecture relies on a framework, established between Ngai and Spillers, that foregrounds the formation of structures of feeling (minor affects) in architectural space (the vestibule). By offering an examination of the courtroom situation, it also demonstrates how photographic evidence becomes, in effect, a component of courtroom architecture. In this capacity, photography plays a decisive role in the relational unfolding of affect among legal personnel, testifying witnesses, and courtroom audiences situated together in the space of the courtroom.

MISDEMEANOR COURTS

One could readily interpret the space of the courtroom as a theatrical space of major affects.[26] However, I turn instead to misdemeanor court, a space of minor offenses—small civil infractions that appear to matter the least. The misdemeanor DV case is thus a critical location of what I will call, drawing from Ngai, a "minor literature" on legal spectatorship: a critical discourse that attends to the production and circulation of minor affects and also describes the talk patterns of court participants and the paperwork about minor infractions that appears in the archives of these trials. I also introduce the metaphor of "irritation," a feeling that is fitting to the situation of DV misdemeanor and civil trials—fitting not only because the term captures the physical pain and suffering of domestic abuse, but also because it describes the experience of legal spectators observing communication in misdemeanor trials for issues such as DV. These spectators experience imbalance, disconcertion, and frustration not over the fact of violence in itself, but in response to the rhythms of its courtroom enunciation, which are pulsating, erratic, and difficult to follow.

Misdemeanor court is a training ground for new law professionals. New attorneys achieve fluency in courtroom procedure. They establish their own routines for trial preparation and finesse strategies for articulating arguments. Misdemeanor courts are professionalization centers for attorneys and de-professionalization centers for other court-involved individuals. They are control technologies that oversee how new attorneys are mentored and monitored by more seasoned lawyers. Jenny Roberts observes that the criminal misdemeanor trial often exposes individuals to major disciplinary and carceral power.[27] Historically, minor offenses have often been met with extreme measures.[28] In *Misdemeanorland: Criminal Courts and Social Control in an Age of Broken Windows Policing*, sociologist Issa Kohler-Hausmann further suggests that the 1970s rise of mass incarceration is currently augmented by the rise of mass misdemeanor justice.[29] During the 1990s experimental policing and criminal court programs evolved from an adjudicative model that decided guilt or innocence in specific cases to a model of policing "concerned with managing people through engagement with the criminal justice system over time."[30] Those arrested under the management model of policing go to what workers in the criminal justice system call "misdemeanorland," a "jurisdictional and physical space" of criminal justice that operates according to new techniques of social control: marking, procedural hassle, and performance. Kohler-Hausmann defines the three techniques in the following way: "Marking involves the generation, maintenance and regular use of official records about a person's criminal justice contacts and behavior for making critical decisions about his or her fate. Procedural hassle entails all of the burdens and opportunity costs attendant on complying with the demands of legal proceedings. Performance means the evaluation of an extended accomplishment, whether it was demanded formally by the court *ex ante* or offered as evidence of responsibility or rehabilitation *ex post*."[31] Unique to the managerial world of misdemeanor courts is that it engages in social control through "sorting and testing defendants into the future by building records based on their law enforcement contacts, evaluating their rule-abiding propensities through measured compliance with a series of procedural requirements, and gradually ratcheting up the punitive response with each successive encounter or failure to live up to the court's demands."[32] The very concepts of management through which misdemeanorland emerges may be situated in the history of racism and social control in US law. Marking, procedural hassle, and performance are all concepts pertaining to the peculiar institution and the process of making and managing slaves. Something of the Southern plantation periodical, replete with slave management techniques described by Stephanie Jones-Rogers's history, remains in Kohler-Hausmann's nuanced description of the regime of mass misdemeanors. As Jones-Rogers's history of slave ownership makes clear, slave management equally entailed the management of feelings and affects belonging to the owner.[33]

In the contemporary United States, misdemeanor DV cases lead to numerous acts of administrative monitoring for defendants who will receive Batterer's Intervention Program, a court-mandated DV education program, and protracted court dates that result in regular forms of administrative monitoring, marking, procedural hassles, and performance evaluations associated with their cases. Domestic violence is thus a new old area of social management and control.

Let us return in more depth to the courtroom encounter between the testifying witness and the photographic evidence of her injuries. The witness lost control of her orientation to her body projected on screen, unable to discern what part of her body was on display. Her loss in orientation was the defense's gain; the case ended in a not-guilty verdict for the defendant. One of the issues upon which the judgment turned concerned the publication (thrown projection) of the evidentiary photographs. In post-trial interviews with the jury, the prosecutor and public defender learned the jury understood that both the prosecutor and witness lost control of the many images the prosecution displayed during testimony. During deliberations, the jury thought they perceived two sets of injuries, one older than the other. The prosecutor's failure to distinguish the two sets of injuries (one of which was reported as having nothing to do with the current matter) confused the jury about which images referred to the pertinent wounds. Here the performance of citizenship–jury service is linked to particular anxious and disoriented attempts to read between the live body and its thrown image in the courtroom's chiasmatic arrangement such that "the representation of anxiety" concerning all legal spectators "oddly becomes dependent on a spatial grammar and vocabulary."[34]

The assistant city attorney violated what I suggest are the haptic customs of law professionals handling domestic abuse cases. Tina Campt encourages a haptic mode of reading photography in order to engage the "sonic, haptic, historical, and affective backgrounds and foregrounds through and against which we view photography."[35] When photographic evidence is published during live court testimony, the image file and witness are sutured together in the performance of memory. The routine of testimony begins with the witness verbally authenticating their image at the time of the events. These are two processes called "publishing" and "authentication," respectively. The witness is bound to their image and equally to any subsequent speech. Legal spectators grapple with the content of the image file and the witness's spoken testimony. The power of the moment when testimony begins is fragile precisely because of the coveted nature of the testimony and its potential to establish legal facts. There is a heavy moment of anticipation. Attorneys establish and coordinate the rhythm of testimony with the witness by acting as a playback mechanism, perpetually starting and stopping the witness's speech. At the same time, attorneys also coordinate the display of the image or images to the jury. Although dominated by spoken testimony—facilitated by rhythmic playback—the talk patterns of the DV trial are cut, disturbed, and interrupted by the parasitic noise of the *image*. Following Michel Serres's work on the parasite in the philosophy of communication, the photograph is not there for the witness; the witness is the object of the photograph.[36]

Publishing and authentication in the courtroom include a fractured moment of semiotic interaction distributed across technologies and legal subjects. The hands of prosecuting attorneys and court officers are endowed with special powers of display. Even so, the hand is a crucial yet often ignored aspect of courtroom thrown projections.[37] Haptic customs of law professionals are hand rhetorics that choreograph the interactions with media interfaces.[38] They condition the possibilities in which the display of visual evidence can and does conflict with live testimony from battered women, creating moments when "eye knowledge" interrupts, frustrates, and vexes the flow of "ear knowledge" of the witness and other spectators. During courtroom testimony haptic customs take three forms: placing images into individual hands, projecting them to everyone at once as in the experience of a cinema or slideshow, and a combination of handing out piecemeal and electronic projection. Projection in the courtroom manifests in the haptic customs of law professionals during image publication and witness authentication.

Attorneys may pass evidentiary photographs in a number of ways, all of them resulting in a moment of disruption, or irritation, of the vestibular system for all spectators. Passing photographs from an attorney to jury members then to court officers marks official, highly charged moments of communicative interaction among law professionals and moments of high attention among court audiences. Publishing images is an intersubjective task performed with the prosecuting attorney who directs the oral testimonial playback. But it is equally a performance that includes the ways photographs disrupt the conceptual space between skin, flesh, body, and photograph during the process of courtroom projection. Skin is the outer layer of living tissue covering the human animal body, while flesh is a combination of fat and muscle tissue interior to the body. Skin appears as flesh when it is seen (or even heard) as broken, scraped, cut, or bruised. Flesh has an in-between quality, consisting of the soft tissue given shape by bone and enveloped by skin. Photography, and its digital circulation, has made the relationship between skin, flesh, and body increasingly plastic. Engaging Ernst Kapp's language, the medium of photography is a projection of the *skin organ*. Photography is a mechanical process that expresses the close relationship of in-between-ness of skin, flesh, and body. When captured by photography, wounded skin achieves another level of materiality, one that is movable, separable, and discontinuous from the body *as if* it were a projection or peeling away of skin. In the courtroom scenario, photographs of wounds projected to the courtroom audience assume a material quality of flesh that is not continuous with the live testifying witness. The witness's experience of something akin to vestibular imbalance and its perception by the courtroom audience would suggest a condition between body-flesh-photograph that is not characterized by immediacy but is a relation made distant from the witness's body due to the disruption caused by projecting multiple, fragmented images of the witness.

In terms of performance, we might think of corpsing as a type of performativity endowed to photography and its subject. Critic and poet David Marriott uses the term "corpsing" from theater and performance to describe how "the promise of a [social] role is meant to accord with the promise of desire" such that "corpsing occurs when desire violates that promise."[39] Corpsing emerges as a possibility given to photographs through the mechanical process of photographic projection. It is precisely the space-expanding aspect of projection and the space-contracting aspect of corpsing that produce

vestibular imbalance as affect. In the witness's experience of disorientation from photographs of herself, one might locate a state of being caught
between the different materiality of word and image. The tactility of the
photograph changes when projected on a screen; the testifying witness momentarily dissolves into suspended agency when seeing the image projected.

What I associate with the psycho-physical experience of vestibular imbalance is a failure to perform the social role of witness that is forced by
the legislative and judicial acts of the Violence Against Women Act and the
Crawford decision. Corpsing, as Marriott argues, becomes apparent in and
outside the theater: "We see it when people fail to live up to, or grasp, their
social roles. Hence the derisive laughter attached to those who forget themselves, or have their pretenses exposed, or who fail to convince us of their
authority."[40] My interest in Marriott's formulation is not about the ways
corpsing is attached to shame, humiliation, or even embarrassment. Rather,
I am haunted by the way the witness's experience of corpsing is mediated
by the image of herself. The very context of the DV courtroom in which
this experience transpires for the witness and the spectator was spatialized
centuries earlier by constitutional law. Corpsing, then, happens within but
also outside the self through material culture such as photography and the
immaterial qualities of legal language.

Perhaps for these reasons prosecutors often circulate evidentiary images
of wounding directly to jury hands in addition to projecting them on screen.
The belief of some attorneys is that in these moments, juries are "holding
the body" of the abused witness.[41] In this technique, each jury member waits
in anticipation for the next image to be passed even while oral testimony
is ongoing. Here, prosecuting attorneys tie their display choices to greater
degrees of empathy in jury members and their own abilities using projection
technology.[42] During evidence authentication and publication, the juries I
observed typically consumed the images without regard for the ongoing oral
testimony of the witness.[43]

In this case, the prosecuting attorney passed images to the jury and manned
the PowerPoint projected slideshow in addition to moving closer to the witness stand to draw on a poster board to help facilitate witness testimony
when she became disoriented. The attorney drew stick figures, providing a
visual reference for the witness to indicate injured body parts. A moment
of shared but oddly placed laughter ensued when the prosecuting attorney
remarked on his poor drawing ability. In this moment attention was directed away from the comparative link being established between projected
photographs and witness and toward the poster board. The movement of

testimony between witness and attorney, the continuously advancing slide-show, and the poster board sketch created multiple and incommensurable views of physical injury, which disrupted the vestibular system of the witness and my own position as courtroom audience member—a testament to the communicability of confusion. Here, a form of vestibular imbalance dominates the sensorium when witness testimony begins and the legal spectator observes and attends to the spoken word and moving image. The publication and authentication of evidentiary images creates confusion in the spectator and testifying witness over where and when to look and how to listen.

Ngai argues that "acts of throwing reinforce the boundary between 'here' and 'yonder' on which the experience of threat depends" such that anxiety and panic are "less an inner reality . . . than . . . a structural effect of spatialization in general."[44] The playback exchange between prosecutor and witness takes time and is a disruptive element of testimony in which the witness loses coordination between her own speaking body and the body represented in the image. Saturated with close-up images, the evidence publication is not smoothly coordinated with the live testimony. It is a falter, a stutter, a hiccup, and does not articulate well in the testimonial record. Here "the logic of 'anxiety' and that of 'projection,' as a form of spatial displacement, converge on the production of a distinct kind of knowledge-seeking subject."[45] My interest lies in the communicable displacement of the witness's anxiety onto the jury and court audience via the "objective mechanism" of courtroom architecture, which includes photographic evidence.[46]

The "suspended agency" that Ngai uses to mark disconcertion, irritation, and confusion as minor affects takes hold as a physical sensation that is well described in psychology. Commonly known as "vertigo" in psychology and neurology, vestibular imbalance is a disruption of the vestibular system, the location and function of the inner ear and brain that coordinate balance and eye movement. After long debate about the diverse etiology of vertigo dating back to Plato, research in the nineteenth through the twenty-first centuries has established a link between vestibular imbalance and panic disorders.[47] Of particular significance for this study is the role of visual influence on the experience of vertigo. *Vertigo visualis* (visual vertigo) emerged as the result of both abnormal and normal perceptual phenomena. Neurologic perspectives associate vertigo with extra-ocular muscle weakness, while the physiological literature supports visually induced vertigo as a normal perceptual phenomenon. Thus, *vertigo visualis* currently describes "*any* visually induced vertiginous symptoms."[48] The significance of vision in orienting subjects in space is borne out in laboratory experiments in which "patients with vestibular disorders appear to be more reliant on visual cues for postural stability than healthy individuals" such that posture control "must rely on other sensory inputs, notably, visual cues, to maintain upright stance."[49] By disrupting the disciplinary boundaries between scientific experiments in proprioception and misdemeanor courtroom activity, we may come to a transdisciplinary understanding of how phenomena such as posture, spatial orientation, and the vestibular positioning of "suspended agency" are shaped in political contexts where affect and architectural forms animate the legal spectator. This line of flight constitutes a dual investment in the visual and audio component of testimonial speech patterns and their influence on the legal spectator, who is also trying to stay on balance during the playback comprising courtroom activity.

MARKING, PROCEDURAL HASSLE, AND PERFORMANCE IN DV CASES

Clearly, defendants are not the only people subject to regimes of criminal court management. Kohler-Hausmann's insights about misdemeanorland are also applicable to the criminal court experiences of VAWA complainants.[50] The VAWA complainant's experience of social control techniques—marking, procedural hassle, and performance—is established not through any offense she has committed, but rather through the visual evidence used to investigate and adjudicate an offense committed against her. Centering photographic evidence in DV cases suggests an underside to misdemeanorland, one in which even victims are socially controlled. In DV cases women are also managed, albeit in ways that vary the meaning of marking, procedural hassle, and performance that characterize misdemeanorland. The policies of VAWA strengthen the national response to the problem of DV by affirming evidence-based prosecution. Mandatory arrest and no-drop prosecution policies effectively engineer the production of photographic evidence, but not through the letter of the law.

Part of what characterizes misdemeanorland is how criminal law "operates as a form of social control without doing the things it is formally set up to do."[51] The primary example of this for Kohler-Hausmann is the fact that legal actors do little adjudicating: there are few convictions and jail sentences made in the misdemeanor courts, but an enormous amount of administrative management of arrested populations. In the case of VAWA, the law does not codify an explicit demand or rule for the production of photographic evidence of DV even as its demands for mandatory arrest and prosecution would appear to make the production of these evidentiary photos a necessity. The Violence Against Women Act is not set up to order or regulate police picture-taking or photographs taken by medical professionals. The production of photographs of abuse and their courtroom circulation operate through *custom*, not law, which is to say, the creation of photographic evidence of abuse is emergent, experimental, and unmarked by judicial authority. In DV cases police picture-taking is expanded, further entrenching images as arbiters of transparency. A key difference of the expansion of police power is that now police vision covers not only the potential terrorist but also images that give spectators access to clear evidence of suffering, and victimhood.[52] VAWA complainants are thus managed through an insidious form of photography, where variations on marking, procedural hassle, and performance pertain to both the testifying witness and photographs of their bodies. These images are insidious because although they appear to merely document the complainant's injuries, the weight of the police, courtroom architecture, formal procedures, and official roles of legal actors has the effect of making the difficult conditions under which these images are created disappear. They also elide the aspects of law that operate through custom.[53]

In Kohler-Hausmann's work, "marking" refers to the number of official contacts the subject has with criminal justice. For misdemeanor DV cases markings are the injuries documented by photography; marking is also present in other aspects of the case files such as the number of domestic incident calls to 911, requests for protection orders, and so on. Casey Gwinn, a former prosecuting attorney and founder of the Family Justice Center in San Diego, California, situates the history of the use of photographic evidence in DV cases in the mid-1980s and early 1990s. It is a history that explains how the VAWA complainant became the subject of photographic documentation, a form of marking, or official contact with the police. I quote him at length:

> When I started doing these cases I rarely saw photographs. Your typical police report which I would get a photocopy of would be a paragraph, maybe two paragraphs. [I] wouldn't have photographs, wouldn't have 911 calls, wouldn't have neighbors' [statements]. Rarely would there be any evidence attached to the police report. At the very beginning of my work we didn't have anything. . . . When I first started virtually everything was dismissed.
>
> The primary focus of pretty much everything that we did was based on whether or not the victim wanted to quote press charges end quote or

prosecute and we asked the victim if she wanted to press charges and if she said no the case would be dismissed and nothing would ever happen. Early at the very beginning when I was first given the case load for the City of San Diego we had a requirement that the victim come in and sign the actual criminal complaint herself if we were gonna file charges against someone and if she didn't come in and sign the criminal complaint herself the charges would never get filed. So that was really the beginning of the solution to not having evidence and not having technology in the assisting us in the gathering of evidence and the documenting of what happened was simply to put all of the onus and all of the responsibility and all of the blame on the victim. And if the victim didn't press charges then it wasn't our fault because the victim wasn't willing to cooperate. And if the victim wasn't willing to come in what could we do? That was pretty much the focus of the whole system right from the very beginning. So right from the beginning the question became, "Well, what evidence does exist, what's out there? What could exist? Theoretically, if you *had* everything that could exist what would it be?" For me, the beginning of all this was I started doing ride-alongs with the police officers. . . .

I was going out there thinking like a prosecutor, thinking like an attorney. I'd get to the scene there'd be an hysterical woman and a very cool, calm and collected guy. . . . I would sort out the scene. . . . I would notice that the victim would have swelling on her face or she might have the beginning of some kind of redness or bruising on her body and I'd say to the police officer, "Are you gonna take a picture" and he'd say "I don't even have a camera. How can I take a picture? I don't even have cameras."[54]

Gwinn is detailing his experience of a time in DV prosecution when little documentation of abuse was available in police files. It is a world in which not only are photographs absent from case files, but the criminal courts are also not electronically networked, making the acquisition of criminal justice information about perpetrators of abuse difficult to cull together. The archive of slavery may surface in Gwinn's statements if we take seriously Ngai's focus on the minor affects and Han's encouragement to attend to the psychic foreclosure accomplished through colorblind fantasy. This is done by attending to how Gwinn calls upon the phrase "the beginning" to articulate a narrative of progress from no evidence of DV to a new norm of photographic evidence included in case files. I highlight the repetition of "the beginning," occurring six times to establish its minor position within the whole of Gwinn's statement. If, as Han argues, colorblind fantasy is a dominant political hallucination that structures how we read both law on the books and innovations in legal theory, then "in the beginning" stands in for much more than the arrival of photographic evidence of abuse and the networking of criminal justice information.[55] "In the beginning" signals a return to the founding premises and repressions of constitutional law. When the history of slavery is read into "the beginning" of contemporary DV prosecution, photography is accompanied by an earlier form of silent witness—the figure of the slave entangled in white domestic struggles. "In the beginning" tells of the discovery of the new custom of entering the camera into the scene of the police domestic disturbance call, but it also reaches farther back to forms of testimony denied to enslaved people and discovered by the Black citizen who emerged in the post-Emancipation era.

A forensic nurse demonstrates another example where an official details his interaction with VAWA complainants through a custom he developed in his forensic practice over time. At the San Diego Family Justice Center, where my ethnographic observations and interviews were conducted, forensic nurses reported how photographic evidence can mediate interactions with VAWA complainants. Unlike sexual assault examinations, photographs of wounds are immediately available to be seen. Although it is sometimes the case that victims do not want to see the photographs taken of themselves, most of the time victims want to see the images. To my question, "Do you use the photographs in that way where you have this practice of showing them, the victim, once you take a picture?," a forensic nurse reported:

FN: If they want to see them. Then yeah.

KM: Do they ever *not* want to see them?

FN: Once in a while, yeah. *And as long as they're going to a safe place, as long in they're in a fairly safe situation if they don't want to see them, that's fine. I'm not gonna shock them unless I think that they need to, to see.* And most of the time they [victims] know that they're sore, but they don't know that there's a bruise, so I'll show them that, definitely. "So that spot where you said you were sore? There is actually a bruise to prove that you're sore." And then you see that they [victims] actually like seeing that information.[56]

In the exchange the forensic nurse discloses a form of customary discretion he has discovered in his practice for deciding whether or not to show the images to the victim and what tone to strike when doing so. It is worth noting the moment when the forensic nurse changes his tense, as if repeating what he often says to victims ("'So that spot where you said you were sore? There is actually a bruise to prove that you're sore'"). This is an aspect of forensic time when the victim's feelings of pain are validated by an official as functioning in court as proof ("'There is actually a bruise to prove that you're sore'"). Forensic time is also a moment when the anxiety of suspended agency transitions into feeling assured ("And then you see that they actually *like* seeing that information").[57]

I want to make clear that in such interactions my interest is not in the positive or negative responses complainants have, but rather in how they are brought into a culture of police picture-taking and its attendant ideology of transparency. These subjects are drawn into new negotiations between the self, their image, and the state investigatory context in which these images are produced. The picture-taking process fosters intimate exchanges between victims, social workers, and forensic nurses who are professionally networked to the police. Though visual evidence is a crucial element of the DV case file, its creation is not an act of law but of police custom. Here I would suggest is an example of how law and culture are not in an exclusively oppositional relationship. Law "on the books" and the enactment of customs that are not "on the books" may establish and entrench power through discursive interplay. The kinds of interiority produced in and as the scene of police photography position VAWA complainants in the genealogy of the modern criminal subject.

Following Jonathan Finn, we can say that photographs of wounded skin are immutable—they attest to violent touch at a specific time and place. Crime, in contrast, is "a mutable social construct" that is historically "bound to conceptions of race, class and gender."[58] The era of increased surveillance and consumer data collection comes into contact with evidence-based practices of DV prosecution. In fact, one could argue that surveillance, data collection, and evidence-based legal practices are of a piece. In this world where data storage meets the collection of visual evidence of abuse, images of battered women are endowed with potential. They become "sites of potential or latent use" whose investigation and interpretation "reflect historically specific conceptions of criminality" and, I would add, victimology.[59] Again, I am less interested in the moral dimensions of creating photographs of abuse. Rather, I want to highlight how this body of images establishes a new trajectory of police photography by inserting its gaze at the victim into its traditional form of the criminal mug shot. This is a new branch in the genealogy of the police looking practice and is the subject of the following chapters. What I want to briefly develop here is a link between photographic evidence of domestic abuse and criminal photography's power-knowledge role in the nineteenth-century pseudoscience of race.

Below the forensic nurse at the Family Justice Center discusses standards for preparing evidentiary photographs for DV prosecutors in a way that opens a window onto familiar forms of measuring the body.

FN: When I [prepare photographs for investigators], I put the color card on there. The color card is for the crime lab. [It] comes from the days of using 35 mm film. When they transitioned from black and white to color photography, there were accusations that they were using color filters to make the bruises look worse.

KM: Do you know how these accusations were articulated?

FN: Defense attorneys.

KM: Ok.

FN: Yeah, So when a case goes to court . . . the defense attorney—all the defense attorney has to do is introduce doubt in the mind of the jury. So, even though they know they are going to get overruled, they'll still get their question out there. Just to see what they can get away with. [Pause.] It's [the use of the color card] a habit that's stuck around and it actually does serve a purpose because the color card has enough different colors on it that you can show that these are the true colors of the bruise. Because a typical bruise can have four different colors in it, easily. Can have yellow can have green can have brown, purple, blue. So, the fact that I'm using the color card says that these are the colors that might come up in these pictures, shows that these are true.[60]

The color card can be situated within the history of documenting and diagnosing criminality. However, instead of measuring the "signs" of criminality on the face of the criminal, the color card is used to measure the signs of criminality on the face of the victim of crime. Color reference cards allow one to check and thereby manage color reproduction of a camera or other imaging system. They are used by photographers to compare, measure, and calibrate cameras to check the color temperature of lighting (the appearance of light emitted from a light bulb).[61] The forensic nurse's color card helps establish more than what and how much color will appear in the images. The idea is that the device also assists all courtroom spectators in the disarticulation between skin color and wounded skin, thereby rendering a clear vision of crime appearing on the skin of the victim. This essential activity of the DV courtroom is explored in this chapter as an unsuccessful example of testimonial evidence authentication where vestibular imbalance was induced in the witness and courtroom audience. The color card is a tool that helps to control the interpretation of photographic evidence. While the spectators' disarticulation of the relationship between skin color and wounds appears to be a less ethically fraught activity than the pseudoscience of reading race using anthropometric devices, I argue it is a deed that remains subsumed within the legacy of race science and the management of Black and Native populations. The Los Angeles Police Departments photographs documenting the 2009 abuse of Afro-Caribbean pop singer Rihanna are a contemporary example of how domestic abuse photography invites the spectator to return to looking practices of scientific racism. The photographs are forms resulting from surveillance practices associated with the management and overseeing of masters over slaves on the plantation, of forensic nurses over rape victims, and of misdemeanor court administrators over individuals with an arrest—all relationships with an element of care built into their disciplinary violence. Rihanna's injuries entreat a negotiation between skin color and skin trauma mediated by camera lighting, forensic nurses, and police photographers who guide the victim's comportment before the camera. Documenting her wounds enacted a photographic regime that controls the hue and brightness of skin color, making the wounds available "to be looked at" legally. Rihanna's case confirmed that evidence of DV relies on norms of visual whiteness to make powerful effects in law.[62]

In this context, the color card's place within the material culture of police photography draws further attention to the iconicity of domestic abuse. Multiple acts of the discernment of violence are mediated by the tool, suggesting the need to discipline an aspect of the visible sign. In the case of DV images, the sign is color. Color is matter whose apprehension by the courtroom spectator must be controlled in order to arrive at a legal decision about violence. Evidentiary photographs are a spatial terrain responsible for regulating color as a natural phenomenon for multiple subjects: the photographer who captures the image(s), the VAWA complainant who authenticates her image, and the jury and courtroom audience who regard testimonial evidence. Theses gazes fulfill the democratic promises of free assembly and trial by one's peers that are guaranteed by the Constitution.

In this chapter, the instance of vestibular imbalance that indicates a failure of coordination between attorney-witness-photograph demonstrates more than women's vulnerability in these courtroom scenarios. This fragile moment of failed evidence authentication before the court also highlights the vulnerable status of this particular body of police images.

Photographic projections collapse the singular concepts of skin, flesh, body, and image in the official and routinized space of courtroom activity. In doing so, these images depicting the live witness may function as what Spillers called the "unacknowledged legislators" responsible for conditioning "how status is made." In contrast to Judith Butler's influential argument about how gender becomes naturalized through the citationality of gender performance, the routines of authenticating, passing, and projecting photographic evidence in space enact a process of ungendering.[63] While it is not my argument that the testifying witness in this case was ungendered, this chapter makes the claim, through Spillers, that the visual evidence was ungendered, detached from the witness's body and returned to flesh. Recall that "ungendering" is the term Spillers uses to describe the violent process of enslavement that did not distinguish between male and female bodies.[64] In terms of DV photography we might think of ungendering as the process whereby the distinctions between skin, flesh, body, and image collapse.

Midway through her essay "Peter's Pans: Eating in the Diaspora," Spillers suggests that we should discover alternatives to understanding (Black) abjection that pivot away from the well-worn critique of identity politics as nothing more than contagious *ressentiment*. In these lines, she returns to her earlier essay, "Mama's Baby, Papa's Maybe" to remind the reader of her oft-cited phrase "hieroglyphics of the flesh." She writes that in this phrase, "I was trying to identify not only one of diasporic slavery's technologies of violence through marking, but also to suggest that 'beyond' the violating hand that laid on the stigmata of a recognition that was misrecognition, or the regard that was disregard, there was a *semiosis* of procedure that has enabled such a moment in the first place."[65] We might see Spillers to have been pointing to how status—subjectivity—accrues to objects (and subjects) thrown or projected into space. She derived a "semiosis of procedure" productive of abject subjectivity from "slavery's technologies of violence."[66] Following Spillers, I have tried to derive the (failed) management of the VAWA complainant to courtroom semiosis. In courtroom semiosis suspended agency and minor affect reign in addition to, or perhaps even instead of, pleasure and terror. In contrast to the major affect and feeling of *ressentiment*, something like suspended agency, minor affect, and the movement of analog and electronic projection may constitute the "unacknowledged legislators" through which the status of the VAWA complainant accrues. Previously, these forms of nebulous and uncertain positioning within and between the self, the instrument of violence, the other, and space had characterized the reproductive economy of plantation slavery and its spatialization and control of Black and indigenous populations. Today, these same elements exist as remainders in the DV misdemeanor courts and the semiosis of evidence publication/authentication. Together they help define the status of the VAWA complainant by and for the legal spectator.

Photographic evidence of abuse is bound to the architecture of the physical courtroom like a keystone. Moments of legal spectatorship prioritize the all-encompassing meaning of the vestibule as a transitional space: from the Middle Passage, to Southern plantations in which slavery is imposed on Black Africans by wounding the flesh, to the transitional space of the architectural vestibule, including the vestibule's anatomical reference of the female gendered body. I prioritize the transitional space of the vestibule in order to bring Spillers's use of the term into conversation with research on vestibular imbalance and its relationship to affect and feeling. In domestic abuse trials, photographic evidence remediates the metaphysics of flesh, initiating a variety of analogical comparisons. Legal spectators attempt to master and are mastered by this "fleshy" matter. By examining the DV courtroom testimony in this case I have illustrated an example of the failure to maintain control in an environment defined by control. As the aforementioned moments from the trial suggest, this visual practice is frequently done through minor affects and all of the politically meaningful uncertainty and confusion they entail.

There is an interface between anxiety and vestibular imbalance. Clinical research has long understood the connection between vestibular and visual systems and the experience of fear and panic. This knowledge circulates largely in the discipline of psychology and human behavior. Ngai's theory of the minor affects helps us appreciate visuality, vertigo, and anxiety outside of the clinical domain of psychological disorders and suggests that these links are germane to the legal domain and the performance of democratic citizenship in the courtroom. Likewise, Spillers's account of the vestibular position of Black people relative to US culture extends the reach of the term from one tracking transitional anatomical and architectural space to the realm of everyday political participation within American domesticity. US courts incorporate the racializing visual practice of reading the flesh instrumental to chattel slavery as a democratic and government feminist looking practice.[67]

The act of sitting quietly in the courtroom offers a view into the transition out of suspended agency through movement. In most US courtrooms, audience seating is divided into two sides, somewhat like a church. They can sit to the left or to the right and regard the operations of the judge, attorneys, witnesses, respondents, stenographers, court officers, and bailiff, facing front. But one can also get up and change seats, as I did one morning during a DV trial. A photograph of the witness was being projected to the jury and courtroom audience by a prosecuting attorney. In pursuit of a different vantage point, I got up and crossed from the left side to right side seating. As I rose, crossed the aisle, and sat down again, some jury members turned their heads to look at me. A minor disturbance, my movement entered into the flow of courtroom communication. The jury saw me seeing another perspective. I then saw the jury seeing me. When they turned their heads back to the visual evidence projected for them, it seemed to me they were not seeing in the same way they had milliseconds prior. My shift in perspective had migrated to a shift among them and back to me.

Changing seats is a freedom to be discovered in the courtroom milieu. It is a freedom borne out of constitutional law and the spatial arrangements of throwing and projecting in traditional courtroom architecture. This freedom belongs to the freedom to assemble but also supersedes this freedom because of the way the courtroom audience participants can reassemble themselves in space, projecting themselves elsewhere within the courtroom communicative milieu. In other words, the courtroom audience is far from a group of people who are passively positioned; rather, they are part of a dynamic ecosystem currently under threat. The courtroom audience is dominated by the fact that 95 percent of misdemeanor cases are disposed with a plea. As the courts continue to advance a managerial model of criminal justice, they promote pleas and seemingly endless monitoring in the form of multiple courtroom appearances. The increased number has a detrimental effect on the presence and purpose of the courtroom audience. By expanding managerial interventions into the lives of arrested populations, the courts are nullifying the constitutionally protected space of free assembly. The stakes of legal spectatorship are to be found here, in the possibility of free assembly in the courtroom and what Nicholas Mirzoeff calls the "right to look," which is above all "a right to the real," a right that does the difficult work of investing in "autonomy, not individualism, or voyeurism, but the claim to a political subjectivity and collectivity."[68] Legal spectatorship seeks a radical position of free assembly or courtroom movement that draws the gaze of the courtroom audience away from their work and back again.

The adjudication and redress of violence are among the most confounding political obligations for citizens. Although codified by the grand narrative of the nation-forming US Constitution, legal spectatorship organizes and encourages subtler micro-analytical approaches to how we see in legal settings. Legal spectatorship observes the process of signification between the subjects and objects of DV courtroom testimony. It also places these observations in dialogue with the legislation that brings the DV courtroom into being and the customs practiced among law enforcement after a long history of perfunctory interventions form these agencies. The ethnographic moments discussed are by no means an exhaustive description of the legal spectatorship of domestic abuse trials. These trial moments illustrate how photographic evidence becomes a site for the production and exchange of minor affects that are constitutive of legal spectatorship.

The testimonial scenario analyzed in this chapter illustrates how VAWA attempts to pursue "universality and unity of the subject of feminism," which is deeply incorporated into governance.[69] Photographic evidence of DV is the absent presence through which VAWA and its enforcement network stabilize the subject of feminism. Yet, in the official context of control and decorum of the DV courtroom my participation in the audience highlights the irritating and frustrating predicament of the legal spectator, who finds one's self in the flow of anticipation of visual evidence of wounding. The inability to attend to the rhythm of official testimony that is simultaneously spoken and visual is not confined to the testifying witness alone. In the courtroom setting, the minor affects of confusion and anxiety are communicable. Although part of the major, time-honored, and official rituals of courtroom activity, the confusion and uncertainty characterizing the minor affects give rise to the performance of some of our most pressing acts of legal spectatorship.

Domestic abuse photography is a relatively new gaze within the corpus of police photography—a body of images historically utilized to forward a pseudo-science of race, civilization, and class disposition. Police photography has revitalized its disciplinary gaze through the production of these documentary images. In the DV trial photographic evidence moves from "here" to "there" in a spatial arrangement comprising a network of customs shared between law enforcement and criminal prosecutors. Battered women are collected within institutional spaces to speak through what are antagonistic relationships with their images of wounding. This is because the images rehearse familiar frames of vision whereby Blackness functions as the technical limit of seeing the color of DV through the use of the camera flesh, haptic, and electronic projection. Ultimately photographic evidence of DV establishes a model of vulnerability located at the confluence of whiteness and femininity. Although misdemeanor DV trials are infrequent relative to other forms of criminal court activity, the images used to prove these cases circulate throughout global culture. We are surrounded by images of battered women that typically embody gender violence as a white feminine body.

In the next chapter, I examine how photographic evidence of DV interacts with similar images encountered in extralegal public settings. The reframing of police vision has led to a new subject of feminism: photographic evidence of DV. Images of battered women exist beyond the courtroom setting, outside of courtroom architecture. They are a normal part of our media-scape seen in magazines, film, television, painting, and theater, including their online occasions. The iconicity of DV images is tied to anti–DV social movements that use tactical media to raise awareness about DV. The rest of this book demonstrates how photographs of DV maintain the domains of law and culture while also destabilizing what makes these two realms of communicative practice distinctive.

4 INCORPORATING CAMP IN CRIMINAL JUSTICE

IN AN ARTICLE ENTITLED "Domestic Violence and the Trauma Surgeon" published in a 2000 issue of *American Journal of Surgery*, two images of battered women are featured (see figure 4.1).[1] The first is a black-and-white close-up image of a Black woman with just over half of her face showing. She stares blankly into the camera as a mascara-stained tear comes to rest at the corner of her lip. At her temple a scar or bruise has formed and connects to her swollen eyelid. The second image, also black and white, features only the torso of a fair-skinned woman wearing an embroidered tank top that reveals a bare arm lined with cigarette burns and bruises. Her face is cut from the camera frame, only a wisp of dark hair indicates that a head was attached to the shoulders whose arms cross the chest and end with a tense grip at the upper arm. A caption reads: "[An] example of recent New York City advertising campaign publicizing availability of support service for domestic violence victims. These photos are of models, not actual domestic abuse victims."[2] The original images, produced in 1999 by British photographer Alastair Thain, advertised legal and social services secured through VAWA. Thain's images draw upon theatrical repertoires of disguise, masquerade, and mask-making. By simulating the physical effects of domestic abuse through

FIGURE 4.1
Amber A. Guth and
H. Leon Pachter,
"Example of recent
New York City
advertising cam-
paign," in "Domestic
Violence and the
Trauma Surgeon,"
*American Journal of
Surgery* 179, no. 2
(2000): 134–40.

cosmetics, the campaign promoted law and policy around DV through the aesthetics of camp.

In this chapter, I explore the mobilization of camp aesthetics to stabilize and control the status of police visual evidence. Following Moe Meyer, whose work radicalized camp as a mode of queer oppositional critique, I explore the incorporation of camp aesthetics into state communications systems and advertising services, including legal recourse to victims of DV. Exploring camp in the context of DV activism also draws on E. Patrick Johnson's invitation to "quare" queer.[3] Quare is a "theory of the flesh" enjoining "theory and practice through an embodied politics of resistance" that is "manifest in vernacular traditions such as performance, folklore, literature, and verbal art."[4] Support services advertising for victims of DV employ a number of aesthetic strategies. This chapter is interested in the particular deployment of cosmetic masquerade to communicate about DV. Examples of support media are explored to understand (1) how make-up is used to simulate DV injury, (2) how faked images reference, implicate, and control the instability of police evidentiary photographs of domestic abuse, and (3) what the incorporation of queer aesthetics as a mode of communicating state policy suggests about law's autopoiesis—the theory that law communicates to itself in its own language.[5] Quare-ing camp aesthetics keeps Black skin and flesh in view as both are evacuated from the technology of DV awareness campaigns. Quare-ing camp also contributes to a range of "camp sensibilities."[6] What is distinctive in this chapter is the emphasis on camp's cosmetic and spatial operation in law and its impact on the visibility of Black queer victims of violence. These discussions bring Spillers's idea of the "hieroglyphics of the flesh" to life in settings in and beyond law.

THE CONTEXT OF LEGAL CAMP

The previous two chapters illustrated the unstable status of both police photography of battered women and battered woman syndrome (BWS), the feminist cybernetic theory of control that sought to explain women's bipolar affect in abusive relationships. Where the previous chapters examined the development of legal spectatorship from the constitutional rights of public assembly and public trial, to the creation of a specific audience for domestic abuse testimony facilitated by choreographed displays of photographic evidence, to the Cycle and Wheel visual heuristics, in this chapter legal spectatorship moves outside the courtroom milieu to extralegal settings. Legal spectatorship is thus not limited to courtroom architecture, sightlines, and acoustics, but includes a larger apparatus of conceptualizing DV through vision.

While keeping in view the instability of police DV images and the unreliability of BWS, the remainder of this book examines more closely the visual elements of photographic evidence of abuse that are salient to legal spectatorship. I move not beyond but beside police photographs that document abuse to explore faked images that simulate visual evidence of abuse in public awareness campaigns. I call this body of images "legal camp." Legal camp uses cosmetics and digital editing to depict physical injury in order to market support services codified by VAWA. In doing so, it transmogrifies the law into an image of itself. One of legal camp's possible guises is art photography depicting battered women. Its characteristic feature is to operate through cosmetic masquerade that attempts documentary realism. Together, police photographs and legally camped DV images suggest realism is not of a singular nature. Rather, photography is multivocal, consisting of multiple forms of realism.[7]

Where police DV photography facilitates abuse testimony through a documentary realist image, legal camp DV images circulate realistically faked images of domestic abuse through social media on- and offline to market support services authorized and expanded through VAWA. Cosmetically faked images expand the concept of realism and with it the territory of legal spectatorship. The creation of campaign imagery to market support hotlines to abused women seeking treatment, protection orders, and other forms of legal recourse relies on hyperrealist photography techniques. These techniques circulate realistic simulations of DV injuries for the purpose of law communication. In this way, the realist photographs became aligned with the camp trace of police DV photography.

When realism is understood as having multiple forms, the looking practices of legal spectatorship move beyond courtroom culture to include public spaces where the subject is exposed to a plethora of art and advertising images that realistically represent DV. Multiple realisms call legal camp into being and suggests its influence upon what Marshal McLuhan called "the global media village."[8] This chapter fleshes out the evolution of legal camp.

Discursively, realness is a matter (*mater*) of queer critique and debate. Camp is a mode of queer communication that signals the terms, or law, of realness and/as performativity. Guided by Margaret Drewal's work on the appearance of the camp trace in corporate America, I suggest that although the legal camp DV image appears to control or signal documentary realness of the police DV photograph, camp returns with ironic vengeance. Drewal asks, "What happens to representation when the signified is reattached to the gay signifier, that is, when it becomes explicitly indexical of the 'gay regard?'"[9] For her, "gay regard" is inaccessible to the heteronormative subject compromised by their participation in the "conspiracy of blindness."[10] The resonance with colorblindness charted thus far in this book illuminates a meeting point between queer and Black critiques of vision. When emphasis is placed in seeing queerly, rather than clearly,[11] the faked DV image camps the very law it seeks to control. A reading of the hieroglyphics of the flesh is indispensable because it calls attention to how cosmetic application of fake injuries enjambs pigment to skin to flesh to body to digital image. Here, what C. Riley Snorton calls "being black on both sides" both secures and disrupts police evidence and its network of creation.[12]

The body of images I am calling "legal camp" refers to the "camp trace" of police DV photography. Moe Meyer defines camp as "the total body of performative practices and strategies used to enact a queer identity, with enactment defined as the production of social visibility."[13] For Meyer, camp

is situated in identity performance and not "some kind of unspecified identification of an ironic moment."[14] This means that not only is camp tied to
queer sociality; it is also crucial to its production. More important, given
that camp is productive of queer sociality, it is always queer and always singular. Camp "can be engaged directly by the queer to produce social visibility in the praxis of everyday life, or it can be manifested as the camp
trace by the un-queer in order" to create "queer access to the apparatus of
representation."[15] Because there are not different kinds of camp, legal camp
is a camp trace manifested by a network of state and private media communication entities. But I also want to suggest, following Snorton, that legal
camp concerns black matter and the Black maternal and therefore belongs
to Black sociality, which is to say, queer, sociality. For as Snorton argues,
"Sex and gender [are] racial arrangements wherein the fungibility of captive flesh produce[s] a critical context for understanding sex and gender as
mutable and subject to rearrangement in the arenas of medicine and law."[16]
Police photography of DV and the fraught customary circumstances of its
production are examples of fungible flesh, albeit captured by the police
camera. Legal camp images of DV are also examples of fungible flesh that
are captured by professional art photographers and include radical uses of
cosmetics for state advocacy and tactical media activism. Legal camp police photography is constitutive of a racial arrangement that asks one to
consider the content of camp and its function in law. This chapter considers
make-up as the camp content of legal camp. It then implicates make-up in
a cybernetic control function in law. Both attributes of legal camp form the
extralegal aspect of legal spectatorship.

I describe an early marketing campaign of domestic abuse support services, an infrastructure of complaint that appeared to enter queer and Black
representation into law. Coming out of VAWA's signing into law, the marketing campaign simulated images of DV to advertise abuse prevention hotlines. I narrate the design of the campaign in order to show an instance of
the production of legal camp, whose attempt at realism mimics DV police
photography. Together, the art photography narratives of this chapter "provide a way to connect the domain of aesthetic realism, where we may ask
how photographs are interpreted as partaking of visual qualia of 'realness,'
with the domain of metaphysical realism (and nominalism), where we may
ask how propositions can be interpreted generally as truthful."[17]

My definition of legal camp clarifies a cultural operation of police photography within legal spectatorship. Realistically faked images of domestic
abuse injuries mimic the kinds of documentary images authenticated and

published to courtroom audiences. I demonstrate this by calling upon the "hieroglyphics of the flesh" to discuss vernacular examples of domestic violence prevention. New media art activism circulating in online and offline archives are discussed as examples of what media scholar Rita Raley calls "tactical media."[18] Raley's account of tactical media locates the emergence of the protest media in relation to postindustrial and neoliberal corporate governance. This chapter explores several examples of tactical media in order to align the question of how to negotiate violent intimacies with techniques of self-fashioning and the beauty industry. Through hyper-realistic simulations of wounds, domestic violence advocates and media activists use cosmetics, photography, and video to educate the public about the legal, cultural, financial, and interpersonal difficulty of repairing and ending violent intimate partnerships. But these forms of tactical media are also deployed to address questions that are raised by the public as they ponder, online and offline, whether or not the anti–domestic abuse activist images are real. On this point I return to path-breaking work on the history of lighting and color photography that oriented toward projecting the white body through film and photography.

Finally, the chapter returns to what the art images reveal about the role of contract and the slave's flesh at play in the multiple viewing sightlines and testimonies encompassing legal spectatorship of domestic violence. The stakes of controlling the influence of the courtroom audience are not limited to the people in a courtroom on a particular day of courtroom action. The courtroom audience is comprised of *any person* who may one day be a participant of the jury or a community member seated in the pews. Despite the decrease in criminal courtroom trials, the courtroom audience is an expansive, future-oriented category, whose potential is the subject of ideological conditioning. Control of the courtroom audience is more than a matter of courtroom rules, decorum, and the idiosyncrasies of presiding judges. Photographic evidence is entextualized as a valuable object of audience attention. This form of control is possible because of photography's promiscuous circulation in different social arenas.

In this sense, photographic evidence of domestic abuse functions as a contract, a tether between the domestic violence victim and VAWA's federal intervention. The Violence Against Women Act authorizes funding to target social service communications to battered women. Though unacknowledged and unanticipated by VAWA, police DV photography mediates courtroom activity during VAWA prosecution. In this chapter, the focus is on images used to communicate VAWA to DV victims. Marketing victim services media is part of the encompassing technology of what Hannah Rose Shell calls "media of reconnaissance."[19] The kind of reconnaissance media under analysis here are components of the domestic violence complaint infrastructure: victim hotlines designed and operated by for-profit, state, and nonprofit entities, specifically the marketing campaigns that advertise hotline services. Marketing campaign images of domestic abuse encourage people to pick up the phone. Such images are iterations of legal camp that provide both the face and the flesh the hotlines aim to target. This targeting occurs through legal camp, a concept I continue to develop in relation to legal spectatorship. Legal camp describes the work performed by queer aesthetics in contracting abused women to engage social services. Legally camped DV photography is the visual mechanism that stabilizes police evidentiary photographs. In the process, VAWA transforms and expands from a law of letters to an image of law that speaks in the mode of queer cultural production and critique. This form of speech implicates the queer cultural object(ive) of realness in buttressing police DV photography and is a citation of the hieroglyphics of the flesh, whereby the concept of "domestic violence," its theories, and material culture are visualized through the camp trace.

Legal camp confirms the incorporation of the camp trace into criminal justice and the infrastructure of DV complaint. By "complaint infrastructure" I mean orders of protection and photographic evidence but also the telephone hotlines that victims of abuse may call for assistance. Marketing domestic abuse complaint hotlines handles the problem of reconnoitering victims of abuse. Since the 1990s, the technical and aesthetic objectives of hotline ads have been targeted toward clear communication to abuse victims. Thus, I am interested in the visual elements of the art photography that would come to represent the hotlines. Through the camp trace of camped DV images, victim hotlines help establish legal spectatorship and the economy of attention delimited by police DV images. Ultimately, the professional uptake and rationalization of visual elements of photographic evidence of domestic abuse demonstrate VAWA's unique capacity, through autopoiesis, to stand as both letter and image of law. Here my analysis extends Han's understanding of the "plural forms of 'letter' that signify formal rule (letter of the law), epistolary correspondence (addressed letter), symbolization of speech's sounds (alphabet letter), and learnedness (man of letters)" to the icon of law (visual evidence).[20] After all, the letter of the law is apprehended by sight as well as sound.

The telephone's history of mediating disembodied authority in contexts ranging from the individual to social and state institutions is instructive.

Avital Ronell highlights the ghostly presence of the telephone in critical theories of technology.[21] By examining the disembodied authorial voices speaking to the schizophrenic, the subject of the Nazi state, and patients under Freudian psychoanalysis, among others, Ronell shows how the telephone is frequently ignored as an object of media theory that would comment on some of the most significant political and social activities. The telephone is an infrastructure collapsing time into space and leading to the expansion of state surveillance, terror, and even manufactured desires for therapeutic immediacy. Ronell observes that unlike the authorial voices of institutional state apparatuses, the voices at the end of domestic abuse victim services hotline have the difficult and ironic task of communicating to victims a message of little immediate relevance and an action that is unlikely to be taken: "Domestic abuse is a crime," and "If you are a victim, seek help." Although the victim services hotline is always on stand-by, its faithful twenty-four-hour availability is directed at unreliable users ensnared in trauma scripts that inhibit the very act of picking up the phone and seeking help. The terrible cycles of learned helplessness and BWS include negation of one's capacities for action that would preserve the self and promote self-determination. Trauma can delay the sense of immediacy necessary to avoid, escape, and otherwise emerge out of violent experience. For traumatized women, the victim services hotline is an infrastructure of complaint whose architecture is shaped around a comminuted image fracture.

IMAGING LAW

In 1999, shortly after the passage of VAWA, battered women were rendered as national objects of distress. Establishing the National Domestic Violence Hotline was a major outcome of the bill's $1.6 billion authorization that also funded grants for law enforcement and new shelters for battered women. Federal funding created new hotlines and increased resources and staffing capabilities to preexisting ones. Through congressional debate, female victims of male violence emerged as the target demographic in a complex marketing problem of audience construction for complaint infrastructure. Though federal dollars helped establish new hotlines and improve others, advertising the resource was underwritten by the probono efforts of major advertising firms and charities. Donations came from local agencies as well as internationally recognized firms.

In New York City, hotline expansion coincided with Mayor Rudolph Giuliani's first year of office. One of Mayor Giuliani's first official projects was to create a subway ad campaign for a hotline (1-800-621-HOPE) run by the nonprofit agency Victim Services. Giuliani turned to one of his advisors, David Garth, a bipartisan political strategist instrumental in the successful mayoral campaigns of both Ed Koch and David Dinkins, for a connection to an advertising firm. Garth knew an executive at Young & Rubicam, the fourth-largest advertising firm in the world.

During the research phase of the campaign, advertising agents studied police photographs of actual victims of domestic violence—photographs that could be used as evidence photography in a domestic violence assault hearing. Their original idea involved a picture of a baseball bat with copy reading, "When his team loses, unfortunately, so does she."[22] The creative team ultimately rejected this design as too misleading in favor of images similar to the ones they studied. The creative process led them back to the original source, images of women's broken bodies that, at least within a professional context, first brought advertising agents within conceptual proximity of "domestic violence." For themselves and their managers, the purest image of domestic abuse became the victim's, made monstrous through injury. Returning to the first images of actual victims they encountered allowed the team to counter the play and subtlety that seemed to contaminate the baseball design. The pursuit of pure representation, a one-to-one correspondence between image and referent, was seconded by the mayor as he informed the account's senior vice president that the "ads have to show women who are afraid to report it [domestic abuse] how serious it is."[23] The senior vice president understood the mayor to mean that the firm had to incite in viewers what he termed, "the gasp factor."[24] The Young & Rubicam team decided the best way to tap into the "gasp factor" would be to simply photograph victims of domestic abuse. Originally, they planned to stake out emergency rooms and clinics in order to access recently injured victims for a photo opportunity.[25] The logistics of such an endeavor were prohibitive, in terms of both setting up camera equipment in a crowded emergency room and potentially exploiting battered women.[26] This was the context in which British photographer Alastair Thain visualized domestic abuse for a 1999 state-sponsored media campaign. His creative articulation of "the gasp factor" advertised VAWA's legal and social services by drawing upon theatrical repertoires of masking through cosmetic disguise. By simulating the physical effects of domestic abuse through make up, the campaign promoted law and policy around domestic violence.

Thain's hotline ads helped establish a network, or cybernetic logic, involving VAWA, photography practices among police and victim advocates, and telecommunications. Cybernetic logic captures "a range of practices and methodologies that render the world legible through processes of capture, digitization, modeling, and prediction" that are affective and spatial.[27] By affixing the ads to the subway advertising space, the campaign became part of the subway architecture, seen daily by traveling spectators. Their location in New York City subways forged an extralegal, but nonetheless municipal, venue of legal spectatorship of domestic violence. The network of VAWA, police photography, and telecommunications created a structure of signification for the "look" of DV and should thus be understood in terms of power and domination. By highlighting the subway campaign and the desire for gasping affect that fueled its design, the state-media communications network disseminated affective and visual codes for police DV photography. As Meyer, who engages Anthony Giddens' theory of power and domination, notes, "Value production is the prerogative of the dominant order, dominant precisely because it controls signification and which is presented by the privilege of nominating its own codes as 'the original.'"[28] Legal camp commits a ruse of rouge to signify blood as the visual code of police DV photography. The faked DV images also rely on light skin to render the code. The campaign images intend to provoke sociality through the astonished gasp.

Within the legal camp trace of police DV photography resides an operation of cybernetic control of what would become coveted visual materials in VAWA cases. As the previous chapters have made clear, VAWA did not anticipate the production of police photographic evidence of domestic violence. The law remains silent on the nature, creation, and protocols directing the circulation of these images in official legal settings. The legislation did, however, mandate the expansion of victim services hotlines. Advertising the hotlines with camped images of battered women affixed a visual code to VAWA. Thain's legal camp photography brought VAWA and police photographic evidence into conceptual alignment. To borrow from the language of computational protocol, the ads signaled to the public the visual materials that would make the machinery of VAWA "go." The rest of this chapter demonstrates that as VAWA transformed from the letter of law into an image of law, it closed a cybernetic loop whereby police DV photographs were controlled through extralegal circulation. We shall see how the appearance of the legal camp trace of police DV photography coincides with a moment when Black and queer flesh are rendered visible in police DV photography just as "values are reassigned in the act of appropriation."[29]

In previous chapters I discussed the live courtroom publication of police photographic evidence of DV, Walker's concept of BWS, the Cycle and the

Wheel, Tomkins's cybernetic lists, Seligman's shuttle-box, and Fanon's use of the Thematic Apperception Test. Whether they be practices, methods, or objects, all of these modeled the effects of power and control, power and domination. Here, the cybernetic logic that I argue gets established between VAWA and images of battered women in public culture is not about modeling DV relationships. Rather, the circuit of control stabilizes visual evidence that had gone unmarked by law. The Violence Against Women Act acquired a visual language in the appearance of the camp trace of police photography, assimilating the "look" of evidence of domestic violence that the legislation called into being but never named as such.

The cybernetic logic or loop is an example of law's autopoiesis, the process wherein law communicates to itself in its own language.[30] Autopoiesis is a communication process in which law settles discrepancies and disappointments in order to stabilize expectations of "what ought to happen." The process is neither linear nor determined by technological or cultural innovation. In terms of VAWA cases, law's autopoiesis is not the result of direct causal links to the instability of police DV photography, BWS, and the Cycle and the Wheel discussed in previous chapters. Nor does it emerge from any conscious decision on the part of legal officials to secure visual evidence in VAWA cases. What I am arguing for, through the additional narrative of the creation of victim hotline ads, is a reading of these events as law's autopoiesis. "Cybernetic logic" is thus the term I use to name law's autopoiesis and further qualify how it stabilizes expectations regarding the distance between photographic evidence of domestic violence and the subjects of this violence. Legal camp introduced the visual codes of police photography into the language of VAWA.

Whether customary or "on the books," the instabilities of photographic evidence, battered women's psychology, and pedagogy tools borne out in legal processes were absorbed into VAWA through the camp trace. Given the ways "law is preoccupied with perfecting legal universality," it should appear as no coincidence that legally camped images of DV perform the work of stabilizing evidence in extralegal settings, cultivating instances of control through a cybernetic loop.[31] The fantasy of legal universality is "written over and through the law's interpretive labors," which manifest throughout US culture.[32] Previous chapters described how visual and scientific evidence of DV were kicked out from legal decision making. While legally camped images of DV are located outside official courtroom spectatorship, they remain within a cultural network of the visibility of battered woman.

Cybernetic logic renders legible the world of DV prosecution—its evidence, the cognitive vulnerabilities of subjects, and information about the quality and eventfulness of abuse. I turn now to extralegal examples of the cybernetic logic by which VAWA stabilizes DV visual and scientific evidence. Returning to Drewal's work on camp, its corporatization leads to forms of residue, through which the slave and techniques of enslavement return. Drewal writes that "when corporate capitalism appropriates Camp in its own interests and then poses as its signifier, then the representation bears only the residue of Camp politics."[33] How might the visual codes of legally camped DV photography perform as the residue of queer and Black identity? What is accomplished for law and culture through the submersion of queer and Black identity within cybernetic logic? Advertising state support services for domestic violence draws viewers into a community of legal spectators through the act of reading skin damage, here indicated by cosmetics. The commodification of images of battered women and the privileged codes of police DV photography are highlighted by the reappearance of Thain's campaign imagery in the medical journal image that opens this chapter. Tactical media examples that circulate in extralegal culture mediate the commodification of domestic violence imagery. In doing so they complete the cybernetic loop of control of photographic evidence of DV.

Most of the examples of victim tactical media use a white feminine body that confirms legally actionable suffering and perceived wounding as an objective of art communication. Suffering is made transparent for law and the public through white skin, pigment, light, and digital apparatus. The same combination of pigment, white skin, and light also informs the image of the Black woman featured in the *American Journal of Surgery* at the beginning of this chapter. Rather than indicate a bruise with red-blue pigment thought easier to discern on white skin, thick black mascara is cleverly smeared down the dark-skinned model's cheek. Mascara leads the viewer's gaze from cheek to eye and back again in wonder about a possible black eye above and the tearful emotional aftereffects of DV. Black pigment is the mark of DV. However, the marks of DV indicated by mascara do not compete with skin color, much less the weighty baggage of domestic racial violence that I seek with the convention, dV. Instead, the tearstained black mascara associates the dark-skinned model with (white) feminine affect. The simulated campaign images are indeed carefully manicured visualizations of DV. The repression of Black queer flesh from tactical media recalls the moments in Darwin's work in the *Expression of the Emotions in Man and Animals*, when his interlocutors report an inability to perceive blushing on Black skin. The inability to perceive blushing upon Black bodies—and the human status that being in possession of shame that blushing confirms—marked the Black as untrustworthy and uncivil.

The poetic work of enjambment returns at this juncture to compress a number of techniques of control: cybernetic logic, camp, colorblind fantasy, hieroglyphics of the flesh, and epidermalization. Each of these is entailed in signification of flesh in/and/as colonial law's quest for universality.[34] The following analyses of victim advocacy and activist media delves further into the ruse of color cosmetics in making available the Black queer trace as slavery's remainder.

ITERATIONS OF COLORBLIND FANTASY

"Color amounts to crime," so says Michael Taussig in *What Color Is the Sacred?*[35] Color suggests truth and authenticity in addition to deception and the synthetic. As German artist Josef Albers (quoted in Taussig) averred in the mid-1970s, "In order to use color effectively it is necessary to

FIGURE 4.2 "The Dress," viral optical illusion revealing differences in color perception. Published online February 26, 2015.

recognize that color deceives continually."[36] The 2014 "dressgate" perceptual dilemma is a colorful example of the strange dialectic between the digital interface and human skin. Searchable online as "The Dress" with a parenthetical "viral phenomena" tag, "dressgate" concerns an optical illusion created when a digital image of a dress appeared to viewers as blue and black and alternately white and gold (see figure 4.2).[37] Besides the excitement over how viewers perceived "The Dress," others rejected its validity as news. Anti–DV activists critiqued the emphasis on perceiving the dress by referencing the black and blue of human skin after being beaten. The Salvation Army South Africa appropriation art demands to know, "Why is it so hard to see black and blue?" Here media form refigures and respatializes a seemingly neutral debate about the scientific discourses on color cognition in the human into the performance of witnessing and legal redress. But witnessing and legal redress of what violence?

Created by the Ireland Davenport advertising agency in 2015, the Salvation Army South Africa advertisement serves VAWA's interest to control visual evidence of DV that the law does not anticipate (see figure 4.3). What interests me here is the use of cosmetics—part of the substance or essence of feminine masquerade—that moralizes social media activity by rerouting the (popular) scientific debate about color expression and its cognitive resolution to the consideration of battered women. One of the most popular genres of media production is the YouTube cosmetic tutorial. In these videos, amateur and professional make-up artists work with pigment, skin,

FIGURE 4.3 Salvation Army South Africa ad hacks "The Dress."

and lighting to contour the face. Through rhetoric of the hand, or what we might recall of the haptic customs of law professionals discussed in chapter 2, they respond to the categories of "ethnic" phenotype and a variety of other epidermal "abnormalities and inconsistencies." If make-up is applied to camouflage imperfections, then legal camp of battered women reverses camouflage as state institutional ritual. Camping the wounds of DV uses the same cosmetic play found in some of the most highly monetized media work on the web, including the beauty industry whose profits increase most during economic downturns.[38] Following Ngai, we can say that the images call attention "to feeling's paradoxical ability to introduce interference in the vey circuits of commerce and communication we have seen it enable."[39] Hyperreal in its composition, epidermal in its fleshy location, legally camped domestic abuse images communicate with genuine evidence circulating as currency in criminal court trials. Legal camp of DV evidence mimics the volatile form of currency characteristic of our era of speculative capitalism.

The advertisement's grasp of normativity through the use of a white model positions Black queer flesh as the hidden text of the advertisement. The use of color cosmetics upon white skin is, to be sure, a form of tactical media of DV victim advocacy, but it is also a hieroglyphics of the flesh steeped in colorblind fantasy. The ad's powerful function as tactical media thrives when Black and queer flesh rise to the surface from repressed subtext. The ad's caption, "Why is it so hard to see black and blue?" questions not merely the cognitive dilemma of (not) seeing color but also the possibility

FIGURE 4.4 Cosmetic tutorial.

of political *social* work toward a broader understanding of DV in the United States that would encompass the history of racial slavery. A radical politics would associate black and blue with the techniques of enslavement, implicating longstanding associations between white femininity and vulnerability that anchor white heteronormative kinship structures in Anglo-American law and culture. As extralegal spectacle, the ad appears to replicate state authority, the marketplace, and police photography customs.

Yet, the surfacing of Black queer flesh announces skin color and the specularity of blood as a significant tension of police DV photography. Representations of DV that deploy color cosmetics and white skin to control and buttress the reliability of this evidence take on a more expansive meaning. This meaning disrupts the control of police DV photography enabled through legally camped images of battered women and suggests we look elsewhere and else-when to conceptualize DV. In the quiet interior moments when one is surfing the web or traveling on board the subway, DV victim advocacy media "transfers" the legal spectator's "containment within the structure of capitalist [state] authority to a possessor and controller of an 'authentic' representative of that structure."[40] In these extralegal settings legally camped police evidence persuades the legal spectator of transparency as a value in law communication where white femininity functions as a model.

MOVEMENT

Of tactical media in the age of capitalism, Raley argues that certain "new media projects provide visual representations of [the] logic of the global market, the transformation of material bodies into statistics, assets, even geometric icons."[41] While speculative capital does not mimic law's truth claims, both forms of currency are equally volatile. Raley's description accords with the concept of legal spectatorship and the aspects of reading skin surfaces in DV criminal trials informing the phenomena of legal camp. The kind of radical use of cosmetics depicted in domestic abuse complaint infrastructure are examples of legal camp. Legal camp appears as feminine masquerade that silently directs, organizes, and conditions legal spectatorship of DV adjudication without ever being entered into live courtroom activity. Legal camp does more than urge one to rethink the ritualistic function of masking practices and the logic and poetics of camouflage. It is a mode of tactical media that irritates while also controlling the closed communication systems of VAWA, art, and the science of BWS.

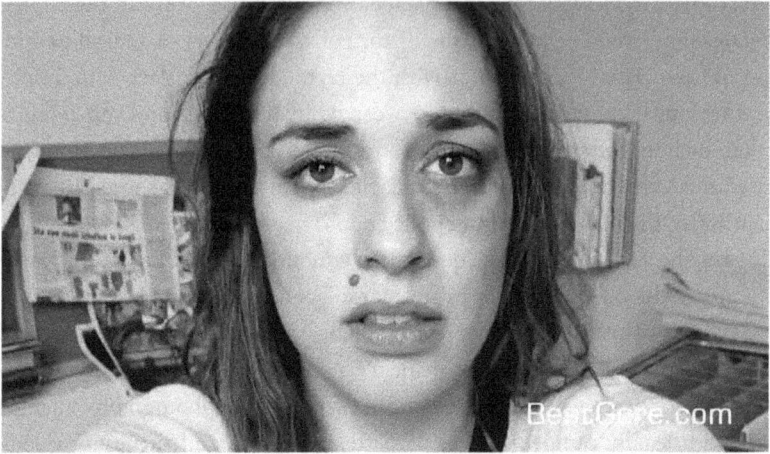

FIGURE 4.5 "One Photo a Day" screen shot of activist with cosmetically simulated domestic violence injuries over left eye.

"One Photo a Day in the Worst Year of My Life" is an activist media public service announcement (PSA) made for Sigura Kusa, a domestic abuse shelter in Serbia. The PSA attests to the global phenomenon of legal camp signifying practice and the triumph of social media. In this media piece, uploaded to Upworthy in 2012, the performer creates a novel digital montage of still digital photography to create a sense of movement. Three hundred and sixty-five still photographs are timed to flash in one minute, simulating the passage of one year. As the images flash, cuts and bruises appear on the performer's face (figure 4.5).

"One Photo a Day" exemplifies the triumph of electronic social media in its contribution to the topos of domestic abuse. The hybrid media performance was taken down due to a controversy about whether or not the media piece documented "real" domestic abuse and then reposted on You-Tube. Bloggers critiqued the piece as a serious and effective public health/social politics media campaign but also wondered about what they were seeing. In other words, they were literally "feeling mediated," on the verge of aesthetic judgment. "One Photo a Day" is an example of a unique gestural engagement with electronic media interface. The performer coordinates her flesh, in radical masquerade, with the screen. The spectator of this social issue media piece discovers a grammar of reading the body that is at issue in the DV trial, as I discuss in chapter 2.

The video deploys an emergent aesthetic convention used by state, for-profit, and nonprofit sectors that locates its rhetorical strength in controlling police photography by cultivating ever-greater perception of the grain of the image through communities of legal spectators who are participants to the scene of subjection.[42] However, it is the video's emphasis on cinematic movement that distinguishes this form of legal camp from the Salvation Army ad and constitutes my focus. Among the media theorists who attend to the relationship between skin and interface, Hanna Rose Shell notes, "Skin serves as a means of identification, as both boundary and interface. Skins are both how an organism appears as distinct from its milieu and the material means of which visual illusionism is possible at all" and further, skin "is a material entity that serves as trace or 'relic' of the whole living animal."[43] Shell's attention to skin as interface confirms the work of hiero-glyphics of the flesh in cybernetic terms. Skin as interface also resonates with Anne Cheng's analysis of the various surfaces characterizing primitive modernism. In her essay "Skins, Tattoos, and Susceptibility," Cheng turns our attention toward a reading practice "that is willing to follow, rather than suppress, the wayward life of the subject and object in dynamic interface."[44] Her practice pivots away from traditional "hermeneutics of suspicion" toward a "hermeneutics of susceptibility" that demand analyses that "step outside of the moral economies of the visual, the categorical, and the criti-cal; to be led by and attend to what the 'objects' have to teach us."[45] In a simi-lar vein, W. T. J. Mitchell famously proposed that we ask pictures "what they want."[46] "One Photo a Day" desires and establishes communication with the DV courtroom and the architectural and acoustic setting of photographic evidence projection. As the video records the appearance and disappearance of cosmetically faked wounds, not only are the guiding hands of forensic nurses signaled, so too are the haptic customs of law professionals. Further, while the video is in dialogue with the most coveted element of the DV case file, it also recalls the science explaining battered women's complex agency. The video uses the static presence of the victim to stage Walker's theory of BWS and the cycles of power and control developed by victim advocates. The more the victim remains fixed within the home, the more wounds appear.

Part of what unites the tactical media examples under discussion here is a shared desire among media artivists to contest the shame within a culture that systematically blames victims for the violence they experience. A sur-face reading of cosmetically simulated domestic abuse suggests some of the imperial desires undergirding Shell's discussion of acts of human mimicry and camouflage and Cheng's illustration of the design practitioners who "*immersed* themselves in skins not their own and, through that inhabitation, constructed themselves as imagined subjects: a mutual pedagogy of erotics."[47] In tactical media about victims of DV the erotic is pedagogical when cosmetics are used to draw attention to the ugly appearance of violence. Here I do not dispute the pleasures of make-up or the access to enjoyment it enables; rather, I suggest the tactical use of make-up to simulate injury is to discover jouissance in color cosmetics and the beauty industry that gives it shape. Amber Jamila Musser's elaboration of the techniques of brown jouissance offers a way to read Black queer flesh into white women's tactical media practices that use make-up to fake wounding. Musser writes, "In thinking with brown jouissance, it is important to remember that this possibility of finding sameness (coalition) begins with locating the self, not only in relation to others, but in relation to violence."[48] The question of DV—its history, inheritance, and the possibility of its redress—has long entailed a struggle with white women and emphasis on the look of the victim in terms of white feminine control. There continues to be a need to read Black and queer flesh into narratives of law and culture to expand what we mean by domestic violence. This is particularly borne out in the incorporation of the camp trace in state media about VAWA. Hyperreal techniques of epidermalization that characterize victim advocacy tactical media share a desire for clear, noiseless transmission befitting the very "moral economy of the visual" and transparency that Cheng wants to challenge.[49] I want to suggest a more radical critique of these media tactics that strive toward an ideal of noiseless transmission. The examples of feminist media practice discussed do the important work of reclaiming the shame that often prevents women from seeking help and escaping abuse. However, in a more radical sense, the use of cosmetics to simulate wounds exposes law's open communication with art according to art's preferred language of perception. Techniques of cosmetic masquerade used in "Salvation Army Dress" and "One Photo a Day" inadvertently establish a baseline for the perception of abuse in acts of legal spectatorship. The baseline is oriented toward an ideal white feminine example of domestic abuse. In cases of misdemeanor abuse the quality of the image and the clarity of its transmission are harder to establish, as I discuss in chapter 2.[50] Legally camped images stabilize police visual evidence, especially its use in digital photography, a format that is always already marked by the possibility it might be faked. In doing so, these images also stand in for the unstable science of battered women's psychology spurned from law.

Across the chapters of this book I have emphasized the minor affects as a way to intervene in the spatial and historical category of domestic violence.

In what follows I continue to analyze the use of movement in victim advocacy media while attending to the disconcertion felt when one's inadequacy as a victim is made public.

Emma Sulkowicz's *Mattress Performance (Carry That Weight)*, begun at Columbia University in September 2014, calls attention to intimate partner violence on the college campus (see figure 4.6). Sulkowicz, an Asian American student, began to carry a twin extra-long mattress wherever she went on campus in the aftermath of her sexual assault. The performance deals with the desire for visual evidence—a form of control—and the inadequacy of the victim's claims before law and her peers in ways that return the legal spectator to the previous chapters' discussions of "what could have been" in courtroom projection of DV visual evidence and the science of BWS. In the aftermath of a rape report that failed to expel the accused rapist from school, Sulkowicz enacted a resistant art performance whereby she began carrying her twin extra-long mattress around campus. The performance was campy, collective, and, having spread to other US campuses, geographically communicable. Twenty to thirty students a week would help her carry her mattress around campus, resulting in news coverage and the hashtag #CarryThatWeight.[51] Andrea Long Chu describes the performance as a *coincidence report* that "finds subjects venturing into the fallout zone of an undetonated event to collect samples of the incident's deformations (coincidences, flukes, misunderstandings) in hopes of finding something that will stick."[52] Sulkowicz's performance did transform into rallies and walks. The mattress, whose size is a standard among college campus dormitories throughout the United States, became a communicative detail; bearing its weight became a posture and a set of moves that indexed the time of live acts and law, ultimately traveling across the country to other universities where students re-performed the work in acts of solidarity. *Mattress Performance* includes an image captioning the rules of engagement in order to condition the mood, tone, and intention of the performers' work. The rules accompanying the performer do the work of instructing subsequent performers in the practice. At the same time, the rules of engagement signal police custody chains by camping the circulation of evidentiary mattress and sheets. Doing so imagines an extended temporality of forensic time into extralegal settings beyond that controlled by police.

Chu further explains that "events promising to furnish expert testimony of structural violence have ended up reneging on their own event-ness without thereby cutting the subject's affective feed. *Mattress Performance* shares with the incidence report, therefore, a certain forensic interest in figuring

FIGURE 4.6 *Mattress Performance (Carry That Weight)*, September 2014: Emma Sulkowicz carrying her dorm mattress across the Columbia University campus.

out what went down, but without the latter's authority, traditionally vested by the police state or someone over in human relations, to fast-track an incident's application for eventual status. Since what's happened only *happens* to have happened, the subject is left with no proof but her own feelings."[53] The reverse may also be true as in the case when the affective feed, as it were, short-circuits between photographic evidence, complainant testimony, and questioning attorney. As I argued in chapter 1, the form of suspended agency occasioned during legal spectatorship suggests that even the event of authenticating photographic evidence, with all its collected evidentiary bits and scraps neatly lined up, can fail, leaving not only the witness but also court audiences in an unexpected affective state. Here the subject's affective feed is dissociated from the event and its material remainders. This book has described the scene of law as one conditioned by the potential for vestibular imbalance. During the special activity of testifying, one's feelings might be rendered unavailable to attach to a source of proof. In such misaligned moments, the image of the wounded self is a proof that will not perform as such.

Mattress Performance plays with something akin to vestibular imbalance by producing the sensation as Sulkowicz pulled, tugged, lifted, raised, and shoved her mattress up, down, and sideways around Columbia University's campus. How awkward and clumsy her movement would have been, whether she was in a hallway alone or jostling among classmates between periods. What so few have been willing to admit of the piece is how Sulkowicz's performance flirts at the edge of physical comedy. The postures taken up in her performance recall Ngai's description of the slapstick routines of the vaudeville-trained comedians "trying to come through a doorway, falling down and getting back up again, collapsing in heaps."[54] Further, "the humor of these local situations usually occurs in the context of a confrontation staged between the small subject and powerful institutions or machines."[55] For Sulkowicz, the violence of rape and the absence of those in institutional authority who would believe her orient woman and mattress, movement and posture, toward camp expression. Ann Pelligrini demonstrates how camp emphasizes smaller social dynamics that undergird larger political struggles. "Camp helps to socialize individual conflict, by providing it with a shared community of interpretation."[56] Sulkowicz's interaction with her mattress at once publicly signaled the private location of her assault and the institutional context of the university in the aftermath of the police decision to decline to prosecute. By physically struggling with her mattress, Sulkowicz carried the weight of an experience that could not be proved in law's traditional settings. In doing so, she delimited alternative domains of redressing not only traumatic experience, but also the difficulty of contracting with VAWA's emphasis on evidence-based claims. The shared community of interpretation exists outside the confines of police investigation or courtroom testimony. The extralegal site of Sulkowicz's performance cites the legal language of Title IX that protects one from being excluded from participation in educational programs and activities and services.

Chu argues for a reading of Sulkowicz's performance as a "study in blue" by reaching back to the blue mood of Black women's strategies for dealing with the effects of antiblackness. I remain uncertain but open to what we might gain theoretically from the association between minor affects and color that does not reference colorism as a mediator of racial slavery. While Chu indirectly links Sulkowicz's performance to Black women performers who vocalize the slave's complaint through blues poetry and song, I wish to consider instead a perhaps uglier feeling, an "off color" reflection more grounded in the logics of camp. Chu notes how scholars demurred from watching Sulkowicz's accompanying film, *Ceci N'est Pas Une Viol*, in which a rape appears to be enacted, because they feared that watching would be sexually arousing. Yet, for those hostile toward Sulkowicz's efforts, the performances in the film may have also led to laughter, mockery, and derision—feelings that might also confirm sexual arousal. Pelligrini is again helpful in explaining camp performance as a spatial claim among the oppressed: "Perhaps, then, camp does not so much 'neutralize the sting' of social disapproval as multiply and extend it. The ethical call of camp extends itself in space, asking the audience to take up its share of the pain—*and pleasure, too.*"[57]

We find another example of camp aesthetics in the liquid interaction between cosmetics, the subject's pose, and photography used in the domestic abuse survivor project *I Survived* (2018) by Dasha Buben. Buben's work with abuse survivors in Bulgaria is part of a growing set of interventions in which the process of planning and taking portraits with subjects has led to unexpected therapeutic results with survivors of abuse. *I Survived* draws on how the camera mediates relationships between strangers and the self. Buben partnered with aestheticians "to help victims of DV regain their self-confidence and feel stronger through a series of portraits" (figure 4.7).[58] Beautification and photography are forms of therapy used with a number of subjects suffering physical trauma—including cancer patients suffering the effects of radiation and chemotherapy, veterans returning home as amputees, and children who undergo cleft palate surgery, among others. Its use among survivors of abuse is a significant example because of the ways these subjects challenge the very legal procedures that organize them through cosmetics and photography.

Survivors of DV have peculiar relationships to vision. The troubled subjects of *I Survived* discover forms of speaking, testifying, and moving that mediate a shift into new status positions of recovery and normalcy. Buben observes that in her initial interactions with photo-shoot participants, "Women came and turned away from the camera. They were scared. I had to shake their hands and talk to them to make them feel safe."[59] This moment of suspended action before both camera apparatus and operator took the form of a physical turn away where the subject's eye contact with the photographer is rerouted away, "over yonder." Resistance also took the form of fatigue where subjects engaged in acts of nonperformance. As Bartleby the scrivener would say, they "preferred not to" be photographed. Elena, a participant in *I Survived*, describes her posture in the following way: "At

FIGURE 4.7 Dasha Buben photographs survivors of domestic violence for the 2018 *I Survived* campaign.

the beginning [of the photo shoot] I felt so tired I could only sit. But then found myself making some poses and enjoying it."[60] As Elena finds pleasure through movement before the camera, she enacts feminine performativity. Moe Meyer might call this movement "camp" and its appearance before the camera a derivative mode of camp, where the straight subject passes through a form of queer embodiment, in a moment of self-renewal. In its derivative mode, camp aesthetics thus repositions the troubled straight subject into normative practices of consumption. But what of the camera operator? In a rare moment, it is the subject of the gaze who throws the photographer into relief and not the other way around. Does the emergence of camp performance appear only in the subject of the photographer's gaze or might the photographer also be implicated in camp performance?

Camp expression extends itself in space in order to share pain with others. The concept of legal camp marks a similar process, one that identifies pain in legal history and procedures and tries to move it outside to extralegal domains. Buben's offer of the handshake to participants of *I Survived* is a gesture that legally camps the endurance of the slave's complaint. Offering the hand works around the fiction of the slave's freedom to contract, now embodied in the domestic abuse survivor free to participate in an intimate photography shoot.[61]

When Buben details how she had to "shake their hands and talk to them to make them feel safe" because the women had turned away from the camera (and from her), she is expressing the emergence of past need for freedom that must be fulfilled before the achievement of present want of performance. Buben finds a social gesture, which she improvises before her photography can take place: a handshake. Touching hands is a social custom that expresses human recognition. The ritual hand offered in greeting, parting, or completion of an agreement is competitive; its performance must occur in mutuality, otherwise recognition is spoiled.[62] Here Schneider's inquiry into what "pulse of multiple time might a pose or a move or a gesture contain" is nothing less than the repertoires of human recognition.

Yet, Buben's incorporation of popular social media tools also reveals the important gestural function of digital media attributes in abuse recovery. *I Survived* asked women to post images from their photography sessions to Facebook. The result was dozens of comments and likes. These digital gestures are part of a return to the traumatic past that needs to be pondered from time to time. Olga Gorbunova, a director at Radislava, where the *I Survived* therapeutic intervention took place, observes: "No matter how hard our psychologists worked with the victims, spontaneous and sincere reactions from the Facebook users often had a stronger and more positive impact on women."[63] For participants, the portrait image could mediate paths of psychic return to trauma. Images of both the wounded and mended self can mediate self-recognition and recognition by the other and, for my purposes, by the legal spectator. These tokens circulate outside court trials as multimedia practices of one's self-care and self-tracking and are witnessed by strangers online.

The work of Buben and Sulkowicz reference the knowledge-making practice of legal spectatorship without being bound by law. Sulkowicz's *Mattress Performance* and Buben's therapeutic photography exist outside of VAWA. Yet their creative products reference law's forensic protocols. Their respective media work emerges from the same conceptual absences of VAWA (unanticipated contract of photography) and the *Crawford* decision (no definition of the testimonial). Their respective citations are extralegal, occurring outside the time of police investigations or courtroom activities. Nonetheless, each makes claims about how we establish the occurrence, or the event, of DV. None of their respective photographs or performances lies squarely within the categories of reenactment, documentation, testimony, artwork, or memoir. Rather, their interventions disrupt not only the stability of genres of photography and performance but also genre's temporal limits, performative goals, and intentions. Domestic violence media projects camp VAWA protocols of evidence production and circulation. According to Karen Crawley, "The irony that attends law's entanglements with cultural texts gives us the opportunity to see law 'in *the scene* of its own destruction' and thus to momentarily escape its thrall, to stand outside law's authority and realize its contingent, and precarious hold on that authority. Through irony's 'double vision' or 'multiple vision,' we witness law's authoritative self-instantiation and at the *same time* perceive it to be a fiction, constructed and vulnerable."[64] Sulkowicz and Buben both produce the very evidence that, in the space of law, could have, would have, and should have performed as proof of their abuse. In extralegal settings and spaces, their photographs and performances deploy camp expression to enact Crawley's idea of "modals of lost opportunities," the perfect continuous conditional grammar of unfulfilled results. Camp's extension into space is necessarily an intervention into time. In these projects, handshakes and "likes," supportive followers and advocates are camp citations of the micropolitics of legal procedure, evidence circulation, and the violent forms of touch that VAWA seeks to redress.

Domestic violence art photography and performance strategies are iterations of legal camp. They highlight the irony at play in legally camped police images of DV. Examining the extralegal performative art strategies for and by abused women demonstrates that "law's sovereign claims are vulnerable because of the ever-present possibility of an improper repetition or 'infelicitous performance.'"[65] As performances of legal camp, Buben and Sulkowicz bring attention to VAWA policy and procedures. That one might be fooled by cosmetically simulated wounds or invited into a scene of subjection to photography through a handshake, that there is a possibility of tumbling out of the solemnity of the mattress performance of "carrying the weight"—these indicate the fate of improper or infelicitous performance shaping VAWA. Legal camp shows that VAWA is marked by conceptual absence, blank spots where no direction, rule, or precedent determines how courtroom testimony is produced across the self and image. The Violence Against Women Act offers no directive on the collection of photographic evidence. Law is silent as to what mood and moves condition evidence collection. Visual evidence collection is a contractual endeavor between women and law's agents. The photographs may be produced under duress or in freedom. Law hides the contractual nature of the exchange of labor between victim and police photographer. If battered women are not free to leave, nor free to remain with their abusers, neither are they free to submit to or refuse pictures of their wounds. Law is conceptually blank in this moment of media production; abuse claimants are vestibular, yet integral, to production. The art photography and performance examined here point toward VAWA's procedural absences and inadequacies.

The Survived & Punished Project (S&P) is a coalition for prison abolition for survivors who kill or otherwise harm their abusers. Its media materials include examples of queer of color feminist tactical media that point to VAWA's procedural absences and inadequacies, similar to the media performances mentioned above but with a significant difference. The tactical media videos of S&P that I describe shortly disidentify with the state's failure to decriminalize the struggles of survivors—from holes in service provision that lead victim-survivors back to abusers to the interruption of kinship and solidarity among incarcerated survivors—even as VAWA aims to protect victim-survivors. Instead, S&P's video project, *No Perfect Victims*, brings the testimony of queer of color feminist survivors to the front stage of critically thinking the routines of state and criminal justice violence perpetrated upon the community.

One of the many immediately noticeable qualities of the videos of *No Perfect Victims* is their pivot away from incorporating the camp trace in criminal justice. Instead these videos are testimonies assembled online, and they work together as examples of Black queer pragmatics. In a time when freedom struggles are increasingly located in Black queer performativity or brown jouissance, in which a joyful elsewhere and else-when is accessed through the pleasures of adornment, cosmetics, fashion, and sex play, the contributors to *No Perfect Victims* pragmatically engage law by transforming their experiences with DV investigation, prosecution, and imprisonment into testimony. The videos of *No Perfect Victims* invest in an alternative form of self-conscious regard through which the performativity of battered womanhood is enacted toward a decolonial future. The videos enact strategies in which Black queer cultural critique employ pragmatic rather than camp aesthetics.

My framing of the *No Perfect Victims* videos in terms of Black queer pragmatics is in keeping with the critique of queer pragmatism formulated by José Muñoz. For Muñoz, the pragmatic organization of contemporary queer activism is something to resist because its strategies and goals are entrenched in straight time and therefore limiting to gay and lesbian political imaginations. The queer pragmatics that organize, for example, pro–gay marriage arguments made by queers is ultimately an attempt to assimilate into straight hegemonic culture rather than deliberating about a future in which queer utopia may be discovered. Queer pragmatics foreclose upon the realization of the "Not-Yet-Conscious" that Muñoz associates with the queer utopian impulse and/as hermeneutics. In *No Perfect Victims*, Black queers engage in pragmatic media-making to deal with their lives as "not-quite-here" due to the unmemorializable history of enslavement and its violent techniques in US law and culture, including colorblind racism. In doing so, they perform bridgework on the way toward the Not-Yet-Conscious, by focusing on the here and now of the criminal justice system and constitutional law that codifies straight time. This bridgework occurs in the present, a concern of Muñoz's thinking on queer pragmatism. He writes, "The present is not enough. It is impoverished and toxic for queers and other people who do not feel the privilege of majoritarian belonging, normative tastes and 'rational' expectations."[66] As I hope to show, the media work of *No Perfect Victims* articulates the scale of pragmatic politics that oscillates between utopian and anti-utopian demands. "To study scale," argue E. Summerson Carr and Michael Lempert, "is to examine how the ideals of social life stand in tension with notions of what is practically achievable" such that scale is considered as "a problem that social actors, as pragmatists in their own right, seek to solve."[67] I argue that Black queer contributors to the video work of *No Perfect Victims* organize their activism around DV pragmatically. These instances of Black queer pragmatism stand in scalar relation to Muñoz's critique.

Nine videos comprise *No Perfect Victims*, each focusing on a particular thematic through which the complexity of VAWA in the larger context of criminal law and mass incarceration may be known. *No Perfect Victims* prioritizes not the police-generated look of DV victimization but the experiences of DV survivors who have been incarcerated. The videos critically link the specific experiences of battered women in the marriage or couple context with those of trans men and women who fought off assault to comprise a broader category of mass incarceration. Slavery is integral to their understanding incarceration. The media work uses extralegal space to circulate the kind of reflection that never occurs in the DV courtroom playback between victim and attorney, the haptic customs of evidence publication or experts on PTSD or BWS. The women before the camera testify to all the intricacies and complexities at which the Cycle and the Wheel can only hint. Put differently, the women flesh out the control narrative of DV. The narratives are historical. In a *No Perfect Victims* video titled "Roots of Survived and Punished," organizer Hyejin Shim observes, "The issues of abuse and intimate partner violence, of gender violence, they often don't get discussed together with the prison industrial complex or systems of policing criminalization in the United States" (see figure 4.8).[68] Black queer and allied feminist critiques of the prison-industrial complex in the United States, found in the work of Angela Davis, Kimberlé Crenshaw, Ruthie Gilmore, Michelle Alexander, Dorothy Roberts, Saidiya Hartman, and Naomi Murakawa, among others, argue that the growth of prisons is linked to criminal justice reform and economic strategies of land valuation that are outgrowths of techniques of managing Black and Brown populations. Shim's point about the relationship between prisons and gender violence also includes the foundational history of slavery, which, Han argues, law leaves un-redressed through colorblind fantasy. The participants of the *No Perfect Victim* videos include women who went to prison for harming their batterers. Their presence on screen incorporates the prison-industrial complex into the narrative of battered women's experience. In these pragmatics, which constitute a scalar difference from the queer anti-utopian pragmatics to which Muñoz calls attention, Black queer women composed concrete utopias that point toward alternative futures. Misty Rojo is a formerly imprisoned organizer. In her video, "Repurposing Prisons," she describes feeling safe in prison, because, in that space, her abuser could not get to her. When she locates her "abolition dreams" in how she would transform prison architecture she resonates with the loophole of retreat where Harriet Jacobs discovered a vexed sanctuary over a century ago. Sharon Richardson's video "Giving Back" offers another example of Black queer pragmatics for and about battered women. She tells her story of starting a catering business that employs formerly incarcerated people. Black queer forays into entrepreneurship harken back to the skills development, house building, and business activities of Black folks in the immediate aftermath of the Civil War and Emancipation Proclamation. Further, the testimonial format of the video recalls Reconstruction-era testimony by Black women, elucidated by Hanna Rosen, where Black women defended against forms of cultural and legal status that would render their selves and their words dishonored. Here, the tactics are not sophisticated media works or data simulations but interviews filmed head-on of Black and queer women.

There are notable refusals enacted in the videos. There is a refusal to linger with evidence circulating in the DV courtroom and its covetous uptake by law professionals on behalf of legal spectators. Like Sulkowicz's work, the videos challenge the wounded image, emphasizing other matters from the scene as the essence of VAWA prosecution. But the videos also suggest that, far from the police image being the *sine qua non* for DV prosecution, it is the history of slavery and its techniques of control that structure US criminal

Hyejin Shim
No Perfect Victims
Convening 2017

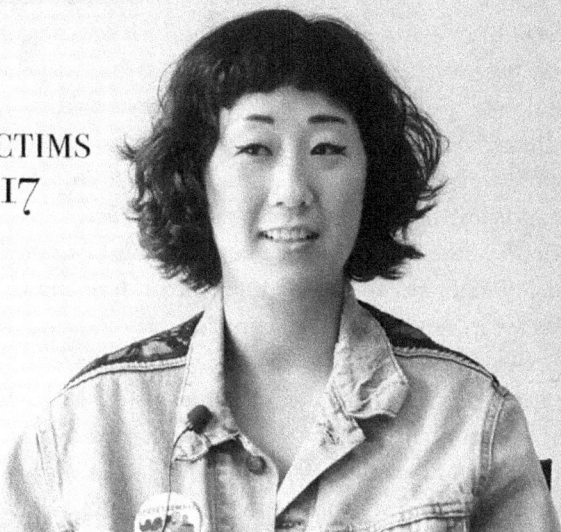

FIGURE 4.8 *No Perfect Victims*: Opening image of Hyejin Shim in *No Perfect Victims* YouTube video.

law and justice mechanisms. Participants invest not in reflections about federal protections offered by VAWA but rather in an etiquette for communicative interaction with DV victims. They also imagine Black queer women's legal defense by Black queer women. A video by Marissa Alexander titled "Being Strategic" explains the active role she played in her trial defense (see figure 4.9). Alexander's case drew national attention for the ways her case intersected and inflected a number of discourses on violence: "Stand Your Ground Law," gun control, DV, and misogynoirism in law and culture.[69] Media coverage of her case positioned her as an unsympathetic victim. In Nicole Fleetwood's discussion of the cultural fixation on images of race and nation, the Black icon is the source of "significance and valuation" particularly among "key black political, social, and cultural figures."[70] *No Perfect Victims* extends Fleetwood's concept of the Black icon by introducing Black queer DV victims who are not celebrities or public figures produced through fandom. Marissa Alexander is infamously known in mainstream culture for firing a warning shot at her abusive ex-husband. The circulation of video testimonies produces DV victims as a plurality that amplifies their dual position as venerated and denigrated images. *No Perfect Victims* mentions the Free Marissa Now Alliance, built by Black queers, including the African American/Black

Women's Cultural Alliance, INCITE!, and the New Jim Crow Movement. Throughout the footage, Alexander and the other participants detail a closed circle of Black and queer women's defense by Black and queer women. I would like to suggest this circle functions as a closed loop that illustrates another way to scale cybernetic logic and Black queer activist politics.

Throughout the different video testimonies, women before the camera disclose feelings that fit within the minor affects that recur in this book. Occasionally, their laughter, smiles, and chuckles awkwardly suffuse the interviews whose content is the grand historical narratives of slavery, police brutality, and rape. The minor affects occur during moments when participants are recounting the failures of advocacy and their geographical, racial, and class intersections. Viewers of these extralegal scenes, whom I am calling legal spectators, and video participants exchange the position of suspended agency. In this way, Black queer pragmatics of *No Perfect Victims* intervene in cybernetic logic by rendering a media practice and methodology that renders Black queer survivor experience as world political history. An alternate theory of control is rendered legible, one that does not participate in the conspiracy of blindness or colorblind racial fantasy.[71] Black queer participants gain control of DV narratives as they occur in law and culture.

Video work in which Black queer testimony of VAWA criminal courts plays a role moves away from the use of camp to signify Black queer identity. Instead these testimonies embrace pragmatic politics to communicate their expertise in living outside the control of VAWA and media representations of DV. The women in these videos are not academically trained ethnographers or lawyers. They are intergenerational survivors of DV (upper case d, upper case v), understood by VAWA and domestic Violence (lower case d, upper case V) as written in the clause guaranteeing a republican government in Article IV of the US Constitution. Through their extralegal setting, *No Perfect Victims* videos imagine legal spectatorship as something on the way toward concrete utopia, one that remakes rationalism toward "an ordering of life that is not dictated by the spatial/temporal coordinates of straight time, a time and space matrix that, unfortunately, for too many gays, lesbians and other purportedly 'queer' people reside in."[72] They do so by showing the reveal codes of VAWA case law and courtroom activity. Constitutional law and courtrooms are special zones in which the spatial/temporal coordinates of straight time live through professional practices of the officials and experts.

My concern in this chapter has been to suggest that the racialization of the wound locates it within colorblind fantasy. Camping the wound in extralegal

MARISSA ALEXANDER
NO PERFECT VICTIMS
CONVENING 2017

FIGURE 4.9 *No Perfect Victims*: Opening image of Marissa Alexander in *No Perfect Victims* YouTube video.

settings can "convert a way of moving *others* to political action ('agitation') into the passive state of *being* moved or vocalized by others for their amusement."[73] I want to be clear on this point that the ruse of rouge operating in this kind of advertising that simulates injuries to raise awareness is not a cruel or necessarily even conscious form of stimulated amusement; rather, it achieves the aesthetic status of "interesting." For Ngai, the "merely interesting" discloses the role of aesthetic judgment in DV prosecution where photographic evidence is central and fraught with ambiguity.[74] The stability of law is at stake in moments of suspension before the images of DV. This is because, on one hand, the state appears to control its own coveted forms of evidence, while media artivists demonstrate that visual evidence of DV is easily compromised. In both instances where subway ads and online videos depict faked wounds to draw awareness about DV, viewers posed questions about realness and authenticity. The antagonism between real/not real has political value for feminism. It may not matter whether domestic abuse injuries are created by the state or by tactical media artivists. I am more interested in the apprehension of wounding itself that "becomes the primary object of" the legal spectator's "quasi-ethnographic fascination."[75]

This is the moment of legal spectatorship when I return to Jackson's claim about the sublime function of Black queer flesh in order to affirm its trace within state and white media activist hieroglyphics of the flesh of DV. Realness and authenticity are Black queer practices of knowing and signifying that were activated both Thain's subway ad and in the Salvation Army take on The Dress dilemma, "One Photo A Day," and many other ads using color cosmetics on predominately white women to simulate DV. Distinctive to these campaigns is that the media activists' tactics reveal a desire for physical indications of DV that return one to Hartman's analysis of the coveted scene of Black suffering and the limits of empathy in unworking hideous social bonds.

Domestic abuse photography circulates DV as a particular "look," one productive of control of police visual evidence in VAWA prosecution. Producing the look as control illustrates the encounter between cybernetic logic and the camp trace in the realm of criminal justice. But I also want to suggest that in their very quality of being faked, legally camped DV images bring the hieroglyphics of the flesh and suspended agency into contact for the legal spectator. In this encounter the legal spectator is in a state of "feeling vaguely 'unsettled' or 'confused,' or, more precisely, a meta-feeling in which one feels confused about *what* one is feeling."[76] When simulated images of domestic abuse wounds are deployed by both the state and tactical media activists, the hieroglyphics of the flesh become entangled in a productive moment in which the legal spectator's suspension at bloodied flesh is the same moment when the racialized meanings of skin color, or, to employ Fanon's language, epidermalization, are at stake.[77] The official DV courtroom and unofficial extralegal setting become public laboratories for experiments in racial looking that cannot be separated from the meaning of domestic violence at the level of social science and constitutional law (DV and dV). For the legal spectator freely assembles in courtroom and public space by right of the US constitution that guarantees a republican form of government, and the interlocking right to a jury trial by one's peers.

CONCLUSION

Often when I talk about this book I am asked about how visual evidence of domestic violence can be improved. The question operates in a context in which networked computing and hypermedia development software promote infinite possibilities for editing photographs, moving images, and sound recordings. Undergirding the possibility of an improved visualization of violence are the marks of a problem-solving and product-oriented sensibility about the packaging and circulation of information. After all, visibility remains crucial to communicating awareness of social problems and imagining what a culture of redress might look like. Asking how to improve the representation of domestic violence is a request for best technical practices for visualizing violence in the courtroom and advocacy spaces. More importantly, it is a desire, a wish, that the persuasive power of visual evidence be fulfilled.

Despite the fantasies stirred by visual evidence, my argument in these pages is not about how or why we need to technically improve images of domestic violence. Before the question of how to improve the image there is an earlier one about how domestic violence came to look and move as it does; how the image of domestic violence came to organize legal and extralegal spaces. Many describe law as a blank space, a zone of nothing where words and arguments await the moment of their written inscription.[1] Legal personalities emerge from the nothing of law. Legal subjects also surface as photography, likewise a nothingness, an absence whose potential awaits emergence through light. To the extent that visual evidence is a container where we locate fantasies of justice, my work in *Legal Spectatorship* is more interested in reflecting on the political settlements forged and sustained through visual evidence, not in how to improve the power of the image or the effectiveness of its courtroom circulation. The book has traced domestic violence, first as a concept in legal writing and then as a body of visual evidence of abuse. I have sought to understand historically how the photograph organizes the space of legal activity and in doing so conditions, for a time, the interiority of those looking at visual evidence.

Thus, one act that sums up the intervention of this book is its refusal to discuss how to improve images of domestic violence or to outline a set of policy recommendations for state or activist tactics. With *Legal Spectatorship* I want to argue something different about domestic violence by inquiring after its appearance in mass communication in federal legislation, judicial decisions, and social awareness campaigns. These include the US Constitution's Domestic Violence Clause, the Violence Against Women Act, and the *Crawford* Supreme Court decision. I explore domestic violence in terms of constitutional, legislative, judicial, and activist mechanics intervening in the condition of being unable to remain yet unable to leave. This work is guided by Black feminist reading practices where flesh, body, and the conquest of physical and psychic space are political priorities that structure radical thought about the thingliness of evidence. Specifically, by attending to the vestibular position of the slave to domestic violence, this book argues that the condition of being unable to remain yet unable to leave is a social and not individual one. In US law and culture, the threat to social and political life posed by domestic violence is incomprehensible without thinking about slavery and the desire to know reproductive freedom.

The arguments contribute a legal, cultural, and media history of the vestibular role of Black fugitivity to how we theorize, research, and know domestic violence—from its first appearance in the US Constitution to scientific research on motivation to social media activism. Whether referring to a threat to national security, a new area of criminal prosecution, or the creation of a largely unacknowledged and therefore unnamed visual pedagogy, domestic violence can no longer have the image of which it seeks to get hold and control. Domestic violence appears as an event only through the mediating effects given to narrative technique. Thus, I maintain that the domestic violence victim and those who advocate and care for them and their families are a part of a centuries-long routine of population management. Despite the work done to demonstrate that domestic violence ignores boundaries race, class, or sexual preference, domestic violence travels under the sign of a white woman with a battered face. She is one half of an intimate couple whom we get to know through statistics, psychology experts, mediated testimony, news reports, and personal disclosures from family and friends. My task in *Legal Spectatorship* has been to show that documentary realism of the DV courtroom can no longer be accessible without the histories of colonialism and slavery. Black freedom struggles haunt the machinations of state and federal legislatures, judiciaries, and activist tactics around domestic violence. Doing so provocatively suggests that slavery figures as the repressed relation of violence adjudicated in the DV court between couples experiencing intimate partner violence.

In my orientation to Black feminism I follow the impulses of Brittney Cooper, Joan Morgan, and Jennifer Nash, each of whom voices concern about the future of the field of Black feminist study. These scholars bring awareness of the institutionalization of Black feminist intellectual history—made possible through the inclusion of Black women within the academy and the best and worst aspects of its disciplinary culture. Nash in particular has posed challenging questions to Black feminism's signature deployment of intersectionality, suggesting the need to surrender the concept in order to feel Black feminism differently. According to Nash, the tradition of Black feminist theory is built on a politics of love where Black women perform the soul work of bearing witness to socially produced, and therefore mutual, vulnerabilities. Because Black feminists' practice of love politics has always explored the condition of linked fate and the related project of witnessing, the field of study promoted a juridical ethic that is deeply invested in the state. This brings Nash to ask a series of questions about the future relationship between love politics, Black feminism, and the state, between intimacy, Black women, and law:

> Is it simply collusion or "cruel optimism" for black feminists to seek engagement with the state? Can we imagine black feminist engagements with the state as taking forms other than seeking redress and demanding visibility? Are there ways to imagine black feminist legal engagement that circumvent the uncomfortable and problematic position of being "at home with the law"? How can black feminists reimagine law as a site for staging productive intimacies and enacting radical vulnerabilities?[2]

Legal Spectatorship is a meditation on visual evidence of domestic violence. Its study of form does the work Nash calls for to reimagine intersectionality as "method/mode/way of conceptualizing movement, time, space and effects of power."[3] The history I detail is guided by the idea of reimagining Black feminist methods and therefore positions the image of domestic violence as the result of numerous struggles, acts of care, and advocacy to help reshape the lives of battered women. I suggest these struggles are illegible without reference to slavery; slavery is the absent presence in research, adjudication, and political activism about domestic violence. When slavery in centered in this way, Black feminism's anti–domestic violence position (its love politics) surfaces as an articulation of Black gendered struggle. This struggle is waged within and beyond the Black community in ways that explode this study's apparent use of battered "women" as a stable term and any assumption that the study pertains only to heterosexual relationship dynamics. In other words, the slave is also a form necessary to reimagine the effects of power intramural to Black life. This means taking Cedric Robinson's observation that "Black opposition to domination has continued to *acquire new forms*" to the limit.[4] The evidentiary photograph is a form constitutive of Black opposition.

There are readers who might conclude the book centers the attention to the image as form in a way that takes the focus off battered women's healing and direct examination of their speech in ways that leave them a step removed from the heart of critical analysis. However, the study of battered women's evidentiary photography is not superficial or uncommitted to their experience. Rather, the book's multiple methods—archival, ethnographic, rhetorical, and semiotic—open several lines of radical intersectional thinking: the victim of domestic violence is produced not only through the punch and abusive words that are thrown but also by the evidentiary image of the self that is thrown in space in the quest for justice. Photographs of battered women's wounded skin are the fulfillment of a centuries-long process of repressing thoughts on the intimacies whereby slavery is instituted and prolonged. The archive of slavery's psychosexual hold is diverted to the category of battered women and the white femininity through which she travels in law and media. Photographs of battered women are a spatializing infrastructure and a remnant of political settlements among the authors of the Constitution who were concerned about the future of slavery and Black people. The images are the descendants of literary and photographic images of escaped slaves whose experiences were authenticated through writing and daguerreotype. Law, scientific knowledge, and activism interact, leading to the collection and positioning of battered women in regimes where they are evaluated by the public through the interplay of photography and a live witness. In this sense, photography becomes a place to go, to inhabit, disperse, and displace colonial and racial intimacy. In order to comprehend the emergence of the battered women as a legal and cultural personality, the particular moment when the slave acquires powers of authentication and testimony about their experience of slavery must be told. By sticking with visual evidence these pages have examined the authenticating role of the literary slave narrative and slave daguerreotype operating in the background of battered women's struggles.

My examination of the history of domestic violence and the production and circulation of photographic evidence has centered mutual vulnerability and witnessing by affording the minor affects a prominent role. My investment in the minor affects comes out of the work of Sianne Ngai, whose books *Ugly Feelings* and *Our Aesthetic Categories: Zany, Cute, Interesting* are deeply suggestive of how to read the minor in all its aesthetic enfleshments and embodiments. *Legal Spectatorship* reads the minor as a set of negative affects that inform the performance of the possible in conditions of unfreedom. The principle of the minor thus also pertains to the written, photographed, and drawn (minor) literatures of freedmen and women recounting their experience of slavery. These affects and the forms and formats in which they are communicated pertain to the condition of suspension experienced psychically and spatially. Suspended agency is an element in Ngai's formulation of the minor affects. Suspension entails a vulnerable form of agency, which, according to Ngai, plays a larger role in discussions of politics and the social than typically thought. I took up suspended agency and the minor affects as a way to reinvigorate Black feminist love politics by identifying in the slave's fugitivity the enormous stakes of suspended agency. *Legal Spectatorship* attends to how suspended agency is worked through by the subject of domestic violence, broadly conceived, to begin with the slave's fugitivity.

The adjudication of domestic violence entails the managed consumption of testimony and the exchange of looks between the alleged victim and jury members, attorneys, judges, and courtroom audience members. Practicing Black feminist love politics in this area of the political and social means confronting new forms of matter produced and controlled by legislative and judicial acts. The Violence Against Women Act (VAWA) and the Supreme Court's decision in *Crawford* are two such acts framing *Legal Spectatorship*. Together, they expand the territory of police photography and its use in managing the confrontation between alleged victims and accused batterers, witnesses and attorneys, witnesses and juries, and so on. Nash locates the future of intersectionality in "imagining legal action that can be individualized,

intimate, and rooted in lived experience."[5] When police photograph battered women, they perform a discretionary legal action that is experienced
as by victims intersectionally.

Intersectionality has received little mention in these chapters. The analytical stakes of my arguments do, however, address the current impasse
between intersectionality and the affects driving feminism, which shaped
the concept around identity, rather than critical analyses of law. Rather
than comment directly on the disciplinary status of intersectionality or of
feminism for that matter, the book analyzes intersectional experience by
bringing a different legal archive into contact with constitutional law, media
objects, formats, literatures, scientific experiments, and architectures. *Legal
Spectatorship*'s analysis of visible evidence of domestic violence theorizes intersectionality outside Kimberlé Crenshaw's initial domain of employment
discrimination and the federal practice of labor law.[6] Through the method
of media archaeology and a reading of constitutional law, the book has taken
up Crenshaw's deployment of intersectionality theory to examine how Black
women experienced visual evidence and the architecture of the DV courtroom. I took the initial position that VAWA and the *Crawford* decision created testimonial scenarios in which photographic evidence mediated the
speech acts of abused women. I also examined how the courtroom speech
act informed activist tactical media strategies about domestic violence. I described the communicative interactions and traced them to the singular appearance of domestic violence in the US Constitution. A new set of media
objects, scientific experiments, sensations, and speech acts illuminated the
vestibular role of the slave and her descendants in the legal theory of domestic violence. The constitutional history of domestic violence would transform
into courtroom adjudication of intimate partner violence and the development of a pedagogy explaining the path of violent intimacy.

Conceptually, intersectionality bears witness to vulnerabilities experienced due to Anglo-American law's inability to read the subject's many
constitutive properties even as law historically endows the subject as property bearing and owning.[7] *Legal Spectatorship* examines this problem anew
by offering a media history of legislative and judicial acts informed by the
shared forms of vulnerability and witnessing to which Black feminist studies are attuned. Throughout the chapters I explored how intersectionality
and the vulnerabilities it exposes before law comment on agency. Thinking
of agency as suspended opened its theorization to space, architecture, sensation, and substance. Suspended agency reveals a subject whose freedom of
movement, insight about feelings, and speech are obstructed. Photographic

evidence, affidavits, court files, and pedagogy tools are objects that contribute to the experience of suspension and its constitutive ugly feelings. Across the chapters, suspension is the condition that demands from victimized people and the people who study them the authentication of experience. Time and again *Legal Spectatorship* finds that the slave is a remnant of conventions and procedures for authenticating evidence in the adjudication and knowledge-making practices of domestic violence. Most of all domestic violence is another way of talking about the status of the social contract.

We now arrive at the tripartite instability of police photographic evidence of DV, battered woman syndrome (BWS), and the Cycle and the Wheel, which critical race theory, visual culture, and media studies are beginning to address: social media and/as contract. Traditional theories of the social contract found in Locke, Hobbes, Rousseau, and Kant conceptualized the humanist project in terms of authority, legitimacy, obligation, and obedience. Carole Pateman's *The Sexual Contract* and Charles Mills's *The Racial Contract* unsettled the tradition and a litany of subsequent scholarly preoccupation with reading class into the social contract. Pateman and Mills illustrate how exclusion and erasure manifest in the practices of misogyny and antiblackness, structure the social contract. In the case of Pateman, the social contract includes activities, alliances, and formations that were made possible by a prior agreement *between men* and that excluded women; in the case of Mills, the social contract was underwritten by agreement between white masters, which excluded slaves. Respectively, both authors explore the ways women and the Black slave and her descendants have been written out of the social contract yet remain integral to its reproduction. Pateman's ideal position holds we ought to do away with contracts entirely, remove them from the social. Another position is to recuperate the contract by investing it with consent. To this end, Mills pragmatically advocates remaking the Rawlsian tradition through a concept of "domination contract," positioning those grouped by the dishonor and exploitation of racialized gender and the colony as the foundation of the social.[8]

Late in *Stolen Life* Moten offers insight about what the domination contract might encapsulate when he imagines the interaction between Betty and Judge Shaw, whose details Sora Han examines in "Slavery as Contract: Betty's Case and the Question of Freedom." His description of a moment of *regard* is suggestive of how Black femininity is a cipher for the quotidian and legal limits of liberal contractual freedom:

> Can we recover what she did not say to [Judge] Shaw; can we excavate what is held in her having been withheld from their exchange, in her

refusal to be party to it, in the obscenity of her objection to the objectifying encounter with otherness? What sociality is concealed from him in whatever what he thought her "face" revealed to him? Her face was not her own but it was a face, and it could be read, he must have thought. Wasn't it a face? Couldn't it be read? Didn't it unconceal? What material amazement is held in the difference that giving and showing embrace? And what do giving and showing withhold? What is withheld in and as their nonperformance?[9]

Han's analysis of Betty's decision to return to the Sweets and the testifying witness(es) discussed in *Legal Spectatorship*'s chapters provide examples of how Black womanhood unsettles the conceptual limitations of free choice and contract. Wonder at Betty's face and its recursion unsettles the now of the domestic violence trial witness, who also appears in Harriet Jacobs's fugitively corpsed body in the loophole of retreat, as the witness who corpses at the sight of her wounded digital image.[10] The political is, for elements of the Black radical tradition, a suspect discourse, a realm whose promise of inclusion through practices of civil contract can neither address nor redress the imposition of Blackness or the liberal concept of freedom it upholds. Where Betty's "choice" exposes a dialectic between freedom (to contract) and slavery, victims of domestic violence expose one between consent (to make photographic evidence) and legal coercion. To imagine a future freedom *from* slavery and the need for forms of consent that Han and Moten might offer as a deconstruction of the social contract tradition would also suggest the limitless production of the violence Mills's domination contract would have to deflect.

Legal Spectatorship has positioned photography as a troubling mechanism/medium of recognition and inclusion into the space of legal adjudication and the fulfillment of the social contract. I ask now, how do photographic acts add further complexity to optimistic and pessimistic, ideal and pragmatic arguments about the future of the contract? In *The Civil Contract of Photography*, Ariella Azoulay documents how people use photography to work through and work on the political and social inequities sown by liberalism and its contracts. She studies the production and circulation of photographs documenting resistance between those near and at a distance from struggles of self-determination, segregation, maiming, and genocide in the Occupied Territories. For Azoulay, people do things with photographs; photos are imbricated in how citizens address each other rhetorically, which is to say politically.[11] The contractual exchange is not only social, but more specifically civil, pertaining to duty and obligation even though these burdens are unevenly born. Contract permeates the ontology of the photograph. Yet, in our era of algorithmic cultures, where more and more communicate through social media platforms through the exchange of images, it is indeed difficult to imagine doing away with photography with the same ease with which Pateman imagines abjuring the social contract as the dominant form—both metaphorical and literal—we use to conceptualize and collectivize the social bond. At the same time, when applied to photography, Mills's pragmatics of retaining the social contract is likely to result in an association between state and corporate photography practices and the rationalizing discourse of photographic realism. Such is the case I illuminate through cosmetically simulated domestic violence injuries produced by corporatized victim advocates.

For Azoulay, the image of rape resists the civil contract she introduces to political theory. She claims there are no images of rape because they are taboo. "The taboo applies not only to direct images of rape, but to an entire gamut of images stained by the term 'rape.' They are all contaminated, and showing them is prohibited."[12] She asks why rape is left outside the field of vision given the frenzy of the real and the pragmatics of social contract that has given us the right to look, and to know. It is possible no one is interested in seeing or attaining images of rape, or it is the case that the desire for rape photography has a mimetic relation to the violence of rape itself. Azoulay argues that "it is impossible to understand why there has been no open, public debate over the question whether such images should be shown and in what way."[13] Ultimately, the absence of rape images prevents us from acknowledging rape as a state of emergency.

One of the ways *Legal Spectatorship* extends Azoulay's position can be seen in its return to the archive of slavery to analyze photographs of domestic violence in legal and extralegal settings. Like the image of the act of rape, images of the act of domestic violence have also been subject to accusations of obscenity that renders them taboo. In 1983 photographer Donna Ferrato famously captured the act of domestic violence between a white, upper-middle-class American married couple.[14] The publication story behind those images is marked by the obscenity and taboo that Azoulay associates with the visual culture of rape. I suggest, through the example of images of domestic violence, that white heteronormativity lies at the heart of *why* the images are obscene and therefore taboo. Members of the Black community have long understood our multi-shaded families to be evidence of acts of plantation rape written upon the skin.

The skin, flesh, and body are areas of inquiry in *Legal Spectatorship* that complicate Azoulay's claims about the absence of rape from the field of vision.

The transition I document, from dV to DV, links the scientific study of violent intimate partnership and the administrative planning of domestic violence courts to origins in chattel slave relations. By working through the archive of slavery, my attention to the courtroom space and networks of handling visual evidence can then detail the ways the state develops around the aporia Azoulay sees in the absence of photographs of the act of rape. Courtroom evolution on domestic violence occurs through strategies of the flesh that perform as civil contracts. Sameena Mulla's ethnography of the rape examination—the probing and scraping of women's flesh to collect and analyze fluids and tissue—is one example that inspires *Legal Spectatorship*.[15] While Mulla's evidence is not presented as photographic media or historicized in terms of the archive of slavery, it nevertheless informs my analysis of visual evidence of domestic violence and its enactment of a civil contract of photography. Both the rape examination and the images of battered women are tactile modes of observation and adjudication; they are strategies of the flesh that stand in for the absent image of the act of rape Azoulay finds elusive. These objects extend how photography mediates Azoulay's theory of the civil contract.

Courtroom architecture conditions the experience of the political and social stakes of the civil contract of photography. The procedural character of visual evidence means its communicative work is largely transactional: evidence is seen with an eye toward a verdict formally achieved. Azoulay's approach to the civil contract of photography, however, involves communicating through images in an extralegal setting where duty and obligation are informally negotiated. Nonetheless, techniques and conventions of authentication I examine in the domestic violence courtroom are part of a communication between legal evidence and public images that appears symbiotic. Common to legal and extralegal environments is that spectators in both environments enact the civil contract of photography through strategies of the flesh. However, by reading visual evidence of domestic violence as flesh, I posit the photograph as irreducible to realist truth claims. This intervention opens up positive law to racial critique.

The fleshy quality of photography, exemplified when physical injuries are passed around or projected as if an extension of the wounded person's body, complicates the meaning of the social contract and its future. Like the courtroom or social media platform, photography is a third space where people experiment and extend the life-world. We might feel the social and civil contract differently through photography.

In chapter 1 I focused on the different ways former slaves narrated their experiences. The periods just prior to and after the Civil War were crucial for transforming the capacities that endowed Black people to communicate about their experience. In an environment of proliferating new media, freedmen and women emerged as bearers of verifiable evidence. As people whose claims to experience were newly endowed with authenticity, freedmen and women influenced the format of abolitionist media. Harriet Jacobs's experience of fugitive maternity offered a view into the garret as a space of suspended agency, the experience of being unable to leave yet unable to remain in place. The daguerreotype taken of the escaped slave Gordon was another example of the slave's experience of suspended agency. Jacobs and Gordon overcame their condition—they sulked and eventually "took to the swamp" in ways that link the flowering of slave insurrection to contemporary domestic violence struggles—DV's legislative and judicial past knowable by returning to the Constitution's Domestic Violence Clause and its drafting history. Both Jacobs's and Gordon's respective escapes would have erupted out of the sulks. Jacobs's flight into the interstitial space of the garret and Gordon's fugitive enlistment in the Union Army are familiar images in Black feminist studies. The circulation of their images—literary in Jacobs's case and photographic in Gordon's—contextualized slave narratives and other forms of abolitionist media in terms of shifting ideas about what, or who, a narrator, observer, and author could be. By reading the affective and physical fugitivity of the slave into the Domestic Violence Clause, the first chapter employed Spillers's notion of an American grammar as a method of reading the US Constitution. This reading enables a deconstruction of images of Black fugitivity and feeling, allowing the theory of domestic violence, as it was formulated by the Constitution, to surface.

Legal Spectatorship further has enacted Black feminist love politics as method by bringing the field to bear on the history of cybernetics. This happens in chapter 2, where I trace a minor literature of Black fugitivity undergirding the work of key civil rights and Cold War psychologists, Sylvan Tomkins, Martin Seligman, and Lenore Walker. By reviewing how these scientists conceived of learned helplessness, affective scripts, and BWS by including and (in the case of Walker) excluding Black people, the chapter establishes the history of slavery within the narrative cybernetics tells itself about itself. Black feminist readings of cybernetics offered in *Legal Spectatorship* excavate the minor literature and minor affects operating in the field. Vulnerability of the colonized and racially enslaved precedes the cybernetic hypotheses, experiments, and conferences and the scientific pioneers whose lives and networks are the obsession of contemporary scholarship on media philosophy and control.

Many critical studies of cybernetics look to the robot and computer to extricate Anglo-Western theories of labor, affect, and the human. Rather than rehearse the trope of the robot and computer as the guiding inspirational media motivating cybernetic theory, I position the fugitive freedom of the slave as a minor history that helps launch cybernetic inquiry. Seligman's behavioral experiment on learned helplessness, Tomkins's narrative of the affective scripts, and Walker's study of battered women's discourse about their experience of intimate partner violence could all be traced to the slave and her descendants, whose experience animated power and control theory. Tracing the development of DV control theory in Cold War science and the place of the slave therein opens the history of cybernetics to Black feminist theorizing. The second chapter pivoted away from previous disciplinary emphasis on the robot and examined how the slave is both central and forgettable in the study of power and control. Seligman's and Tomkins's theories of power and control offered a scientifically reproducible perspective into Black people's experience of DV. They translated Black experience into behavioral concepts that would explain social and political crisis. Put simply, white scientists examined in chapter 2 conceived of slavery's afterlife and abolition in the social science laboratory.

As Black freedom struggles provide the structuring examples for scientific research on affect and motivation, the work of Black authentication surfaces anew. Nineteenth-century conventions invented by freedmen and women to authenticate their experience appear outside the literary context; they continue to proliferate across new media forms and disciplinary boundaries. Black experience authenticated psychological research in the civil rights and Cold War contexts even as Black people were either excluded from scientific research protocols or displaced by animals. By making this point, I intend to do more than encourage multiculturalism in science. Rather, by tracking down the subterranean ways Black freedom struggles enable scientists to produce work authentically, I locate an abolitionist scientific protocol that rebels against the myth of the human undergirding the social sciences.

My description of the DV courtroom has revealed a space for the circulation of a peculiar body of images and affects. Photographs of battered women are projected to multiple lines of sight in the courtroom. They are live projections where the substance of photography and skin appear and are thrown as one. But they are also historical projections of constitutional law, specifically the Domestic Violence Clause and its deep anxieties harbored in the drafting of the clause about Black insurrection. The case described positions witnesses in these cases in the context of "misdemeanorland," where the tentacles of the criminal courts reach out to manage more than petty criminal offenders; they also manage their victims. Here the minor affect emerges again as a "low level victim" whose availability and appearance are managed by the misdemeanor courts. Reading what happens to testifying witnesses at the misdemeanor level reveals a major flaw of the lower courts. Evidence in misdemeanor DV courts is characterized by the suspension of affect and knowledge they create in the spectator about the content of the image. Yet such cases and the evidence they circulate make up the bulk of the court activity and expose respondents on both sides to increased state management.

Photographs are crucial forms of paperwork in the DV courtroom. Their elevated status derives from their ontology as techno-scientific objects, their participation in structuring the master narrative of science. By tracing the authentication of evidentiary photographs of the wounded self, chapter 3 showed how the image translates the scientific work of Walker's theory of BWS. Visual evidence of wounding conveys the narrative of BWS with greater immediacy. Projected images of injured skin move across the sightlines of courtroom space. They speed up the cyclical process BWS explains, analogizing an exchange of passive-aggressive feelings between intimates through an icon that is thrown. Evidence in the misdemeanor case discussed did not fail alone as if in a vacuum. The relationship between visual evidence of domestic violence and Walker's feminist theory of power and control is one of inheritance. The inheritance extends far beyond photographic evidence and Walker's theory to the moment in the Constitution where domestic violence and the guarantee of a republican form of government are legally inscribed. The moment of testimony and the cycle of abuse it analogizes failed according to historical conditions befalling the enslaved.

A criticism of my arguments about mass communication of visual evidence of domestic violence may be that the approach ascribes too much power to the state. *Legal Spectatorship* focuses on the state's engagement in media-making and its uptake by social services and advocates at an exciting moment when many Black feminist thinkers engage Spillers's flesh-body distinction in ways that theorize beyond the state and its projects of humanity, normativity, and recognition.[16] Nash articulates the stifling sense of Black feminist lingering upon the question of representation and our longing for recognition outside controlling images that mythologize Black femininity and maternity. However, visual evidence of domestic violence is a new controlling image emerging in the criminal courts, one whose history is outside the boundaries of critical public discussion. In response, *Legal Spectatorship* has followed the spatialization of the DV courtroom through law's incorporation and transformation of legal writing about slavery and the science of human motivation. Taking seriously the contemporary spatialization of the DV courtroom and its choreographies also means tracing the encounter between legal communication about domestic violence and its extralegal counterpart. To do so is to understand how the archive of slavery informs media practices in places where slavery appears to have no bearing, treating the process of spatialization of the DV courtroom as a space to think about visual evidence of domestic violence ecologically.

Recent Black feminist theories provocatively affirm skin and flesh as staging ground where controlling mythologies of Back women are unsettled through play. Playful and sincere strategies of the flesh are at work in anti–domestic violence media campaigns. The fourth chapter develops a reading of white feminist tactical media examples where the absent presence of black skin from the DV courtroom returns like a boomerang to unsettle not only the controlling image but the camera as a philosophical tool deployed as ideological state apparatus.

Chapter 4's final arguments about the extralegal production of evidence illuminate the afterlives of courtroom aesthetics. Police photography of battered women circulates beyond the DV courtroom; though outside the closed system of legal procedure, its afterlife remains tethered to law's reduction of domestic violence to an icon. Though its "look" largely depicts white feminine injury, this book points to how black skin delimits how injury can be seen in visual evidence. As matter, black skin confounds the form and content that structure the experience of domestic violence photography. As narrative, Black rebellion from slavery also disrupts the story hegemonic images of battered women can tell.

Thus, while it is important to look for and affirm strategies of the flesh that manifest from outside state power and law's autopoiesis, a process whereby law moves to maintain the status quo in the face of its disruption, my critique of tactical media examples of anti–domestic violence activism suggests how the creative techniques and gestures deployed actually reify state power and its narrow understanding of what constitutes evidence of domestic violence. Domestic violence is a look, one that disrupts testimonial narrative. Writing the ecological relationship between visual evidence and tactical media responses to domestic violence does the more radical work of deconstructing evidence as production. The ecology may at first appear to reinforce state power in terms of how law and culture interact to secure evidence. However, by revealing the closed communication circuit between police DV photography and activist simulations of DV, chapter 4 returned to the real business of illustrating how the visual eviscerates law, rather than upholding a symbiotic relationship between the two.

This book has examined visual evidence in the context of formal, highly circumscribed movements and testimonial acts of the domestic violence courtroom. While it has considered a relatively small body of photography, the explorations and concepts developed to read, critique, and historicize visual evidence are useful for understanding the historical dynamics of authentication and testimonial speech acts. The interventions made in these pages are a step toward analyzing the media forms emerging to capture testimonial speech about traumatic experience, from workplace microaggression to sexual harassment and assault. Strategies of the flesh deployed in domestic violence courtrooms and extralegal settings have given way to algorithmic means of authenticating experience. If the civil contract of photography mediates the escape from and displacement of the threat of domestic violence, then Twitter, Instagram, and other social media accounts are emerging loopholes of retreat.

The #MeToo movement, for example, draws attention to how the problem of intersectionality in US law and culture is sustained by the property established in and as whiteness, developed by Cheryl Harris's widely influential essay "Whiteness as Property."[17] Sora Han has noted how "few have appreciated Harris's focus on how modern property law administers classical forms of property, *including intangible things*."[18] Harris's essay ties a theory of white subjectivity to Enlightenment theories of property as they were weaponized through settler colonialism and chattel slavery. The insights of the essay are profound for communication, media, and object relations theory because Harris demonstrates how property rights are conferred through the exchanges of administrative tools (slave codes, apportionments, paperwork, classification schemes) and rhetorical strategies. According to Harris, such techniques engendered "economic hegemony of black and Native American people."[19] Whiteness and property rights are produced through conventions of authentication mastered by whites who use the conventions to both dismiss the other's capacity to hold property while also reifying the ontology of being property for the other. When Harris is read for the ways the ideology and tools of property-making can administer even "intangible things," social media tools are added to the litany of forms whereby whiteness is propertied in the US contemporary. Thus, my analysis of domestic violence photography extends to the intangible space of the Internet, for it, too, is where modern property law administers whiteness as a shield against the other.[20]

Started in 2006 by Tarana Burke, the MeToo hashtag addressed the silence among women and girls victimized by sexual violence and harassment. The hashtag, #MeToo, was used by Alyssa Milano, a white actress who hoped to move victims, allies, and advocates into discourse against remaining silent in the wake of the sexual assault scandals involving Harvey Weinstein, Bill Cosby, Jeffrey Epstein, and Donald Trump. Obviously, these men should not function as a list of "bad eggs." For their violence occurred in an ongoing context of nation-building that secures white patriarchy institutionally and intergenerationally, from school to office to factory floor, from cradle to grave in ways that compromise everyone. Burke's identity as the founder of the #MeToo movement encompassed concerns within Black feminism about the larger issue of how white women who are positioned as ideal representations of the sympathetic victim dominate awareness campaigns, advocacy, and legal redress in sexual harassment, even as they, too, are seldom believed. Raising controversy about the attribution of the #MeToo movement (from Milano back to Burke) is part of how Black feminist love politics practices its work on vulnerability. As a result, Black and Brown women made vulnerable to erasure within #MeToo were in excess of Burke.

Legal Spectatorship establishes a media history, informed by critical race and visual culture studies, that contextualizes the kind of speech and media practice represented by the #MeToo movement. As persuasive rhetoric, the social and political stakes of #MeToo concern the entwined problems of affect, media, and their valuation in and as space. First, there is the difficulty of negotiating the feelings associated with victimization that conditions reproductive unfreedom. Burke sought to end the silence of victims who suffer from the kinds of ugly feelings associated with suspended agency, a condition of being unable to reckon with current and past situations of sexual violence and harassment. Second, in its brevity, #MeToo's mere six characters cultivates extralegal forms of testimony online. Those who retweet #MeToo issue a public complaint that may circulate without direct assistance by the state or even the care of social service advocates, family, and friends. The hashtag moves beyond the no-drop prosecution and mandatory arrest policies of the Violence Against Women Act. It also moves past the image of battered woman controlled by the police and secured through tactical media activism that cosmetically simulate wounding. In this sense the hashtag activism of #MeToo locates the stakes of testimonial speech in constitutional law, specifically the critique of the Domestic Violence Clause *Legal Spectatorship* affords.[21] #MeToo circulates as extralegal testimony in opposition to the *Crawford* decision. Third, the movement challenges the origins of social media in white supremacy and colonial and military conquest. It establishes and holds space for Black feminist feelings, concerns, and speech acts. This maneuver returns the project of Black feminism to Crenshaw's original intentions for the concept of intersectionality in which law is positioned at a metaphorical junction between how discrimination operates and what Zakiyyah Iman Jackson and Riley Snorton refer to as the "blackened" subject of legal rights.[22] Employment and discrimination law read male employee victims as Black and female employee victims as white and directs its liberal capitalist redress options toward these populations. Consequently, Black women appear unaffected by discriminatory laws and policies that structure reproductive unfreedom; they are vestibular to the legal work of employment discrimination law. Black women lose out on monetary and other forms of redress for discrimination. More damaging is how the incomprehensibility of Black women's complaints before law, including the kinds of affective labor performed in nonprofit organizations such as Burke's, develops labor law through their absence.

Of course, #MeToo, and #SayHerName hashtag activism are part of a broader social movement globally known as "Black Lives Matter." Black Lives Matter organizing is also informed by the arguments this book makes about the theory of domestic violence in US law and culture. Patrisse Cullors, Alicia Garza, and Opal Tometi circulated the hashtag in 2013 after the murder of high school student Trayvon Martin. They started the campaign with the purpose of creating a network for theorizing Black social life and death within an ongoing enterprise of judicially sanctioned murder. From a media studies perspective informed by Black feminism, #BlackLives Matter rearticulates the relationships analyzed in network theory for Black freedom struggles. Where network theory studies the structure of social relationships making their findings manifest through graphical representations, #BlackLivesMatter has an a priori reading of the structure of social relationships as colonial and racial. The ethical force of its reading restructures and critically manifests social relations not as graphical abstraction but in the real. In other words, participants of Black hashtag activism escape to the intangible space of the Internet. They extend the interstitial space of Harriet Jacobs's loophole of retreat to online places where whiteness currently properties itself. The immediacy of the fervor with which BLM hashtag activism efforts were lampooned and rebuked confirms the Internet as a hegemonic space for the administration of white property, including its economic schemes and the supplementary function of aesthetics.

My hope is that *Legal Spectatorship*'s discussion may extend to the problem of authentication and testimony beyond photography to the intangible space of online communication. Increasingly, digital tools translate and transform the traditional means of witness testimony. The development of digital information escrow technologies is an exemplary site where the influence of photographic evidence may be shifting toward the cybernetic body that archives testimony by logging in to an escrow device. The investigation of sexual harassment and assault is an emerging testing ground for escrow technologies that victims who are attached to corporatized total institutions such as colleges, universities, and company towns can record negative experiences, ranging from microaggression from colleagues to harassment to rape. Allegation escrow technologies intervene in the paralyzing eruption of minor or negative affects. Like police photography of battered women, escrow devices organize an intangible space for victims who are not sure they are victims. By logging a disturbing event anonymously and electronically, the escrow contributor experiments with time and what it might mean to identify as a victim of rape, harassment, and microaggression in the absence of any official or mandatory reporters who typically hear and bureaucratically process abuse claims. The experiment with allegation escrow technology does not prioritize investment in rights discourse. Rather than initiate legal proceedings, contributors invest in an infrastructure of complaint. They invest in an intangible space-time to think and feel their experience. Similar to hashtag activism, the allegation escrow algorithmically gathers the complaints logged by others who attest to the same experience.

Future scholarship might explore the investment in complaint infrastructures in ways allowing us to feel Cheryl Harris's insights about property in new ways.[23] It might also examine the transformation of victim testimony in the wake of emerging escrow technology use. *Legal Spectatorship* has explored the ways photographic evidence mediates testimony in ways that appear to settle authorial conflicts between science and law. The force of allegation escrows lies in how they release individual complaints once those complaints are algorithmically matched to a shared perpetrator. Possibilities for new forms of assembly and solidarity are therefore realized through ledger devices. Solidarity and assembly are forms of togetherness and sociality that are estranged from the history of police photography. Where visual evidence organizes numerous spaces for state power to throw images in a strategy of emphasizing and thereby control the look and demeanor of both crime and victimization in all of their colonial and racial guises, the escrow device may signal a shift away from the image. This shift imagines a subject who may be uncertain of their feelings, but is nonetheless empowered to authenticate their pain by tying their claim, and all of its vexations, to that of another.

CODA

This book is completed in a moment of seizure and transmogrification of the meaning of domestic violence. The arguments in *Legal Spectatorship* have detailed the ways slavery and Black insurrection center the historical meaning of domestic violence, despite the hegemonic use of the term to describe and abbreviate the paperwork circulating in courtroom settings where violence between intimate partners is adjudicated. Black rebellion against enslavement and the plight of battered women are linked to the condition of being unfree to remain and unfree to leave the state of violent coercion. The dominant condition in which we find ourselves, which encompasses a state of being (unfree), applies equally to the global coronavirus 2019 (COVID-19) pandemic. Unseen and largely unanticipated, COVID-19 is a global scourge whose proliferation across the US landscape led to a lockdown of businesses, government offices, schools, recreation, and leisure centers. The terms "lockdown" and "shelter in place" offer a vocabulary at once aggressive and gentle that analogizes the conflicting interpretations of data on the pathogen made by the highest level of government and public health officials. All manifestations of evidence—from data to information to knowledge to understanding—are rendered certain; they are riven by conspiracy theories and corruption. Or, more accurately, all forms of evidence are rendered uncertain except statistics on domestic violence during COVID-19, whose evidentiary claims are ironically conditioned by the phenomena of under-reporting, the *absence* of numbers. By way of a final remark, I want to suggest another beginning, another translation of visual evidence of domestic violence and emerging strategies of the flesh used to authenticate experience in the context of plague.

Connections between the US pandemic lockdown and domestic violence were made early on in public discourse. Declines in victim hotline use and other social services evince that the lockdown increases household tensions that violently and cyclically erupt because family members are confined to the home together. "The most dangerous place for a woman to be is her own home."[1] As reports make clear, domestic violence advocacy in the time of COVID-19 occurs through hotline services, where victims steal away to secretly get help over the phone. This form of telecare reveals the cybernetic future of domestic violence—its public advocacy and judicial culture operating at a distance. Power and control are intensified by confinement—the condition of being unable the remain yet unable to leave examined in this book through the slave's fugitive freedom.

Soon after published reports of the likely uptick in domestic violence during the time of COVID-19, the figure of the slave and her descendants returned to haunt the proliferation of the virus. The disproportionate movement of the pathogen throughout the bodies and communities of Black people displaced intimate partner violence as the inconvenient truth revealed by the plague. Effects of the COVID-19 pandemic on Black respiration and the state-sanctioned murder of George Floyd by asphyxiation evacuated the breath in at least two senses: "I can't breathe" encapsulates the weight of policing upon Black lives while also marking respiratory failure, one of several disproportionate outcomes related to the virus among Black folks.[2] The collision between aggressive pathogen and a state-corporate response prioritizing capitalist wealth management through police use of force also intersects with the structure of social service advocacy. This intersection evacuates psychophysical space, which is necessary to sustain the work of advocacy. As social workers man domestic violence hotlines from home, they have less space for distance from the pain and suffering of victims they listen to for a living. During the pandemic the need to decrease office contact has led to many hotline workers manning the call centers alone on rotating shifts. Overall, "hotline workers, who once counted on the commute between office and home to decompress from stressful professional lives no longer have that sense of separation."[3] "Bystander trauma" and "compassion fatigue" are a few names for a form of consumption that spreads outward, in the wake of domestic violence. These psychophysical conditions are constitutive of what Christina Sharpe calls "the weather." Regarding weather, "anti-blackness is pervasive as climate"; it "necessitates changeability and improvisation; it is the atmospheric condition of time and place" that "produces new ecologies."[4] The exhaustion and inability to decompress from holding the trauma of others coupled with the spatial demands of pandemic resonate with the Black life-death enunciation, "I can't breathe." Domestic violence has many atmospheres.

EVEN A BROKEN CLOCK IS RIGHT TWICE A DAY

In response to national demonstrations in the spring of 2020 against antiblackness and its particular figuration in the cop killer, Republican Senator Tom Cotton published an op-ed in the *New York Times* that reminded Americans of the constitutional demand for military force to address the protest. Though the senator referenced Article IV, Section 4—"the federal government has a duty to the states to 'protect each of them from domestic violence'"—he failed to engage the centrality of the history of and Black rebellion to the legal language of domestic violence.[5] This failure enlivens Cotton's subtler goal of locating antiblack racism squarely in the Democratic Party, rather than a world-making attribute of US constitutional law. In two examples, Republican presidents invoked the Insurrection Act, allowing the deployment of federal troops domestically to protect "the people" from rioting: President Dwight D. Eisenhower in 1957, federalizing National Guard troops mobilized at Little Rock's desegregation riots, and President George H. W. Bush in 1992, responding to the aftermath of the Rodney King police brutality verdict. In both instances Republican Party leaders deploy state power to quell race riots.

Cotton's argument establishes a genealogy of Republican federal action in matters of racial justice in an attempt to rationalize President Donald Trump's threats of military involvement against Black insurgency, which were reignited in 2020 after the murder of George Floyd by police. The senator, cottoning up to the Trump administration, draws an equivalence between white race rioters of the 1960s and BLM protestors and allies, who are the contemporary manifestation of Black abolitionist freedom struggles. The result is a rhetorical reversal whereby white race rioters of the civil rights era exchange positions with BLM protesters sixty years later.

I am drawn to the photographic evidence used to buttress Cotton's argument to "send in the troops." Included in the piece are two 1962 images, one of US federal troops walking and a second depicting angry white rioters protesting the arrival of James Meredith, a Black student who would integrate the University of Mississippi. Through the idea of legal spectatorship, I have argued that the subtleties of legal language should be brought into explicit conversation with photography's analytic arsenal. The concept suggests that photographs be read for more than their indicia of genre. Beyond a concern for particular styles of composition and categorization is the fact that photographs can operate as authenticating bodies; the movement of photography through projection in space allows images to stand in for the live testimonial presence of the persons and things depicted. The arguments by Senator Cotton constitute a deployment of legal spectatorship that illustrates the concept's imbrication in antiblack politics that I work against.

A closer look at the layout of the page suggests a Black insurgent reading that *Legal Spectatorship* has tried to offer, one that imbricates the law's letters and the projection of feeling and flesh through photography. Two separate crowds of white men are depicted side by side; in one image white soldiers carry guns, in the other white men stand with mouths agape, vociferously mocking their outrage at a Black man sharing intellectual space with them. What reader, what membership to what community does Cotton assume for his *New York Times* op-ed? The senator is willfully ignorant of the fact that Blackened people have little to no trust of *either* group of white men. The tradition of US law and culture is to shield the property of whiteness in the men on both the left- and the right-side images. Here the camera apparatus comes to mind as a model for historical political reversals Cotton stages between the Democratic and Republican Parties. The critical student of colonialism and antiblackness will not shy away from the resemblance between Cotton's rhetoric and the mechanics of the camera that invert the image upside-down and left-right. Up is down; right is left.

In this moment men and women post images of themselves with wounds sustained during the BLM protest. Some are self-portraits; others are captured by nearby protesters and bystanders. Images of maiming—shot-out eyes and burned flesh—that depict the effects of police rubber bullets on the body are common pictures posted online.[6] The injuries depicted in BLM protest imagery inform spectators how to read the rubber bullet, thereby contributing to the visual literacy of documents of state injury. Associating the wounds with a particular instrument also asks spectators to consider what the police have in their arsenal and the legal maneuvers, which include the very reforms for which many activists and lawmakers fight so hard, developed that ultimately keep diverse forms of police force in place.

Such photographs contribute to the long multimedia history of civil rights photography, descending both from literary narrations by former slaves who took to the swamp and the white surveilling gaze of the slave daguerreotype. But I also suggest that images of wounding at the hands of police return us to the question of domestic violence and the scientific theories and teaching tools developed to explain its psychophysical effects upon the subject. Black folks who assemble under the sign of BLM are subjects of visual evidence of domestic violence in its original conception, drafted in the US Constitution, and its psychological conception established in the laboratory. They remain conditioned by the state of being unable to leave and unable to remain. With nowhere else to go, they retreat into the third space of photography. But this may be a loophole of a different sort.

RETHINKING SOCIOTHERAPY

At this point we must apply the repressed question ostensibly belonging to the battered woman's psychology to BLM protesters: Why do they go back? Why do Black insurgents and their allies keep coming back? What kind of subject or legal personality is represented in the images and those who regard them? How, in a time of pandemic, when being Black is a morbidity indicator, do protesters continue to risk infection by taking to the streets? What does the image of Black wounded protesters who are called into assembly by numerous video recordings of lynched Black folks symptomatize of Black insurrection *as a social role*?

"When the civic sphere has succumbed to mass torture and restraint, only decolonial violence can redeem civil life by offering the mind a way out."[7] The images of BLM organizing against antiblackness point toward a reconsideration of Frantz Fanon's sociotherapy (*socialthèrapie*) and its possible relationship to the attempt at a civil contract seen in the study of authentication of domestic violence and undertaken in this book. Social media and photography are thus constitutive of decolonial violence, albeit in another form; their work is psychophysical, affective. Through his clinical practice Fanon reworked the asylum, changing its weather conditions from a carceral power-knowledge of abnormality to a critical understanding of subjection that tends toward amnesty and sanctuary. The distinction is subtle as both senses of the word "asylum" concern spaces of enclosure for populations that mark the boundary between civilization and the abnormal, racial. Postcolonial theorist Ranjana Khanna observes that through sociotherapeutic experiment Fanon learned "the importance of introducing the outside habitat into the asylum" in order to reproduce a traditional "important site of everyday living in the asylum itself."[8] Social media production and courtroom spectatorship are important sites of everyday living. What would it mean to reorient Fanon's experimental work in the clinic toward the fleshy projections of social media and the courtroom milieu? The goal of excavating the political history of domestic violence cannot be a list of technical recommendations for how best to capture wounds or display evidence to the courtroom milieu. Instead, we might be centered by a Black fugitive desire to read photography and its spatialization of the decolonial violence, which has always been domestic violence. Social media is another milieu in which to inhabit madness.

NOTES

Introduction

1 See Corrigan, *Up against a Wall*; Andrus, *Entextualizing Domestic Violence*; Trinch, *Latinas' Narratives of Domestic Abuse: Discrepant Versions of Violence*; Lemon and Perry, "Admissability of Hearsay Evidence."

2 See Crenshaw, "Mapping the Margins"; Davis, *Violence against Women*; Roberts, "Criminal Justice and Black Families."

3 Han, *Letters of the Law*, 23–24.

4 Han, *Letters of the Law*, 17.

5 As Carrie Rentschler explains, "*Law and order* signifies a political ideology vis-à-vis crime that focuses on crime control and the containments and warehousing of those deemed criminal" (emphasis in original). See *Second Wounds*, 33.

6 Testimony at VAWA congressional hearings implicated police and court practices in the escalation of dangers facing women who sought legal action from violent partners. This exposed many instances of orders of protection—court documents that safeguard individual(s) from harassment by another by controlling the amount of personal contact and space that must exist between parties—that had gone un-honored once women crossed state lines, as well as many stories about the police's routine lack of response to domestic incidence calls and their frequent ineffectiveness when they did respond to emergency calls. The Violence Against Women Act measures removed police discretion, a significant source of power, from the process of investigation in domestic violence cases: it instituted

a "no-drop" policy that requires police to pursue charges, provided there is evidence of probable cause, with or without the victim's consent, and it also introduced "mandatory arrest," stipulating that police responding to domestic disturbance calls arrest abusive partners. Effectively, VAWA policing reforms invigorated the institutional and juridical production of contemporary domestic abuse claims. Together, these policies represent what Sally Engle Merry calls a "regime of domestic violence governmentality" embedded within law and order criminal reform ("Spatial Governmentality and the New Urban Social Order," 16). See also Merry, "Governmentality and Gender Violence in Hawai'i."

7 *Crawford v. Washington* 541 US 36 (2004).

8 *Crawford* involved the admissibility of hearsay testimony in the context of a married couple, Michael and Sylvia Crawford, who confronted Kenneth Lee for allegedly raping Sylvia Crawford. Michael Crawford stabbed Lee and claimed self-defense, saying that Lee had drawn a weapon that initiated the stabbing. Lee avowed no weapon was present. Upon police questioning, Michael Crawford said he was not sure if Lee had a weapon, but he believed he did so at the time of the confrontation. Sylvia Crawford, when questioned, initially reported that she did not witness the attack but upon further questioning claimed that she did in fact see the struggle and that Lee indeed employed no weapon. At trial, Sylvia Crawford could not be compelled to testify against her husband under the state of Washington spousal privilege law, which held that spouses cannot testify in court without the consent of the defendant spouse. Prosecutors sought to introduce Sylvia Crawford's testimony as evidence that Michael Crawford had no reason to believe that he was in mortal danger from Lee. Generally, because the statement was made out of court it would be excluded from evidence on the ground of hearsay. The court, however, allowed Sylvia Crawford's statement to be admitted on the basis of its reliability, assured by Michael Crawford's statement. Michael Crawford's defense counsel objected to the admission of Sylvia Crawford's statement on the grounds that Crawford would not be allowed to cross-examine Crawford without abnegating spousal privilege. To admit Sylvia Crawford's statement without confrontation violated the Confrontation Clause secured by the Sixth Amendment. The statement was allowed into evidence, and Michael Crawford was convicted. Crawford's conviction was overturned by the Washington court of appeals and later reinstated by the Washington Supreme Court, with the US Supreme Court ultimately agreeing to hear the case in November 2003. *Crawford v. Washington* swiftly and dramatically intensified the burden of prosecutors to prove their cases. Writing for the majority opinion, Justice Antonin Scalia argued that "the Framers would not have allowed the admission of testimonial statements of a witness who did not appear at trial unless he was unavailable to testify, and the defendant had not had a prior opportunity for cross-examination." *Crawford v. Washington* 541 US 36 (2004). Previously, hearsay evidence could be admitted by making exceptions to the hearsay rule. Under *Crawford*, prosecutors need the physical presence of the witness in court in order to prove their cases.

9 Lyon, *Surveillance Studies*, 14.

10 On this point I follow Han's citation of the work of Vicky Labeau and her reading of Frantz Fanon, where he specifies how he understands fantasy's relationship with Lacanian notions of "the real." Labeau, "Psycho-Politics."

11 Simone Browne's emphasis on the convergence between surveillance and antiblack racism is helpful for linking the forms of witnessing of enslaved people to contemporary forensic technologies. See Browne, *Dark Matters*.

12 See Moore, "Held in the Light."

13 Here I am inspired by the work of Bruno Latour and actor network theory. See Latour, *The Making of Law*.

14 See Brownmiller, *Against Our Will*.

15 See Sokoloff and Dupont, "Domestic Violence at the Intersections of Race, Class, and Gender."

16 See Crenshaw, *Say Her Name*. See also Threadcraft, "North American Necropolitics and Gender."

17 Threadcraft, *Intimate Justice*.

18 Han, *Letters of the Law*, 2.

19 Marriott, "Inventions of Existence," 313; emphasis in original.

20 Marriott, "Inventions of Existence," 298; emphasis in original.

21 I am grateful to Allen Feldman for his discussion on this point.

22 *On Racial Icons*, 4; emphasis in original.

23 Fleetwood, *On Racial Icons*, 1.

24 Courtney R. Baker, *Human Insight*, 7.

25 Baker, *Human Insight*, 7.

26 Brown, *The Repeating Body*, 8.

27 Following Cudjoe, Brown writes, "Caribbean literature boasts a history of art being connected to acts of structured rebellion" (*The Repeating Body*, 170). Both writers suggest any discussion of Black literature is impossible without a conception of (literary) resistance. See also Cudjoe, *Resistance and Caribbean Literature*.

28 The literature on forensic technologies and the racialized surveillance of women addresses a number of techno-cultural dilemmas facing victims of violence. See Das, "The Act of Witnessing"; Dubrofsky and Shoshana Magnet, *Feminist Surveillance Studies*; Corrigan, *Up against a Wall*; White and DuMont, "Visualizing Sexual Assault"; Campbell et al., "The Impact of Sexual Assault Nurse Examiner (SANE) Program Services on Law Enforcement Investigational Practices: A Mediational Analysis," *Criminal Justice and Behavior*.

29 Schaefer, "The Spectators as Witness?," 1, 5.

30 Other relevant histories of marriage dissolution during slavery include Basch, *Framing American Divorce* and *In the Eyes of the Law*; Manfred, *The Road to Reno*; Coryell et al., *Negotiating the Boundaries of Southern Womanhood*; Grossberg, *Governing the Hearth*; Hartog, "Marital Exits and Marital Expectations"; O'Hear, "Some of the Most Embarrassing Questions"; Stevenson, "Distress and Discord in Virginia Slave Families"; Daniels and Kennedy, *Over the Threshold*.

31 Schweninger, *Families in Crisis in the Old South*.

32 Schweninger, *Families in Crisis*, 99.

33 Schweninger, *Families in Crisis*, 100, 195n3.

34 Jones-Rogers, *They Were Her Property*, 61–62.

35 There is a point of speculative tension between Schweninger and Jones-Rogers. Their respective histories support two different profiles of white womanhood in the plantation South that are suggestive of the conditions of white women as a class. In Jones-Rogers's history slave-owning white women are empowered, capable of extreme, premeditated, and vicious violence against slaves—the kind of violence it is difficult to read and write about. Profligate white husbands are found desperately trying to gain access to their wives' income generated by slaves. Yet, a variety of legal documents including marriage contracts, pre- and postnuptial agreements, and wills create permanent enslaved income for white women that their husbands cannot appropriate. Jones-Rogers reports that despite how desperate husbands are to assume control of their wives' property, there was little to no physical force, no "domestic violence" between white couples disagreeing about money even though such disagreements were part of the pattern of their lives. Schweninger, for his part, presents copious analyses of marriage disputes, divorce documents, and other court papers between white slave-owning couples in which physical violence is mentioned as a dominant form of communication. Domestic violence was rampant in Southern slave-holding society. White men were physically disciplining their wives in ways indistinguishable from punishments traditionally meted out to slaves. White women in Schweninger's text appear without power but are increasingly motivated to divorce in the pre–Civil War years. The question that must be asked of both texts is, where, in Jones-Rogers, is the domestic violence one would expect given its frequency during the period; and, where, in Schweninger, is white women's violence against slaves, given its rampancy during the period?

36 See de Silva, "Toward a Black Feminist Poethics."

37 See *Farmer and Planter, DeBow's Review* (New Orleans, LA, 1868–80); *Southern Agriculturalist* (Charleston, SC, 1841–46); *Southern Cultivator* (Augusta, GA, 1843–).

38 Jones-Rogers, *They Were Her Property*, 68.

39 Jones-Rogers, *They Were Her Property*, 63; emphasis added.

40 My work here is indebted to Sara Ahmed's phenomenological approach that draws on a politics of disorientation in *Queer Phenomenology*.

41 Moten, *Stolen Life*, 250.

42 In addition to the entire corpus of Dubois's scholarship, I am thinking here primarily of anthropologist and writer Zora Neale Hurston's coverage of the 1952 murder trial of Ruby McCollum. McCollum stood trial for killing Dr. C Leroy Adams, a white doctor and senator-elect who repeatedly raped McCollum and forced her to bear his child. The trial and treatment of McCollum by the judge and an all-white jury provide an important case study of Black women and clemency rights and the topic of Black women and "paramour rights." Hurston

covered McCollum's trial in the *Pittsburgh Courier*. For work on Black life worlds by Black anthropologists, see Beale, "Double Jeopardy"; Bolles, "Anthropological Research Methods"; Gwaltney, *Drylongso*.

43 In this sense this chapter speculates on the intellectual successors of German philosopher Ernst Kapp's thinking on philosophy of technology and networks to demonstrate how ideas of freedom and the slave were made vestibular to Cold War era social science even as they continued to be central to concurrent civil rights–era politics. See Kapp, *Elements of a Philosophy of Technology*.

44 Allissa V. Richardson shows that while bystander recordings of Black death and dying have not done much to radically change US policing, the use of video has mobilized many Black Americans to use smartphone technology toward civil rights work and forms of protest. See Richardson, *Bearing Witness While Black: African Americans, Smartphones, and the New Protest #Journalism*.

45 The "ugly feelings," also known as minor affects, are negative affects (e.g., irritation, confusion, consternation) whose negative flow is characterized by the absence of noncathartic release. Ngai suggests political theory consider building politics around the underacknowledged significance of minor affects. See Ngai, *Ugly Feelings*.

46 See Kohler-Hausmann, *Misdemeanorland*.

47 For work on governance feminism, see Halley, *Split Decisions*. See also Halley et al., *Governance Feminism*.

Chapter One. Authenticating Domestic Violence

1 In *Reconstructing Womanhood*, Hazel Carby observes numerous acts of subversion of the cult of True Womanhood committed by the narrative arguments in *Incidents in the Life of a Slave Girl*. Jennifer Larson, who follows Carby's analysis of Jacobs's indictment of the cult of True Womanhood, further analyzes its key tenets: purity and submission. Focusing on the actions of white women in Jacobs's text, Larson demonstrates that "any actions by actual slave mistresses that may have been labeled as 'passive resistance' can be revised to 'active acceptance' for they had the power to reject the cult of True Womanhood's charge of submissiveness, and protect the purity of slave women, rather than continue to abuse it." Within the white married couple Black women occupied a vexed and vulnerable position. See Larson, "Converting Passive Womanhood to Active Sisterhood," 746. Yet, white women's understanding of the concept of victim of violence was oriented away from rather than in solidarity with Black female slaves, according to Barbara Omolade in *The Rising Song of African American Women*. But the garret has also been thought as a space of possibility where a modicum of happiness and relief could be discovered. In "Between the Rock and the Hard Place," Gloria T. Randle develops the psychoanalytic dimensions of Jacobs's estrangement from her own mother that is replicated in her estrangement from her own children and the role of her grandmother, her mother's twin, in mediating maternal absence and presence that nurtures

Jacobs's own maternal strength. The garret's evocation of tropes of Christian death, resurrection, transcendence, and ascension is, according to Georgia Krieger, an affirmation of Jacobs's skillful deployment of religious rhetoric to connect with guilty audiences reading her work (see Krieger, "Playing Dead"). In a similar vein, Valerie Smith considers the materiality of affect in space by focusing on the relationship between Jacobs's narrative of feeling in the garret in terms of the sentimentalism organizing the modern novel during the same period (*Self-Discovery and Authority*). As Isabel Soto affirms, *Incidents* "endorses freedom and agency as viable goals, or alternatively demystifies them" ("'The Spaces Left,'" 31). Collectively discussions of the garret and Jacobs's positioning within it mark the distinctions between freedom and its material and maternal realities.

2 *Oxford English Dictionary*.

3 Theories of sulking behavior abound in the psychological and psychoanalytic literature. The sulks are overwhelmingly conceptualized in terms of the Oedipal parent-child relationship. Psychoanalysis in particular assumes a disciplinary approach to sulking such that the psychoanalytic milieu helps the child over-come the need to seek attention and reparation by manipulating relationship dynamics through the performativity of withdrawal. Sulking is an indicator of the child's development of an entitlement complex. For examples of approaches to sulking grounded in parent-child relations, see Hardecker and Haun, "Approaching the Development of Hurt Feelings in Childhood"; Bonime, "A Psychotherapeutic Approach to Depression"; Barnett, "On Aggression in the Obsessional Neuroses"; Caparrotta, "Oedipal Shame, Rejection, and Adolescent Behavior Development"; Donald J. Cohen, "Enduring Sadness"; DeLia, "The Achilles Complex."

4 I am referring here to arguments made by Davis, *Women, Race and Class*, as well as Harris, "Whiteness as Property"; Alexander, *The New Jim Crow*; Gilmore, *Golden Gulag*; Murakawa, *The First Civil Right*.

5 On the question of public housing, see Shabazz, *Spatializing Blackness*.

6 Haley, *No Mercy Here*, 7.

7 Haley, *No Mercy Here*, 7.

8 The work of Darlene Clark Hine, Saidiya Hartman, Sarah Haley, and Sora Han are exemplary for the ways they consider the utterability of Black women's complaint. Saidiya Hartman examines how law legislated the terms of enslave-ment but endowed the master class with the everyday power of managing slaves. In this way, law buttressed and naturalized slavery as a kinship relation between master and slave. Hartman's intervention crosses between law and culture, such that the variety and depth of Black cultural expression in moder-nity is always already conditioned by slave law and the absolute power of the master. The legal history of contract is brought to bear on the question of slavery through Sora Han's analysis of Betty's case, an enslaved woman who, upon being transported North by her masters, was involved in a legal fight to free her from her masters. After testifying to Judge Lemuel Shaw, Betty "freely"

elected to return with her masters south. Han's description raises the question of the entwinement of freedom, choice, and contract in a condition of simultaneously being unable to leave and unable to remain. Darlene Clark Hine attends to Black women's discourse, describing a "culture of dissemblance" that developed during Reconstruction among Black women to cope with assaults upon sexuality. Dissemblance is pattern of speech that performs discretion and circumspection about matters of sexuality, especially the experience of rape. Hine raises the question of the particular rather than universal subject in the history of sexuality by addressing the discursive relationship between the reproductive exploitation of Black women and modernity. Hine's theory of the culture of dissemblance is linked to Black women's strategies of self-protection and assimilation post-Emancipation. For her part, Sarah Haley examines the legal and cultural battleground through which conceptions of humanity were discovered post-Emancipation. Black women's sexual exploitation was a key element of how slave conditions were retooled into the carceral regime of Jim Crow violence, whereby the formerly enslaved were transitioned from slave to criminal convict. Haley illuminates how the gendered and racial contours of Black women's incarceration, whether on the chain gang or as domestic laborers in white households, buttressed white femininity. Each contributes a theory about the afterlife of slavery that traverses law and culture. See Haley, *No Mercy Here*; Han, "Slavery as Contract"; Hartman, *Scenes of Subjection*; Hine, "Rape and the Inner Lives of Black Women."

9 According to legal historian Jennifer Mnookin, the use of photography in law sparked a political debate about photography in which two competing discourses about the medium emerged. The first view understood photography as an exceptional form of evidence, one secured by its mechanical reproduction of the world. Following the idea of "nature's pencil," this perspective suggested that the process of photography resulted in a complete and truthful transcription of nature; the mechanism of photography and the materiality of the image became a primary location of objectivity under this view. The second view understood the photographic image as a technology whose workings are inseparable from human intervention and therefore a rejection of the idea of pure, unmediated representation. The two perspectives resulted in two evidentiary perspectives. In court cases, judges sharing the view that photography replicated nature truthfully treated photographic images as primary evidentiary objects, while judges of the opposing view treated images as inferior evidentiary materials. Settlement on the issue came from the 1881 case of *Crowley v. People*. In this matter, the courts neutralized the hierarchy of evidence created by the two competing perspectives of photography. *Cowley* made photography analogous to traditional visual representational forms—maps, paintings, drawings, diagrams, and models. By arguing that photographic images were not different from earlier media forms, the opinion created a legal precedent on photographic evidence by inventing a pedigree for the new technology. *Cowley v. People*, [1881] 83 N.Y. 464. Through the use of analogy to earlier technologies of representation,

judges gave photography a legal history. See Mnookin, "The Image of Truth."
See also Golan, *Laws of Men and Laws of Nature*. For a study of analogy as
it relates to the documentation of history by the photographic apparatus, see
Silverman, *Miracle of Analogy*.

10 Mnookin, "The Image of Truth," 12.

11 Brown's notion of the repeating body is informed by an interdisciplinary body
of feminist scholarship that includes Hammonds, "Black (W)holes"; Hartman,
"Venus in Two Acts"; hooks, *Ain't I a Woman?*; Keeling, *The Witches' Flight*;
Spillers, *Black, White, and in Color*; Gordon, *Ghostly Matters*; and many others.

12 For work on this perspective on the method of media history, see Gitelman,
Always Already New.

13 Here I am thinking of Fleetwood, *Troubling Vision*.

14 I am thinking here of Lisa Gitelman's media history of automatic writing
devices (e.g., phonographs and typewriters) emerging in the nineteenth century
in her book, *Scripts, Grooves, and Writing Machines*.

15 Cooper, *Beyond Respectability*, 12.

16 Neary, *Fugitive Testimony*.

17 Neary, *Fugitive Testimony*, 10.

18 Neary, *Fugitive Testimony*, 9.

19 Neary, *Fugitive Testimony*, 9.

20 Rosen, *Terror in the Heart of Freedom*, 235.

21 Article IV, Section 4 is also known as the "Guarantee Clause." The use of either
term appears dependent on which aspect of the sentence is emphasized, the
guarantee for a republican form of government or federal protection against
domestic violence.

22 Domestic violence has a long history of naming. Its multiple iterations in
social science, literature, law, and policy include "uxoricide," "wife murder,"
"wife abuse," "wife beating," "domestic abuse," "dating violence," "teen dating
violence," "date rape," and "intimate partner violence." The many categories of
violence listed above inform statistics on risk and protective factors for women
and children as a result of exposure to domestic violence. We know a great
deal about domestic violence as an index of biopolitics. The numbers account
for age, social class, the onset of initial violence, warning signs, and the timing
of abuse. Each of these terms and their statistics seek greater specificity on the
legal character of the partnership, the nature of intimacy, the location and measure of violence, and even the age of abused and abuser. None of these terms
includes the slave's sociocultural-economic condition.

23 Stein, "The Domestic Violence Clause in New Originalist Theory." Stein argues
against Balkin's self-proclaimed originalist argument against the use of the
"Domestic Violence Clause" to refers to spousal abuse in "Framework Originalism and the Living Constitution."

24 See Bybee, "Insuring Domestic Tranquility." See also Finkelman, "Affirmative
Action for the Master Class."

25 See Stein, "The Domestic Violence Clause."

26 Stein, "The Domestic Violence Clause," 133n16. See also Farrand, *The Records of the Federal Convention of 1787*, 3:467.

27 Stein points out that "during the founding period, as today, the word 'domestic' had a meaning of 'belonging to the house,' and another, derivative meaning of 'not foreign'" ("The Domestic Violence Clause," 132). See also Johnson, *Dictionary of the English Language* (1755).

28 Jacobs, *Incidents in the Life of a Slave Girl*, 569.

29 Jacobs, *Incidents in the Life of a Slave Girl*, 613.

30 See Philips, "The Proportions of Paradox," 35.

31 Foucault, *Discipline and Punish.*

32 Foucault, *Discipline and Punish*, 201.

33 James, "The Womb of Western Theory," 268. James argues that Captive Maternals are biological or socially feminized into caretaking and consumption; further, James describes Captive Maternals and Black Matrix as "unfamiliar terms that point to the limits of theory that rationalizes the avoidance of interstices or gaps in the world through the consumption of maternal lives and bodies" (256). As one in a line of enslaved Black mothers, Harriet Jacobs is both Captive Maternal and the offspring of the Black Matrix, who "remain disproportionately disciplined, denigrated, and consumed for the greater democracy" (256).

34 Best, "Neither Lost nor Found," 151.

35 The sculpture mediates my speculative approach to how the sensation of vertigo might have been induced in Jacobs and recurring in contemporary victim abuse testimony mediated by photographic evidence. Jacobs's sensations are suggestive of a key object of the vestibular system—balance—and the cycle of disorientation and reorientation between her and the garret structure. The idea of balance and its daily disruption and readjustment by Jacobs's body in space was not merely physical, nor a phenomenon confined to her time and the authorial power of slave narrative. Once translated into a published form, Jacobs's narrative of confinement offers clues about the conventions of testimony governing victims of domestic violence.

36 Copeland, *Bound to Appear.*

37 Hartman, *Scenes of Subjection.* Hartman's book opens with a consideration of the anti-slavery epistle of white abolitionist John Rankin to his brother. Rankin imagines himself and his family in the position of enslaved Black people for abolitionist persuasion. For Hartman, Rankin's persuasive rhetoric raises the following problem: "The purpose of these inquiries is not to cast doubt on Rankin's motives for recounting these events but to consider the precariousness of empathy and the thin line between witness and spectator. In the fantasy of being beaten, Rankin may substitute himself and his wife and children for the black captive in order that this pain be perceived and experienced. So, in fact, Rankin becomes a proxy and the other's pain is acknowledged to the degree that it can be imagined, yet by virtue of this substitution the object of identification threatens to disappear" (17).

38 Hartman, *Scenes of Subjection*, 19.

39 Green-Barteet, "The Loophole of Retreat."

40 Jacobs, *Incidents in the life of a Slave Girl*, 567–68.

41 In using the term "performance" to think through Jacobs and sensation in the garret, I am reliant upon McMillan, *Embodied Avatars*.

42 Charles Babbage, considered the "father of the computer," offers a fascinating example of the interrelationship between control and feedback mechanisms and the archive of slavery. In the *Ninth Bridgewater Treatise, A Fragment*, written in 1838, Babbage offers a description of the atmosphere as "one vast library, on whose pages are for ever written all that man has ever said or woman whispered" (112). The air is a sea of particles acting, reacting, and recording the sum of man's deeds. While poetic, Babbage's description of atmosphere and/as history suddenly terminates with reference to the Negro and the hellish atmosphere of the slave ship. As a whole, the *Treatise* is a scientific paper that draws from Babbage's own theoretical work on calculating machines to suggest the existence of scientific law and design in nature. The elaboration of the calculating engine is interrupted by a curious extract from a naval report on the horrors of slave trade vessels and the "poor Negro souls" who are thrown overboard in the insurance scams occasionally perpetrated by owners of slave trade vessels. The *Treatise*'s ninth chapter, "On the Permanent Impression of Our Words and Actions on the Globe We Inhabit," offers some confirmation of the resonance of slavery in the contemporary moment, its many afterlives and repeating bodies:

> *The men are chained in pairs*; and, as a proof they are intended so to remain to the end of the voyage, *their fetters are not locked, but rivetted by the blacksmith*, and as deaths are frequently occurring *living men are often for a length of time confined to dead bodies*; the living man cannot be released till the blacksmith has performed the operation of cutting the clench of the rivet with his chisel; and I have now an officer on board the *Dryad*, who, on examining one of these slave vessels, found *not only living men chained to dead bodies, but the latter in a putrid state*. And we have now a case reported here, which, if true, is too horrible and disgusting to be described."—*Parliamentary Paper*, 1832, B, pp. 170, 171, as quoted in the *Quarterly Review*, Dec. 1835. When the ink was scarcely dry on the paper on which the remarks in the text, suggested by a former description of the atrocities of the slave trade, was written, the following paragraph caught my attention: "SLAVE TRADE.—His Majesty's ship *Thalia*, 31, Captain R. Wauchope, has captured on the coast of Africa, two slave vessels—one the *Félicité*, 611 slaves; the other, the *Adalia*, with 409 slaves. It appears the latter vessel had been chased by the boats of one of our cruizers, and to avoid being come up with she threw overboard upwards of 150 of the poor wretches who were on board, besides almost all her heavy stores."—*Western Luminary*, May 1837. (Babbage, *Ninth Bridgewater Treatise*, 117–18)

The filth and putrefaction of living slaves chained to dead ones often tossed from the ship may be read for its commentary on the horrors of slavery. But they may equally be read as an example of the economic waste entailed in the slave trade and the reorganization (and re-racialization) of labor through the Industrial

Revolution, including various engines of calculation. Babbage, whose Analytical Engine lay the groundwork for the mechanical computer and cybernetic systems, published his treatise four years prior to Jacobs's escape from the Flints. That the *Treatise* blends theories on the calculation machine with observations of the horrors upon the slave ship specifically and the insurance laws underwriting the slave trade more broadly accords with legal spectatorship. This is because Babbage is offering an extralegal observation of a horrifying scene of legal rationale and practices of slave trading. For Babbage and others conceiving of the emancipation of reproductive labor and a science of autonomous machines, the plan to reform the movement and activities of the craftsman's workshop and factory floor passed through the example of the wasted slave. Likewise *Incidents* offers many details about the workings of racial capitalism, particularly how the slave's physical energy is manifested, consumed, and exploited. Inside the garret, the labor of racial capital is also wasted.

43 Crary, *Techniques of the Observer*, 27.

44 Crary, *Techniques of the Observer*, 27.

45 Crary, *Techniques of the Observer*, 5.

46 Crary, *Techniques of the Observer*, 24.

47 See Ngai's discussion of vertigo as aversion in her chapter on anxiety in *Ugly Feelings*.

48 Crary, *Techniques of the Observer*, 4.

49 Visual artist Carrie Mae Weems has produced a multimedia intervention upon Gordon, whose scars are famously known as "The Scourged Back" daguerreotype. Weems's photography series, *From Here I Saw What Happened and I Cried*, offers another example of representational static that positions contemporary art within the constitutional trajectory of the domestic violence clause. Weems's series remixes and recirculates slave daguerreotypes culled from the Louis Agassiz archives located at Harvard University. The work was exhibited from 1995–1996, on the heels of the ratification of VAWA. Amber Musser reads Weems's images for the ways they disclose the artist's own performance of witnessing the experience of enslaved Black people. She cogently argues that the series provides a window into the operation of what she calls "brown jouissance" in relation to the voice and witnessing. Brown jouissance lies in a psychic movement between the violence of photographic objectification and the opacity of the interior voice. Weems conjures Black ancestors "so that the relationship between spirituality and interiority is made manifest even as these photographs illustrate a history of black bodies as commodities" (*Sensual Excess*, 96). In Musser's formulation brown jouissance can be seen as the experience of the difference between these two meanings, which shatters the viewer. The care Weems enacts upon the Agassiz archive is a strategy of the flesh that recovers a semblance of personhood, individuality, and interiority for the people represented as specimens by layering context over the daguerreotype. Mediated by Weems, the slave daguerreotypes may be the platform through which brown jouissance erupts.

50 The image of Gordon was also attributed to photographer Chandler Seaver Jr. of Boston. Philadelphia-based McAllister & Brother circulated pirated versions of the image.

51 See Collins, "The Scourged Back"; Silkenat "'A Typical Negro'"; Wood, *Blind Memory*; Strick *American Dolorologies*; Emberton, *Beyond Redemption*; Abruzzo, *Polemical Pain*.

52 Collins, "Scourged Back."

53 Abruzzo, *Polemical Pain*, 201.

54 Strick *American Dolorologies*.

55 Silkenat specifies that "while more than 50 versions of the scourged back exist in archives and museums the only copy of the photo that became 'Gordon as He Entered Our Lines' was sold in a private auction in 2008, and no copies of the photograph that served as the basis for 'Gordon in His Uniform' have been located" ("'A Typical Negro,'" 174).

56 Silkenat, "'A Typical Negro,'" 169.

57 Rogers, *They Were Her Property*.

58 *Harper's Weekly*, "A Typical Negro," 430.

59 Silkenat, "'A Typical Negro,'" 183n1.

60 Hartman, "Venus in Two Acts."

61 In "Venus in Two Acts" Hartman employs "critical fabulation" as a way to write speculatively on the archival presence, which is to say absence, of Black women in their own language.

62 Jones-Rogers, *They Were Her Property*, 121.

63 Snorton, *Black on Both Sides*, 71.

64 Definition used by Jennifer Morgan in "*Partus sequitur ventrem*," Morgan quoting Camilla Cowling,'s *Conceiving Freedom: Women of Color, Gender and the Abolition of Slavery in Havana and Rio de Janeiro*. For more scholarship on Black women's negotiation of racial inheritance, see also Morgan, *Laboring Women* and Johnson, *Wicked Flesh*.

65 "Scenes from Memphis, Tennessee—During the Riot—Shooting Down Negroes on the Morning of May 2, 1866," *Harper's Weekly*, May 26, 1866, 321.

66 Rosen, *Terror in the Heart of Freedom*, 62. See also Richards, *"Gentlemen of Property and Standing"*; Gilje, *Rioting in America*.

67 "Visit of the Ku-Klux," *Harper's Weekly*, February 24, 1872, 157.

68 The Ku Klux Klan was founded in 1865 in Pulaski, Tennessee.

69 "Visit of the Ku-Klux."

70 "Visit of the Ku-Klux."

71 Rosen, *Terror in the Heart of Freedom*, 224.

72 Rosen, *Terror in the Heart of Freedom*, 224.

73 Rosen, *Terror in the Heart of Freedom*, 224.

74 Gitelman, *Scripts, Grooves and Writing Machines*, 1.

75 Gitelman, *Scripts, Grooves and Writing Machines*, 4.

76 Vismann, *Files*, 72.

77 The quotation comes from Saidiya Hartman's "Venus in Two Acts," where she employs a new writing practice—critical fabulation—to trace the presence of Black women in the archive of slavery, an archival task made almost impossible because their lives are historically mediated by the writing of the master class. The full passage in Hartman reads:

> In this incarnation, she appears in the archive of slavery as a *dead girl* named in a legal indictment against a slave ship captain tried for the murder of two Negro girls. But we could have easily encountered her in a ship's ledger in the tally of tidbits; or in an overseer's journal—"last night I laid with Dido on the ground"; or as an amorous bed-fellow with a purse so elastic "that it will contain the largest thing any gentleman can present her with" in *Harris's List of Covent Garden Ladies*; or as the paramour in the narrative of a mercenary soldier in Surinam; or as a brotherl owner in a traveler's account of the prostitutes of Barbados; or as a minor character in a nineteenth-century pornographic novel" ("Venus in Two Acts," 1).

78 Rosen, *Terror in the Heart of Freedom*, 2–3.
79 Vismann, *Files*, 123.
80 Rosen, *Terror in the Heart of Freedom*, 233.
81 See Parsons, "Midnight Rangers."
82 Rosen, *Terror in the Heart of Freedom*, 112.
83 Rosen, *Terror in the Heart of Freedom*, 209.
84 Rosen, *Terror in the Heart of Freedom*, 215.

Chapter Two. Battered Women in a Cybernetic Milieu

1 Gilroy, *The Black Atlantic*.
2 Gieser and Stein, "Overview of the Thematic Apperception Test," 5.
3 In 1956 Fanon presented results of the TAT conducted with Algerian psychiatric patients. The TAT, designed at Harvard Psychological Clinic under psychologist Henry A. Murray in 1938, is "a projective test in which the subject is exposed to a series of situations, or panoramas" (Bullard, "The Critical Impact of Frantz Fanon and Henri Collomb," 227). The TAT images enable the projection of affective scripts. The description reveals that the logic of the test is distributed across gender codes, picture theory, and what Ngai calls "ugly feelings" (in her book by that name), which track affects such as confusion, disconcertion, and concern. Yet the "ambiguous black and white pictures" return us not merely to Ngai's important work in affect theory but to the interpretive lens through which we might read Black women's peculiar freedom struggles before law and, in particular, the enduring case of Betty and Reconstruction-era rape claims, discussed previously.

The test employs images for subjects to regard and seeks to elicit spontaneous oral response. As Alice Bullard describes, "The Murray-Morgan TAT was designed so that the individual performing the test views a set of panoramas and spontaneously organizes each into a drama. The intent of the test is that the dramatic scenes and lines of force that emerge express the self in dynamic relation to the tableaux. The governing theory behind this test is that recurrent patterns in an individual's responses indicate various, usually hidden, motive forces of the personality" ("The Critical Impact of Frantz Fanon and Henri Collomb," 228). Gieser and Stein further remark that the TAT's "aim is to tap 'root fantasies' of the personality; its focus is on evoking emotion; *and its element of ambiguity is designed to best produce projective processes*" (*Evocative Images*, 18; emphasis added). The images are a remarkable feat of visualizing and drawing vagueness and ambiguity, which I suggest are characteristics of minor affects, or "ugly feelings," that condition the practice of legal spectatorship discussed in chapter 1.

Images of solitary individuals and groups engaged in ambiguous communicative interactions are mediating elements of the TAT instrument. Each picture is meant to pull for factors of personality and group dynamics such as interpersonal relations, achievement motivation, aggression, moral judgment, reality testing, anxiety/depression, sexual identity, delay of gratification, and self-concept. While these factors are singular, the instrument overwhelmingly pulls for them in combinations. For examine, in Card 4 of the TEMAS ("Tell-Me-A-Story-Test"), a multicultural version of the TAT, "An angry father is threatening the mother. The two sons and two daughters are standing by the mother. A girl lies in a bed with her face covered" (Costantino and Malgady, "The Tell-Me-A-Story-Test," 195). The design intends "to pull for interpersonal relations, aggression, anxiety/depression, and moral judgment" (Costantino and Malgady, "The Tell-Me-A-Story-Test," 195). Though the images depict private scenes or scripts of vague meaning, what is clear is the indoor or outdoor location of the action. The psychotherapeutic logic is to depict the entirety of the lifeworld. This is important for theorizing how the TAT tracks the domestic sphere and the violence it conditions and is conditioned by. The instrument presents perplexing scenarios that depict *in medias res* the moment of action, the moment where freedom exists. The TAT is thus a psychotherapeutic instrument that returns us to the ambivalence of Betty's ostensibly free act before law and women testifying in the domestic violence courtroom. The TAT image is also a major element of projection we can source in Kapp's philosophy of technology and the antebellum context of his writing.

4 Eve Kosofsky Sedgwick's develops the concept of triangulation in *Epistemologies of the Closet*.

5 Franklin, *Control*, xxii.

6 Adelman, *Figuring Violence*, 4.

7 Adelman, *Figuring Violence*, 4.

8 In 1967 at the University of Pennsylvania Psychology Department, graduate students Martin E. P. Seligman and Steven F. Maier proposed the theory of "learned helplessness" to explain the loss in voluntary agency in animals after repeated exposure to physical trauma. Working in the area of animal learning, they came to the theory as a result of several torture experiments on rats, dogs, cats, and fish in which it was consistently discovered that a deadly form of

passivity set in when animals learned that their self-initiated actions had no influence on their environment. In his experiments, Seligman administered random and varied electric shocks to dogs confined to a shuttle-box. Under these conditions the animals naturally tried to escape, although to no avail. After prolonged administration of the shocks that occurred despite voluntary escape actions, the dogs adopted a submissive and passive position that continued even after they were shown how to exit the shuttle-box. Over the course of the study, Seligman and fellow researchers found themselves dragging the animals to the exit, eventually resulting in the restoration of the dogs' voluntary escape reaction. Seligman conducted his study with older and younger dogs, finding that the earlier the animals experienced the administration of shock, the longer it took to reestablish the voluntary capacity to avoid danger and harm. See Peterson, Seligman, and Maier, *Learned Helplessness*.

9   Walker, *The Battered Woman Syndrome*, xvi; emphasis added.

10 Peterson, Seligman, and Maier, *Learned Helplessness*, 9.

11 Peterson, Seligman, and Maier, *Learned Helplessness*, 229.

12 In *Shame and Its Sisters*, Eve Sedgwick and Adam Frank offer a condensed version of Tomkins's two-volume tome on the human affect and motivation system, *Affect, Imagery, Consciousness*. Published in 1962, the original text covers Tomkins's major psychological and experimental work and was a contribution of many decades of stops and starts in the making. Tomkins's theories are mobilized for his cybernetic influence on affect as feedback system, which stems from his reworking of Freud's theory of the drives that subsequently illustrated the freedom of affect. Unlike the Freudian drives, affect is organized by seemingly endless degrees of freedom. Affect wants to be free. The prodigiousness of affect theory for contemporary cultural criticism centers on this principle. In contemporary cultural theory, affect is the way around or through stagnant elements of poststructuralist thought. Combined with cybernetic feedback, affect circulates in and through the other and is constitutive of the social bond. Where poststructuralist and deconstructionist theories ascribe a hegemonic notion of power that makes the ends of capitalist statecraft inevitable, the freedom of affect offers an approach that emphasizes the micro and interpersonal circuits through which meaning-making becomes possible. In Tomkins, affective scripts develop as the subject negotiates the social world.

13 In the biographical sketch of Tomkins in *Shame and Its Sisters*, psychologist and friend Irving E. Alexander notes that the writing of the negative affects, specifically the complex of shame-humiliation and Contempt-disgust and anger were the most challenging and time-consuming to produce. Alexander remarks that in Tomkins's own life "overt anger was not an acceptable response to [his mother's] ministrations. Indeed, the overt expression of anger as an affect eluded him intellectually" (Alexander, "Sylvan Tomkins," 262). Tomkins's writings are replete with examples drawn from his own family experiences. He called these examples "nuclear scenes," and they informed the regulation of affect into nuclear scripts. Negative affect entered into Tomkins's relationship to

his mother, described overall as "nurturant, loving and protective," through an insufficient supply of mother's milk—Tomkins's hunger was supplemented by a wet-nurse—a situation that, Alexander remarks, induced shame in Tomkins "for demanding more than his due" (Alexander, "Sylvan Tomkins," 262). Tomkins's father "was a vigorous, excitement-oriented, lavish person, mesomorphic in structure and orientation. Winning, overcoming, and conquering were strong values for him. Any failure to exhibit these attributes by his son was likely to bring on shame-producing behavior from taunts about gender inadequacy to physical humiliation, like a slap in the face" (Alexander, "Sylvan Tomkins," 263).

14 Tomkins, *Affect, Imagery, Consciousness*, 1: 411–12.

15 Tomkins, *Affect, Imagery, Consciousness*, 1:412–13.

16 Tomkins, *Affect, Imagery, Consciousness*, 1:x.

17 Stoever, "Transforming Domestic Violence Representation," 487.

18 Stoever, "Transforming Domestic Violence Representation," 504.

19 Han, *Letters of the Law*, 55.

20 Tomkins, *Affect, Imagery, Consciousness*, 1:408; emphasis added.

21 Tomkins, *Affect, Imagery, Consciousness*, 1:409; emphasis added.

22 At the height of civil rights struggles and student protests, Tomkins became discouraged with the psychology program at Rutgers University's Livingston campus. He retired in 1975, in part because he "became increasingly disenchanted by the apparent lack of interest shown by the students in anything other than practical, concrete problems" (Alexander, "Sylvan Tomkins," 259). Tomkins's formulation of bipolar affect was the very issue Walker was studying in the same department. That she would make such similar theorizations as both Seligman and Tomkins, whose research was ongoing at the University of Pennsylvania and Rutgers, respectively, and formulate them as the BWS suggests a missed opportunity among these three cybernetic thinkers.

23 Sheila Jasanoff examines the ways courts influence the production of science, arguing that "one cannot fully comprehend the place of science and technology in American political life without closely attending to their deployment in the legal process" (*Science at the Bar*, xvi). Jasanoff details how law regulates science and technology through legal disputes that arise about matters such as scientific expertise, mistreatment of experimental subjects, moral and religious opposition, and so on. This chapter reverses Jasanoff's claim that science is shaped through legal events. While it is true that law manages the production of scientific knowledge and authority, it is also true that scientific knowledge powerfully influences the intricacies and intimacies of legal procedure and argumentation. The science of the human motivation system laid the groundwork for the control of legal spectatorship and ultimately the development of courtroom audiences through photographic evidence.

24 Faigman, "The Battered Woman Syndrome and Self-Defense"; Schuller and Vidmar, "Battered Woman Syndrome Evidence in the Courtroom."

25 See Maguigan, "Battered Women and Self-Defense"; Koss et al., *No Safe Haven*; Gangé, *Battered Women's Justice*.

26 Bricker, "Fatal Defense"; Stubbs and Tolmie, "Race, Gender, and Battered Woman Syndrome"; Schneider, *Battered Women and Feminist Lawmaking*.

27 Baker, "Complex Agency of Battered Women Who Kill," 51.

28 Donovan and Wildman, "Is the Reasonable Man Obsolete?"

29 Bochnak and Krauss, *Women's Self Defense Cases*.

30 Allard, "Rethinking Battered Woman Syndrome."

31 Posch, "The Negative Effects of Expert Testimony"; Johann and Osanka, *Representing Battered Women Who Kill*.

32 Convincing juries of BWS as a legal defense has led courts and the public to condemn the majority of battered women who kill their abusers to the prison industrial complex. A model dubbed "battered woman syndrome survivor theory II" emerged in the 1990s out of studies of domestic violence that focused on the nonpassive survivor behaviors exhibited by battered women. These were, in most cases, battered women who killed or were otherwise physically aggressive toward or defended themselves against abusive partners. In the early 1990s Schuller and Vidmar suggested that juror misconceptions about domestic violence invigorated the science of BWS and its discursive circulation via expert testimony. Citing Cynthia Gillespie's *Justifiable Homicide*, they argue that "given the potential interplay between jurors' beliefs and the lack of fit between the woman's actions and the existing laws of self-defense, establishing that a woman's behavior was reasonable can be a formidable goal for the defense to achieve" (Schuller and Vidmar, "Battered Woman Syndrome Evidence," 277). In their account of early research on BWS, Schuller and Vidmar show that the role of expert testimony supplemented jurors' lay beliefs about domestic violence. This alternative account recognizes the complex agency demonstrated by abused women without equating agency with freedom. Expertise on BWS in this stage of the model provides a "social framework" for assessing the actions and states of mind of abused women on trial for killing their partners.

33 Callahan, "Will the 'Real' Battered Woman Please Stand Up?"

34 Faigman, "The Battered Woman Syndrome and Self-Defense," 619.

35 See Frye v. United States, 293 F. 1013 (1923) and Daubert v. Merrill Dow Pharmaceuticals, Inc., 113 S. Ct. 2786, 2795 (1993). In 1993 *Daubert* rejected the general acceptability test of evidence for expert testimony previously established in *Frye*. Under the current *Daubert* precedent, judges must themselves be convinced of the validity of a given scientific research upon which expert testimony is presented. See Golan, *Laws of Men and Laws of Nature*.

36 Golan, *Laws of Men and Laws of Nature*, 19

37 Ibn-Tamas v. United States, 407 A.2d 626 (D.C. 1979) at 638.

38 State v. Martin 666 S.W. 2d. 895 (Mo. Ct. App. 1984). See State v. Leaphart 673 S.W. 2d. 870 (Tenn. Crim. App. 1983) for a case similar to *Martin*.

39 Faigman used Buhrle v. State 627 P.2d. 1374 (Wyo. 1984) to support the requirement that expert testimony supports the science at issue in the self-defense claim and not to advocate for the defendant.

40 State v. Hawthorne, 470 So. 2d. 770 (Fla. Dist. Ct. App. 1985).

41 Faigman and Wright, "The Battered Woman Syndrome in the Age of Science."
42 See Lisa Cartwright's chapter on "experiments of destruction" in her *Screening the Body*.
43 Seligman's laboratory studies were examples of what Lisa Cartwright has called "experiments of destruction" because they reflected the dominant paradigm of producing scientific knowledge by penetrating the interior space of a living body.
44 Cartwright, *Screening the Body*, 46.
45 See Buhrle v. State of Wyoming.
46 Gallagher, *Ibn-Tamas v. United States* at 907.
47 Cartwright, *Screening the Body*, 18.
48 Cartwright, *Screening the Body*, 20.
49 American Psychiatric Association, *Diagnostic and Statistical Manual*, section on Diagnostic Features of Post-Traumatic Stress Disorder.
50 It has not been my intention to establish feminist advocates for battered women and advocates for the *Daubert* standard as mutually exclusive. It is certainly possible to engage the *Daubert* standard as an Aristotelian question of "good law" and inquire into the contours of medico-legal experiences of battered women.
51 Jackson, "'Theorizing in a Void.'" Jackson's essay offers a much needed return to the racial underpinnings of Kant's and Burke's respective conceptualizations of beauty, the sublime, judgment, and accounting. She writes, "For Burke, the sublime is a property of a thing, and for Kant (of the third *Critique*), it is a judgment of a thing, but for me, the sublime function of the black *mater*(nal), which I am calling black femininity, is an antecedent to both perception and knowledge of a thing in a post-1492 context" (628).
52 Jackson, "Theorizing in a Void," 629.
53 Spillers, "Mama's Baby, Papa's Maybe," in *Black, White, and in Color*.
54 Crenshaw, "Mapping the Margins."
55 Hammonds, "Black (W)holes and the Geometry of Black Female Sexuality."
56 Keeling, *The Witch's Flight*.
57 Wallace, *Black Macho and the Myth of the Superwoman*.
58 In "'Theorizing in a Void,'" Jackson uses the phrase "invisible companion" in reference to Evelyn Hammonds's discussion of how black holes are detected. The full passage reads: "As Hammonds instructs, one detects the presence of a black hole by its effects on the region of space where it is located, as in the case of observing a binary system in which a visible star circulates an *invisible companion*. The existence of a black hole is not seen optically but rather is inferred from its ability to distort the orbiting star. The forces observed within the system could not be produced solely by the visible star, but instead gesture toward that which withdraws from direct empirical observation" ("'Theorizing in a Void,'" 633; emphasis added).
59 Fleetwood, *On Racial Icons*, 2.
60 Fleetwood, *On Racial Icons*, 13.
61 Jackson, "Theorizing in a Void."
62 Jackson, "Theorizing in a Void," 628.

63 See Bullard, "The Critical Impact of Frantz Fanon and Henri Collomb," 234.

64 These values encoded in the TAT also include the gender dynamics at play in making scientific knowledge about the individual's capacity for agency, control, and motivation used to design the instrument. Though Jungian psychologist Christiana Morgan originated many of the images, Cecelia Roberts is only recently credited with inspiring the TAT's development under the institutional stewardship of Henry Murray (Bronstein, "The Mail"; Bullard, "The Critical Impact of Frantz Fanon and Henri Collomb"). Morgan requested that she be removed as principal investigator of the experiments after receiving many questions about the test that she could not or would not field. Researchers involved in the TAT's development valued the test as a whole and the design of its specific components differently (Bullard, "The Critical Impact of Frantz Fanon and Henri Collomb"). Saul Rosenzweig, a psychologist who worked with the TAT at Harvard Psychological Clinic during Murray's and Morgan's tenure, offers the following account of Morgan's disappearance from scientific credit attribution:

> One of the significant conclusions that can be drawn form the correspondence between [Christiana] Morgan and myself [Rosenzweig] is that she was the major contributor to the construction of the TAT. The evidence for this conclusion includes the following: (a) She is named in the authorship line of the 1935 basic article (C. D. Morgan & Murray, 1935). (b) In a letter dated March 27, 1935, she indicated that she was taking the initiative in finding a publisher for TAT. She wrote "this spring I am going to see if Houghton Mifflin will publish a set [of TAT images].' (c) She, rather than Murray, was doing the active collaborative research with me. (d) It was Morgan, not Murray, who was invited to speak at the psychology department colloquium at Worcester State Mental Hospital. (e) Finally, she was clearly responsible for six of the drawings that constituted the pictures of the 1943 published series. The question remains as to why, in publishing the manual in 1943, Morgan was not mentioned by Murray as one of the authors. (Rosenzweig, "Pioneer Experiences," 43)

In the development of the TAT, the attribution of scientific authorship and credit to the pioneering white male occurs in the same moment that the instrument acquires its logic of a universal, rational subject. For example, Henry Murray, presumed inventor of the instrument, attributed great diversity among research subjects' personal beliefs. The initial TAT subjects were all male college students from Harvard. "Given the realities of who was able to pursue university degrees in the 1930s, an in-built norm of whiteness can be assumed" (Bullard, "The Critical Impact of Frantz Fanon and Henri Collomb," 228). In other words, there is a match between the identity of the assumed main creator of the TAT and the identity of the subjects of analysis. Revealed here is how the development of scientific instruments, particularly instruments meant to test personality, involves acts of projection on the part of the scientist.

65 As Fanon presented his TAT experiments at the 1956 French-language conference of "Medécins Alienistes and Neurologistes," an annual psychiatry conference, with coauthor, Dr. Charles Geronimi, he illustrated the vestibular position

of the colonial subject whose life and customs disrupt the logic of the TAT by existing at its conceptual border. Bullard quotes from the Fanon-Geronimi study:

For example, in response to 3 BM (a card depicting a person of indeterminate sex, sketched from behind): "I don't know if it's a girl or a boy. I think it's a girl. I don't know what she's doing. I don't know what to say. I don't understand. Maybe he's sick. He has a headache (I'm tired. She sighs). . . . Or another response, this time to Scene 11 (an indistinct mountain pass, with a dragon- or dinosaur-like creature in the upper left): "One might say it's the sea, but it is blue or green and this is black. This isn't the sea, it could be a village (she turns and turns the scene) you might say it's an airplane, a boat, but it isn't any of these. I don't understand" (Bullard, "The Critical Impact of Frantz Fanon and Henri Collomb," 235).

See Fanon and Geronimi, "Le T.A.T. chez les femmes musulumanes."
66 Franklin, *Control*, xiii.
67 Franklin, *Control*, xiv.
68 Franklin, *Control*, xvi.

Chapter Three. Authenticating Testimony
in the Domestic Violence Courtroom

1 It should be noted that while domestic abuse comprises a significant amount of the courtroom arraignment docket, domestic abuse trials, including images, are a relatively infrequent occurrence. This accords nonetheless with my argument about the importance of the minor affects.
2 Baker, *Humane Insight*, 14.
3 Ngai, *Ugly Feelings*, 222.
4 Spillers, "Peter's Pans: Eating in the Diaspora," in *Black, White, and in Color*, 4. The full passage reads:

The marking, the branding, the whipping—all instruments of a terrorist regime— were more deeply *that*—to get in somebody's face that way would have to be centuries in the making that would have had little to do, though it is difficult to believe, with the biochemistry or pigmentation, hair texture, lip thickness, and the indicial measure of the nostrils, but everything to do with those "unacknowledged legislators" of a discursive and an economic discipline. To that extent, the critique of "identity politics" has positioned the wrong objects in its sights: it needs to ask, more precisely, how *status* is made and pay attention to *that* because *that* is the dialectic that plays here. (4, emphases in original)

5 Baker, *Human Insight*, 9.
6 Rosen, *Terror in the Heart of Freedom*.
7 Here I am of course referring to the law *partus sequitur ventrem*, a foundational slave law that determines that the slave's status is lifelong and follows the gendered conditions of the mother. The writing on *partus* is extensive. For some crucial literature from colonial to the contemporary incarnation in

mass incarceration see Morgan, "*Partus Sequitur Ventrem.*" See also Roberts, "Criminal Justice and Black Families" and "The Social and Moral Cost of Mass Incarceration in African American Communities."

8 Mulla, *The Violence of Care.*

9 Hartman, "Venus in Two Acts."

10 At the same time, there is a growing literature on how the expression of anger and rage—specifically, Black anger and rage—is not tolerated in democratic political discourse. See Grier and Cobbs, *Black Rage*; Thompson, "An Exoneration of Black Rage." For a discussion situated outside the United States, see Canham, "Embodied Black Rage."

11 In addition to the grand affects, capitalism is a companion grand narrative used to theorize Black enslavement. My work throughout this book is to attend less to the workings of capitalism and more to the idea of sovereignty.

12 Spillers, *Black, White, and in Color*, 207.

13 Spillers, *Black, White, and in Color*, 207.

14 Spillers, *Black, White, and in Color*, 206.

15 Foucault, *Discipline and Punish*, 26.

16 Ngai, *Ugly Feelings*, 212.

17 Ngai, *Ugly Feelings*, 12.

18 Ngai, *Ugly Feelings*, 36.

19 Bowers, "The Normative Case for Normative Grand Juries." See also Simmons, "Re-Examining the Grand Jury: Is There Room for Democracy in the Criminal Justice System?"; Ryan, "Juries and the Criminal Constitution."

20 Simonson, "The Criminal Court Audience in a Post-Trial World."

21 Emerling and Gardner, "Architecture!," 296.

22 Stierli, "Architecture and Visual Culture," 313, 314.

23 Feigenson, "The Visual in Law," 13.

24 For other examples, see Mirzoeff, *The Right to Look*; Resnik and Curtis, *Representing Justice*; Robles-Anderson, "The Crystal Cathedral."

25 Vismann, *Files*, xii.

26 For examples of this argument that bring together law, theater, and performance, see Auslander, *Liveness*; Byers and Johnson, *The CSI Effect*; Conquergood, "Lethal Theater"; Feigenson and Spiesel, *Law on Display*; Sherwin, *Visualizing Law*.

27 Roberts, "Crashing the Misdemeanor System."

28 Gonzalez Van Cleve, *Crook County*.

29 Kohler-Hausmann, *Misdemeanorland*.

30 Kohler-Hausmann, "Managerial Justice and Mass Misdemeanors."

31 Kohler-Hausmann, *Misdemeanorland*, 5.

32 Kohler-Hausmann, *Misdemeanorland*, 5.

33 Jones-Rogers, *They Were Her Property*.

34 Ngai, *Ugly Feelings*, 215.

35 Campt, *Listening to Images*, 8.

36 Serres, *The Parasite*.

37 See Mulla's discussion of the hands of forensic nurses in *The Violence of Care*.

38 Repertoires of touch and gesture have a long history in the pedagogy of non–typically ordered communication and the political education of the oppressed. See John Bulwer's 1644 *Chirologia and Chironomia* for an example that informed the hand rhetoric for deaf language.

39 Marriott, *Whither Fanon*, 322.

40 Marriot, *Whither Fanon*, 322.

41 Public Defender Susan Clemens, 2010: personal communication.

42 Attorneys also reported that in passing each individual image, one risked creating boredom among the jury.

43 Another instance of this technique of "holding the body" can be found during initial VAWA investigation and case preparation for defense attorneys, who are part of the network of offices of the misdemeanor court. During interviews with Legal Aid, attorneys disclosed that once in possession of photographic evidence, they typically sit in their office looking at the images, asking themselves "What happened here?" Frequently these attorneys walked the image down the hallway to their colleagues, seeking an additional pair of eyes to construct a narrative. Handing the images to a colleague charges the color content of the images with narrative promise for the defense's case. In such encounters the photograph mediates the construction of a narrative between colleagues, and not one between defense attorney and defendant. In these exchanges photographic evidence functions as if the complaining witness and defendant were participants in the conversation with the attorneys. Moments like this help further establish particular qualities of photographic evidence within the misdemeanor court, even as colleagues might remark that the injuries look so terrible as to be appropriate for a felony-level prosecution. Recalling the architectural implications of Vismann's argument about files, these practices of walking photographs down the hall and handing them to colleagues are forms of professional vision that occur in specific architectural settings.

None of this should give the impression that defense attorneys engage with photographic evidence in the same ways as prosecuting attorneys. While it is the case that defense attorneys engage in a similar practice of 'holding the victim's body" among one other, they do so with quite different objectives concerning the fate of their clients. The hands of defense attorneys are not endowed with special powers of display. In my interviews, defense attorneys disclosed that after conferring with colleagues about the photographs, they spent little time examining them again, preferring to "put them away and forget about them." Marking, which is relevant to both district attorneys and Legal Aid attorneys—two opposed communities of practice—is pertinent here and returns one to Kohler-Hausmann's insights about the role marking plays in the managerial model of criminal justice. Defense attorneys are highly aware of the number of previous encounters, or administrative marks, in the misdemeanor courts their clients often have. As a result, their attention is directed principally toward minimizing what they call the "exposure" of their clients to further administrative marking and, most important, jail. The marks to which they are primarily attuned are not the witness's wounds captured by photographs, but rather the number of appearances and court-mandated assignments through which the defendant is gradually exposed to jail time and removal from the communities to which they belong. Photographic evidence is not the locus of attention for defense attorneys. They are focused on administrative marks, resulting in jail exposure, that accrue to defendant's records rather than the mark of injury stored in evidentiary photographs. In DV cases when defense attorneys win, they have often overcome photographic evidence. Ironically, their defense practice operates at a distance from the preoccupations of visual evidence.

44 Ngai, *Ugly Feelings*, 212.

45 Ngai, *Ugly Feelings*, 215.

46 Ngai, *Ugly Feelings*, 221.

47 Balaban and Jacob, "Background and History of the Interface between Anxiety and Vertigo."

48 Mallinson, "Introduction to Visual–Vestibular Mismatch," 18, emphasis added; Bronstein, "Visual Vertigo Syndrome."

49 Redfern, Yardley, and Bronstein, "Visual Influences on Balance," 87.

50 The misdemeanor courts are fertile ground for an encounter between Black Studies and the minor literature. Anthropologist Savannah Shange's work on the discourse of school "push out" among Black girls is an excellent example of Black Studies of minor affect. "Push out" is an individualizing carceral gaze organizing public school discipline whereby Black youth's self-expression and ways of knowing are viewed as suspect, contagiously detrimental to themselves and other students. Shange takes up Spillers's flesh-body distinction as a hermeneutic for understanding the resistant methods Black girls in public school systems create to negotiate their freedom dreams in the wake of push out. When Shange argues that Black girls are "bureaucratically destroyed" through school push out," she hints at the dead seriousness of a minor strategy of abjecting Black youth through a carceral gaze where the concern, interest, anxiety, disconcertion of school agents with regard to Black students subtly but surely result in pushing youth out of public institutions of learning. The "ugly feelings" manifested about Black students serve to route them away from established academic pathways and professionalizing networks of higher education that open the child's life to salaried professions, home ownership, financial security—traditional markings of reproductive freedom in the US body politic. By criminalizing students early on in their education, agents of white supremacy—teachers, administrators, teachers' assistants, janitors, and so on—work to deskill young Black people. When school administrators target the physical and affective comportment of the Black child for the purpose of mainstream social control, they enact school pushout as a form of disavowal and dishonor in a minor key. The process of socially controlling Black youth need not occur through murderous rage and acts of terror; they can also occur through the flow of Ngai's conceptualization of the minor affects in which perpetrators of school push out appear to be merely demonstrating interest,

concern, irritation, and anxiety about the behaviors of Black students. The results, while seemingly slow and subtle, are devastating for Black futures. Further, marking, procedural hassle, and performance are all present in the systematic work of push out in public schooling. Thus, one ought to view push out as an institutional management technique wholly in league with municipal strategy at work in Kohler-Hausmann's conceptualization of misdemeanorland. See Shange, "Black Girl Ordinary," as well as *Progressive Dystopia*.

51 Kohler-Hausmann, *Misdemeanorland*, 4.

52 See Moore, "Held in the Light."

53 A question emerges here about the silence in law and the possibility of justice, which has been addressed by Marianne Constable in *Just Silences*. In this book Constable argues that law is not simply or "just" silent on matters; sometimes law's silences are rightful. Constable suggests that examples of justice can be found in law's silences.

54 The ride-along is an ethnographic practice whereby lay people or legal actors voluntarily accompany police on their patrols. The volunteer consents to assume responsibility of any risks and/or injuries incurred associated with joining police on their assignments.

55 Han, *Letters of the Law*.

56 Tom Collins, 2009: personal communication.

57 Tom Collins, 2009: personal communication (emphasis added).

58 Finn, *Capturing the Criminal Image*, 50.

59 Finn, *Capturing the Criminal Image*, 51.

60 Tom Collins, 2009: personal communication.

61 For critical studies of color balance techniques in photography, see Roth, "Looking at Shirley"; and Winston, "A Whole Technology of Dyeing." See also Winston, *Technologies of Seeing*.

62 To be sure, the norm of visual whiteness of the DV victim is a familiar argument derived from techno-cultural analyses of white femininity and/as significa-tion. See Dyer, *White*; Mulvey, Visual Pleasure and Narrative Cinema"; Gaines, "White Privilege in Looking Relations."

63 Butler, *Gender Trouble*.

64 Spillers, *Black, White, and in Color*.

65 Spillers, *Black, White, and in Color*, 21; emphasis in original.

66 Spillers, *Black, White, and in Color*, 21.

67 See Halley et al., *Governance Feminism*.

68 Mirzoeff, *The Right to Look*, 1.

69 Butler, *Gender Trouble*, 4.

Chapter Four. Incorporating Camp in Criminal Justice

1 Guth and Pachter, "Domestic Violence and the Trauma Surgeon." The photo is called "Figure" and has the following caption: "Example of recent New York City advertising campaign publicizing availability of support services for

domestic violence victims. These photos are of models, not actual domestic abuse victims."

2 Guth and Pachter, "Domestic Violence and the Trauma Surgeon," 138.

3 Johnson, "Quare Studies."

4 Johnson, "Quare Studies," 4.

5 Luhmann, *Law as a Social System*.

6 Kathryn Bond Stockton explores a sense of camp sensibility through the idea of "dark camp." Stockton develops examples of dark camp through the work of Toni Morrison and Eldridge Cleaver, among others, suggesting the way Blackness and camp interact to keep "the violent edge of [antiblack] debasement visibly welded to camp caprice." *Beautiful Bottom, Beautiful Shame*, 37–38. The genealogy of scholarship on camp includes Susan Sontag's (in)famous universal characterization of camp taste in "Notes on Camp," published in 1964. See also Meyer, *The Politics and Poetics of Camp*; Isherwood, *The World in the Evening*; Pelligrini, "After Sontag."

In *Beautiful Bottom, Beautiful Shame*, Kathryn Bond Stockton contests Meyer's claiming of camp as a form of explicitly queer aesthetics and communication, pointing out that camp cannot be solely produced and exchanged in the purity of queer but is rather produced, "born of swtichpoints" in which social signs are transferred from one group to its dialectical other. Stockton goes on to confirm the absence of racial critique in his work and edited volume, *The Politics and Poetics of Camp*. However, I would draw attention to the Meyer's thought-provoking essay on Blackness, camp, and circuits of the African diaspora in *Archaeology of Posing*, chapter 5: "Rethinking 'Paris is Burning': Performing Social Geography in Harlem Drag Balls." Meyer's engagement with audience reception of knowledge and interpretive frames of Blackness and African cultures would complicate any notion that Meyer excludes the "Negro question" from both camp and queer culture. The chapter takes up *Paris Is Burning* and offers important critiques of famous discussions of the film by bell hooks and Judith Butler (see hooks, "Is Paris Burning?"; and Butler, "Gender Is Burning."

7 In his writing on realism and indexicality, anthropologist Christopher Ball makes the following observation, which is vital to existence and work performed by police DV photography and legally camped police images:

In the eras of both film-based and digital photography, and to a different degree and with differing consequences in documentary and art photography, the role of indexicality in establishing the veracity of the image has been paramount in photo theory. There is a need, however, for expanding the ways we think about indexicality in photography. In addition to the familiar concepts of the trace, citation, reference, social diacritics, interactional cues, and artists' intentions, the indexicality of photography may be better understood through appeal to less direct, or more densely mediated, modalities of indexicality. These include qualia (hypostatically abstracted—nesses), dicentization (the upshifting of icons into indexes of contiguity), and propositionality (the assertion of messages subject to truth claims). All of these have a place in the indexical and broadly semiotic analysis of the production, circulation, and reception of photographs. We may ask, what are the connections between these various indexicalities and the ideologies of realism (or various realisms) to which qualia, dicentization, and propositionality contribute? To begin to answer this question it is germane to consider semiotic approaches to realism alongside examples where the fidelity of the photograph as directly indexical of reality is challenged. This challenge is found again and again in the suspicion of manipulation. ("Realisms and Indexicalities of Photographic Propositions," 154–55)

I am grateful to Lily Chumley for introducing me to Ball's work. See Ball, "On Dicentization."

8   For subsequent work on McLuhan's concept of the global village, see Birkle, Krewani, and Kuester, *McLuhan's Global Village Today.*
9   Drewal, "The Camp Trace in Corporate America," 172.
10 Drewal, "The Camp Trace in Corporate America," 151.
11 I am thankful for the humor of Hentyle Yapp for this turn of phrase.
12 Snorton, *Black on Both Sides.*
13 Meyer, "Introduction," *The Politics and Poetics of Camp,* 5.
14 Meyer, "Introduction," 5.
15 Meyer, "Introduction," 5.
16 Snorton, *Black on Both Sides,* 11–12.
17 Ball, "Realism and Indexicalities," S159.
18 Raley, *Tactical Media.*
19 Shell, *Hide and Seek.*
20 Han, *Letters of the Law,* 96.
21 Ronell, *The Telephone Book.*
22 Pogrebin, "Madison Avenue Creates Stark Ad about Battering."
23 Pogrebin, "Madison Avenue."
24 Pogrebin, "Madison Avenue."
25 Pogrebin, "Madison Avenue."
26 Pogrebin, "Madison Avenue."
27 Franklin, *Control,* 43.
28 Meyer, "Introduction," 11. See also Giddens, *The Constitution of Society.*
29 Meyer, "Introduction," 15.
30 Autopoiesis is a difficult concept to grasp; it is part of a complex vocabulary used to describe communication systems as self-organizing through an encounter with difference. Many communication systems may influence law, but they cannot be law. The response of law to outside communication is internal to law; it is law's operative closure. Operational closure, however, does not mean the evacuation of openness, and by extension, a limitation to openness to change. Law may respond to its own environment; this is how law as a social system is able to learn through the process of structural coupling. Structural coupling occurs when operationally closed systems encounter and mutually perturb each other. Based on experiments of destruction, Lenore Walker's adaptation

of learned helplessness to BWS is an important example of how law stabilized itself from the intrusion of social science communication into unity. The unity of law is simply the fact of law's operative closure, its autopoiesis. Operative closure is subsumed under the concept of autopoiesis. The autopoiesis of law stabilizes expectations. Of course, organized religion and morality may also stabilize expectations, or, what ought to happen. However, law's autopoiesis is unique in that it organizes all its communications and environment precisely in terms of "legal/not legal." As Luhmann observes, "There is no other authority in society which can proclaim: this is legal and this is illegal" (Luhmann, *Law as a Social System*, 100). The binary legal/not legal is a code. Law's autopoiesis, otherwise known as operative closure, stabilizes expectations by stabilizing its code. Yet, code also requires application, otherwise law communication would go no further than the mere designation of its own code. Legal/not legal is a binary stabilized by programs. Programs derive from law's previous observation of its own code. Programs are the rules for allocating legal/illegal and "what is right or wrong with respect to them" (Luhmann, *Law as a Social System*, 118). They are how law responds to previous coding, and thus they play a crucial role in the time-binding work of law.

Luhmann's theory depends on the activity of self-observation for law to perceive its earlier coding, its conditioning of time. Law's code, legal/illegal, is the work of second-order observation. Second-order observation concerns the "observation of the making of distinctions," or, a process of observing the (first-order) observers (Nobles and Schiff, "Introduction," 34). In second order observation, the focus is on observing *how* observers observe. When Luhmann writes that justice is "a formula for observation intended for the use of courts, for which legislators only supply new test material over and over again," he brings together the idiom of systems theory; that is, its communications, and the environments where law communication occurs (Luhmann, *Law as a Social System*, 229). Law has environments. Its primary environment, courtrooms, is a closed operational context where self-observation occurs. What is discovered through autopoiesis is that environments are defined by the decisions that are made therein. Nobles and Schiff, "Introduction."

31 Han, *Letters of the Law*, 73.
32 Han, *Letters of the Law*, 73.
33 Drewal, "The Camp Trace in Corporate America," 150.
34 Tiffany Lethabo King's use of the shoal to tack back and forth between Black and Native formations in US culture is an equally generative way to spatialize techniques of the flesh. See *The Black Shoals*.
35 Taussig, *What Color Is the Sacred?* 18.
36 Taussig, *What Color Is the Sacred?* 18.
37 As of this writing, a few special issue journals within the neuro-scientific community are planned on the dress in addition to publications that are already circulating. Of those that have been published, scientists argue that the dilemma involved illumination and color, specifically the "special ambiguity of

blue." See Lafer-Sousa, Herman, and Conway, "Striking Individual Differences in Color Perception"; another study cites the conditions under which the colors perceived could be "flipped," see Witzel, O'Regan, and Hansmann-Roth, "The Dress and Individual Difference"; another considers the distribution of color within the dress relative to the distribution of natural daylights and how the brain resolves unchanging objects under changing illumination. See Hugrass et al., "Temporal Brightness Illusion."

38 In personality psychology and economic theory, the "lipstick effect" describes the counterintuitive increase in women's cosmetics spending during economic recessions, when consumers are more likely to be risk averse. The theory originated to describe women's increased lipstick purchases to regulate their moods during the Great Depression.

39 Ngai, *Ugly Feelings*, 68.

40 Drewal, "The Camp Trace in Corporate America," 153.

41 Raley, *Tactical Media*, 142.

42 The moral spectator, as developed by Lisa Cartwright, informs the concept of legal spectatorship. One is a moral spectator before one becomes a legal spectator through the interacting rights of the First and Sixth Amendments of the US Constitution. See Cartwright, *Moral Spectatorship*.

43 Shell, *Hide and Seek*, 36.

44 Cheng, "Skins, Tattoos, and Susceptibility" 101–2. See also, *Second Skin*.

45 Cheng, "Skins, Tattoos, and Susceptibility," 102.

46 Mitchell, *What Do Pictures Want?*

47 Cheng, *Second Skin*, 166.

48 Musser, *Sensual Excess*, 14.

49 Cheng, *Second Skin*, 167–68.

50 At this point, questions of lossy transmission and glitch aesthetics make an intervention. Normally, recordings on one media are transcoded—converted into other coded representational formats. Lossy formats are those that contain audible traces of previous transcodings. For example, Jonathan Sterne describes the MP3 player as a "lossy" format that easily reveals transcodings from other formats. See Sterne, *MP3: The Meaning of a Format*. Glitches are points of inspiration for creative interventions that move us toward an "outside of knowledge," a phrase media artist Rosa Menkman uses to emphasize the necessity of glitch for critique. In terms of glitch aesthetics that push us to the limits of thought, I suggest that the circulation of camped domestic abuse photography unsettles the fleshy evidence—especially in misdemeanor cases—that is the core value, or currency, of domestic abuse trials and moments of testimony. Glitch is defined in several ways. Principally, a glitch is "an interruption that produces visual or sonic effects" (Schlesinger, "Go Play Outside!," 94). See also Menkman, "Glitch Studies Manifesto." The information technology industry defines a glitch as something to be repaired, while media and visual culture studies view it as a positive potential for intervention into techniques and technologies of control. Though this second view is more promising politically and socially, it

ignores an embodied definition of glitch, one that acknowledges the historical reality of race, the social fact that "black bodies *do not live in the same space
as other, white bodies*; they are, quite simply barred from the intercorporeity"
constitutive of *human* subjectivity" (Hanson, *Bodies in Code*, 151). Before we
can appreciate the glitch as good, we must first appreciate the glitch as *a good*,
a product of value in racial capitalism. To suggest a natural progression from
hyperrealism to discourses of compression, glitch aesthetics, and lossy transmission is all too tidy.

51 Hia, "Carrying That Weight." See also Kaplan, "How a Mattress Became a
    Symbol."

52 Chu, "Study in Blue," 303.

53 Chu, "Study in Blue," 303.

54 Ngai, *Ugly Feelings*, 294.

55 *Stuplimity* is Sianne Ngai's portmanteau of "stupefy" and "sublime." Stuplim-
    ity combines the feelings of stupefaction and sublimity to encapsulate our
    mediatized modern condition that is characterized by a simultaneous feeling
    of boredom and overwhelming hyperawareness. Ngai suggests "the shocking
    and the boring" are dispositions that "prompt us to look for new strategies of
    engagement and to extend the circumstances under which engagements be-
    comes possible." Ngai, "Stuplimity," 9. Ngai's discusses the stuplime movements
    of slapstick comedians: "Such fatigues can also be darkly funny, as Beckett's
    Molloy, Buster Keaton, Harpo Marx, and Pee-Wee Herman remind us by their
    exhausting routines: running endless laps around a battleship, trying to come
    through a doorway, falling down and getting back up again, collapsing in heaps.
    Significantly, the humor of these local situations usually occurs in the context
    of a confrontation staged between the small subject and powerful institutions or
    machines." (*Ugly Feelings*, 294).

56 Pelligrini, "After Sontag," 179.

57 Pelligrini, "After Sontag," 179; emphasis added.

58 Isachenka, "Domestic Violence." See also Dunja Djudjic, "This Photographer
    Helps Survivors of Domestic Violence."

59 Isachenka, "Domestic Violence," 2018.

60 Isachenka, "Domestic Violence," 2018.

61 To be sure, Buben is working in the Bulgarian context and with white women.
    My argument about the slave's complaint and freedom to contract holds, none-
    theless, due to the history of white slavery in the Balkans and its significance
    to the formation of racial slavery in the Americas; this also includes Bulgaria's
    contemporary participation in human rights law, which, like that of the United
    States, centers on freedom and the rights-bearing subject. Buben's therapeutic
    photography camps the scene of police investigative photography.

62 Hillewaert, "Tactics and Tactility." For more work on touch and tactility, see
    also Meyer, Streeck, and Jordan, *Incorporeality*.

63 Isachenka, "Domestic Violence," 2018.

64 Crawley, "The Critical Force of Irony," 201.

65 Crawley, "The Critical Force of Irony," 190. See also Austin, *How to Do Things with Words*.

66 Muñoz, "Queerness as Horizon," 458.

67 Carr and Lempert, *Scale*, 10. My thanks to Lily Chumley for bringing my attention to this work.

68 Shim, "Roots of Survived & Punished."

69 *Misogynoirism* is Moya Bailey's portmanteau of "misogyny" (meaning hatred of women) and "noir" (the French word for "black") to refer to antiblack racist misogyny. Moya Bailey traces the contestation of sexist prejudice and discrimination targeted specifically at Black women through Black feminist uses of digital platforms for social movement work. See Bailey, *Misogynoir Transformed*.

70 Fleetwood, *On Racial Icons*, 1.

71 This argument resonates with Laura Wexler's use of the term "photographic *anekphrasis*" to describe "an active and selective refusal to read photography—its graphic labor, its social spaces—even while, at the same time, one is busy textualizing and contextualizing all other kinds of cultural documents" (*Tender Violence*, 58). Wexler argues that photographic *anekphrasis* occurs within nineteenth-century histories of photography.

72 Muñoz, "Queerness as Horizon," 461.

73 Ngai, *Ugly Feelings*, 32.

74 For more work on the status of interesting in aesthetic judgement, see Ngai, *Our Aesthetic Categories*.

75 Ngai, *Ugly Feelings*, 32.

76 Ngai, *Ugly Feelings*, 14.

77 For a description of suspension as it relates to the embodied experience of racial and class difference, see Ngai's discussion of Nella Larsen's *Quicksand* where she tracks the protagonist's emotional responses while traveling aboard a segregated train (*Ugly Feelings*, chap. 4).

Conclusion

1 See Goodrich's "Iconography of Nothing." See also Dayan, *The Law Is a White Dog*; Han *Letters of the Law*.

2 Nash, *Black Feminism Reimagined*, 122.

3 Nash, *Black Feminism Reimagined*, 115.

4 Robinson, *Black Marxism*, 5; emphasis added.

5 Nash, *Black Feminism Reimagined*, 127.

6 Crenshaw, "Mapping the Margins."

7 For work on law's role in ascribing property to the subject, see Harris, "Whiteness as Property."

8 Pateman and Mills, *Contract and Domination*, 80. See also Pateman, *The Sexual Contract*; and Mills, *The Racial Contract*.

9 The full passage in Moten reads:

Can we recover what she did not say to [Judge] Shaw; can we excavate what is held in her having been withheld from their exchange, in her refusal to be party to it, in the obscenity of her objection to the objectifying encounter with otherness? What sociality is concealed from him in whatever what he thought her "fac" revealed to him? Her face was not her own but it was a face, and it could be read, he must have thought. Wasn't it a face? Couldn't it be read? Didn't it unconceal? What material amazement is held in the difference that giving and showing embrace? And what do giving and showing withhold? What is withheld in and as their nonperformance? What remains unowned? What if to be free from slavery is to be free of slavery? What if freedom is (a condition) of slavery? What if the condition of the slave in general, or "generally speaking," is that she is chained to a war for freedom, chained to the war of freedom, to the prosecution of freedom as war, to the necessity, in freedom, that freedom imposes of the breaking of affective bonds, the disavowal, in entanglement, of entanglement? What if freedom is nothing more than vernacular loneliness? (*Stolen Life*, 250–51)

10 For an insightful analysis of contract that centers the condition of enslaved Black women, see Han's "Slavery as Contract." See also Fred Moten's lecture, "Blackness as Nonperformance," given at the Museum of Modern Art's Afterlives series for its furthering of the genealogy of Betty's case first examined by Aviam Soifer and reinvigorated by Han (https://www.moma.org/calendar/events/1364, accessed March 20, 2020).

11 Azoulay, *The Civil Contract of Photography*, Introduction.

12 Azoulay, *The Civil Contract of Photography*, 260.

13 Azoulay, *The Civil Contract of Photography*, 242.

14 See Moore, "Photographie Fèminine."

15 See Mulla, *The Violence of Care*.

16 For example, Amber Musser explores strategies of the flesh in art photography and lesbian pornography that lead to identity-shattering eruptions of feeling she terms "brown jouissance." Also, for Jennifer Nash the analysis of racialized pornography locates "technologically and historically embedded" pleasures produced in and for Black female bodies. Black ecstasy, like brown jouissance, prioritizes how Black and Brown sexual pleasure create loving social and political practices. The exploration and expression of Black queer joy, pleasure, and love circulate radical communication because of the ways public media systems and state apparatuses typically ignore or outright refuse these life-affirming practices. Fleshy practices detailed by these scholars draw our attention to alternate ways of knowing and living in/with/as/through the body. See Musser, *Sensational Excess*. See also Nash, *The Black Body in Ecstasy*.

17 Harris, "Whiteness as Property."

18 Han, *Letters of the Law*, 87; emphasis added.

19 Harris, "Whiteness as Property," 1714.

20 Here we might consider the relationship Han draws between Harris's discussion of whiteness as shield and Frantz Fanon's titular figuration of the "white

masks" in *Black Skin, White Masks*: "For it was one of Fanon's tasks in *Black Skin, White Masks* to meditate on white culture's symbolic reliance on phobic fantasies of blackness." Han, *Letters of the Law*, 88.

21 For an excellent discussion of #MeToo hashtag activism as counterpublic from the discipline of communication and cultural studies, see Jackson, Bailey, and Welles, *Hashtag Activism*.

22 See Snorton, *Black on Both Sides* and Jackson, *Becoming Human*.

23 Moore, "The Digital Rape Complaint."

Coda

1 Selvaratnam, "Where Can Domestic Violence Victims Turn during COVID-19?"

2 The phrase "I can't breathe" became a Black Lives Matter slogan after the "accidentalized" murder by chokehold of Eric Garner while being arrested by New York City police, July 2014. For work on the relationship between COVID-19-related Black morbidity and the afterlife of slavery, see Strings, "It's Not Obesity. It's Slavery." See also Strings, *Fearing the Black Body*.

3 Kelley, "Who Bears Witness to a Hidden Epidemic?" Cotton, "Send in the Troops."

4 Sharpe, "The Weather."

5 Cotton, "Send in the Troops." Article IV, Section 4 reads, "The United States shall Guarantee to every State in this Union a Republican Form of Government, and shall protect each of them from Invasion; and on application of the Legislature, or of the Executive (when the Legislature cannot be convened) against domestic Violence."

6 Associated Press, "Florida Police Heard in Video Laughing about Shooting Rubber Bullets."

7 *Whither Fanon*, 185.

8 Khanna, "The Lumpenproletariat, the Subaltern, the Mental Asylum," 139.

BIBLIOGRAPHY

Abruzzo, Margaret Nicola. *Polemical Pain: Slavery, Cruelty, and the Rise of Humani-
tarianism*. Baltimore, MD: Johns Hopkins University Press, 2011.

Adelman, Rebecca. *Figuring Violence: Affective Investments in Perpetual War*. New
York: Fordham University Press, 2019.

Ahmed, Sara. *Queer Phenomenology: Orientations, Objects, Others*. Durham, NC:
Duke University Press, 2006.

Alexander, Elizabeth, *The New Jim Crow: Mass Incarceration in the Age of Colorblindness*. New York: New Press, 2012.

Alexander, Irving. "Sylvan Tomkins: A Biographical Sketch." In *Shame and Its
Sisters: A Sylvan Tomkins Reader*, edited by Eve Kosofsky Sedgwick and Adam
Frank, 251–63. Durham, NC: Duke University Press, 1995.

Allard, Sharon Angella. "Rethinking Battered Woman Syndrome: A Black Feminist Perspective." *UCLA Women's Law Journal* 1 (1991): 194–207.

American Psychiatric Association. *Diagnostic and Statistical Manual of Mental
Disorders*, 5th ed. Arlington, VA: American Psychiatric Association, 2013.
https://doi.org/10.1176/appi.books.9780890425596.

Andrus, Jennifer. *Entextualizing Domestic Violence: Language Ideology and Violence against Women in the Anglo-American Hearsay Principle*. Oxford: Oxford
University Press, 2015.

Associated Press. "Florida Police Heard in Video Laughing about Shooting Rubber Bullets." *Huffington Post*, July 2, 2020. https://www.huffpost.com/entry
/florida-police-video-laughing-rubber-bullets_n_5efdbe1fc5b6ca9709a2006.

Auslander, Philip. *Liveness: Performance in a Mediatized Culture*. London: Routledge, 2008.

Austin, J. L. *How to Do Things with Words*. Oxford: Oxford University Press, 1975 [1955].

Azoulay, Ariella. *The Civil Contract of Photography*. London: Zone Books, 2008.

Babbage, Charles. *Ninth Bridgewater Treatise, A Fragment*. New York: New York University Press, 1989.

Bailey, Moya. *Misogynoir Transformed: Black Women's Digital Resistance*. New York: New York University Press, 2021.

Baker, Carrie N. "Complex Agency of Battered Women Who Kill." In *Survivor Rhetoric: Negotiations and Narrativity in Abused Women's Language*, edited by Christine Shearer-Cremean and Carol Winkelmann, 42–63. Toronto: University of Toronto Press, 2004.

Baker, Courtney R. *Human Insight: Looking at Images of African American Suffering and Death*. Urbana: University of Illinois Press, 2015.

Balaban, C. D., and R. G. Jacob. "Background and History of the Interface between Anxiety and Vertigo." *Anxiety Disorders* 15, nos. 1–2 (2001): 27–51.

Balkin, Jack M. "Framework Originalism and the Living Constitution." 103 Nw. U. L. REV. 549,552 (2009).

Ball, Christopher. "On Dicentization." *Journal of Linguistic Anthropology* 24, no. 2 (2014): 151–73.

Ball, Christopher. "Realisms and Indexicalities of Photographic Propositions." *Northwestern. University Law Review* 103, no. 2 (2009): 549–614.

Barnett, Joseph. "On Aggression in the Obsessional Neuroses." *Contemporary Psychoanalysis* 6, no. 1 (1969): 48–57.

Basch, Norma. *Framing American Divorce: From the Revolutionary Generation to the Victorians*. Berkeley: University of California Press, 1999.

Basch, Norma. *In the Eyes of the Law: Women, Marriage, and Property in Nineteenth-Century New York*. Ithaca, NY: Cornell University Press, 1982.

Beale, Frances M. "Double Jeopardy: To Be Black and Female." *Meridians* 8, no. 2 (2008): 166–76.

Best, Stephen. "Neither Lost Nor Found: Slavery and the Visual Archive." *Representations* 113, no. 1 (2011): 150–63.

Birkle, Carmen, Angela Krewani, and Martin Kuester. *McLuhan's Global Village Today: Transatlantic Perspectives*. New York: Routledge, 2016.

Blake, Nelson Manfred. *The Road to Reno: A History of Divorce in the United States*. Westport, CT: Greenwood Press, 1977.

Bochnak, Elizabeth, and Elissa Krauss, eds. *Women's Self Defense Cases: Theory and Practice*. Charlottesville, VA: Michie Company, 1981.

Bolles, Lynn A. "Anthropological Research Methods for the Study of Women in the Caribbean." In *Women in Africa and the African Diaspora*, edited by Rosalyn Terborg-Penn, Sharon Harley, and Andrea Benton Rushing, 65–77. Washington, DC: Howard University Press, 1987.

Bonime, Walter. "A Psychotherapeutic Approach to Depression." *Contemporary Psychoanalysis* 2, no. 1 (1965): 48–53.

Bricker, Denise. "Fatal Defense: An Analysis of Battered Woman's Syndrome Expert Testimony for Gay Men and Lesbians Who Kill Abusive Partners." *Brooklyn Law Review* 58 (Winter 1993): 1379–1437.

Bronstein, A. M. "Visual Vertigo Syndrome: Clinical and Posturography Findings." *Journal of Neurology, Neurosurgery and Psychiatry* 59, no. 5 (1995): 472–76.

Bronstein, P. "The Mail." *New Yorker*. October 11, 2004.

Brown, Kimberly Juanita. *The Repeating Body: Slavery's Visual Resonance in the Contemporary*. Durham, NC: Duke University Press.

Browne, Simone. *Dark Matters: On the Surveillance of Blackness*. Durham, NC: Duke University Press, 2015.

Brownmiller, Susan. *Against Our Will: Men, Women, and Rape*. New York: Simon and Schuster, 1975.

Bullard, Alice. "The Critical Impact of Frantz Fanon and Henri Collomb: Race, Gender, and Personality Testing in North and West Africans." *Journal of the History of Behavioral Sciences* 41, no. 3 (2005): 225–48.

Bulwer, John. *Chirologia and Chironomia*. London: Tho. Harper, 1644.

Butler, Judith. "Gender Is Burning: Questions of Appropriation and Subversion." In *Bodies That Matter: On the Discursive Limits of "Sex,"* 81–98. New York: Routledge, 1993.

Butler, Judith. *Gender Trouble: Feminism and the Discursive Limits of Sex*. New York: Routledge, 1990.

Bybee, Jay S. "Insuring Domestic Tranquility: Lopez, Federalization of Crime, and the Forgotten Role of the Domestic Violence Clause." *George Washington Law Review* 66 (1997): 1–83.

Byers, Michelle, and Val Marie Johnson. *The CSI Effect: Television, Crime, and Governance*. New York: Lexington Books, 2009.

Callahan, Renée. "Will the 'Real' Battered Woman Please Stand Up? In Search of a Realistic Legal Definition of Battered Woman Syndrome." *Journal of Gender and the Law* 3 (1994): 117–52.

Campbell, Rebecca, Deborah Bybee, Kathleen D. Kelley, Emily R. Dworkin, and Debra Patterson. "The Impact of Sexual Assault Nurse Examiner (SANE) Program Services on Law Enforcement Investigational Practices: A Mediational Analysis." *Criminal Justice and Behavior* 39, no. 2 (2012): 169–84.

Campt, Tina. *Listening to Images*. Durham, NC: Duke University Press, 2017.

Canham, Hugo. "Embodied Black Rage." *Du Bois Review: Social Science Research on Race* 14, no. 2 (2017): 427–45.

Caparrotta, Luigi. "Oedipal Shame, Rejection, and Adolescent Behavior Development." *American Journal of Psychoanalysis* 63, no. 4 (2003): 345–55.

Carby, Hazel. *Reconstructing Womanhood: The Emergence of the Afro-American Woman Novelist*. New York: Oxford University Press, 1990.

Carr, E. Summerson, and Michael Lempert, eds. *Scale: Discourse and Dimensions of Social Life*. Berkeley: University of California Press, 2016.

Cartwright, Lisa. *Moral Spectatorship: Technologies of Voice and Affect in Postwar Representations of the Child*. Durham, NC: Duke University Press, 2008.

Cartwright, Lisa. *Screening the Body: Tracing Medicine's Visual Culture*. Minneapolis: University of Minnesota Press, 1995.

Cheng, Anne. *Second Skin: Josephine Baker and the Modern Surface*. Oxford: Oxford University Press, 2010.

Cheng, Anne. "Skins, Tattoos, and Susceptibility." *Representations* 108, no. 1 (Fall 2009): 98–119.

Chu, Andrea Long. "Study in Blue: Trauma, Affect, Event." *Women and Performance: A Journal of Feminist Theory* 27, no. 3 (2017): 301–15.

Cohen, Donald J. "Enduring Sadness—Early Loss, Vulerability, and the Shaping of Character." *Psychoanalytic Study of the Child* 45 (1990): 157–78.

Collins, Kathleen. "The Scourged Back." *History of Photography* 1, no. 1 (1985): 43–45.

Constable, Marianne. *Just Silences: The Limits and Possibilities of Modern Law.* Princeton, NJ: Princeton University Press, 2005.

Costantino, G., and R. G. Malgady. "The Tell-Me-A-Story-Test: A Multicultural Offspring of the Thematic Apperception Test." In *Evocative Images: The Thematic Apperception Test and the Art of Projection*, edited by L. Gieser and M. I. Stein, 191–206. Washington, DC: American Psychological Association, 1999.

Cooper, Brittney. *Beyond Respectability: The Intellectual Thought of Race Women*. Urbana: University of Illinois Press, 2017.

Copeland, Huey. *Bound to Appear: Art, Slavery, and the Site of Blackness in Multicultural America*. Chicago: University of Chicago Press, 2013.

Corrigan, Rose. *Up against a Wall: Rape Reform and the Failure of Success*. New York: New York University Press, 2013.

Coryell, Janet L., Thomas H. Appelton Jr., Anastatia Sims, and Sandra Gioia Treadway. *Negotiating the Boundaries of Southern Womanhood: Dealing with the Powers That Be*. Columbia: University of Missouri Press, 2000.

Cotton, Tom. "Send in the Troops." *New York Times*, June 3, 2020.

Cowley, Camilla. *Conceiving Freedom: Women of Color, Gender, and the Abolition of Slavery in Havana and Rio de Janeiro*. Chapel Hill, NC: University of North Carolina Press, 2013.

Cowling, Camillia. *Conceiving Freedom: Women of Color, Gender, and the Abolition of Slavery in Havana and Rio de Janeiro*. Chapel Hill: University of North Carolina Press, 2013.

Crary, Jonathan. *Techniques of the Observer: On Vision and Modernity in the Nineteenth Century*. Cambridge, MA: MIT Press, 1990.

Crawley, Karen. "The Critical Force of Irony: Reframing Photographs in Cultural Legal Studies." In *Law's Popular Culture and the Metamorphosis of Law*, edited by Cassandra Sharp and Marett Leiboff, 183–206. Abington: Routledge, 2016.

Crenshaw, Kimberlé. "Mapping the Margins: Intersectionality, Identity Politics and Violence against Women of Color." *Stanford Law Review* 43, no. 6 (1991): 1241–99.

Crenshaw, Kimberlé. *Say Her Name: Resisting Police Brutality Against Black Women*. New York: African American Policy Forum/Center for Intersectionality and Social Policy Studies, 2015.

Cudjoe, Selwyn. *Resistance and Caribbean Literature*. Athens: Ohio University Press, 1980.

Cvetkovich, Ann. *Depression: A Public Feeling*. Durham, NC: Duke University Press, 2012.

Daniels, Christine, and Michael V. Kennedy, eds. *Over the Threshold: Domestic Violence in Early America*. New York: Routledge, 1999.

Darwin, Charles. *The Expression of the Emotions in Man and Animals*. New York: Oxford University Press, 1998.

Das, Veena. "The Act of Witnessing: Violence, Knowledge and Subjectivity." In *Violence and Subjectivity*, edited by V. Das, A. Kleinman, M. Ramphele, and P. Reynolds, 205–25. Berkeley: University of California Press.

Davis, Angela Y. *Violence against Women and the Ongoing Challenge to Racism*. Latham, NY: Kitchen Table, 1985.

Davis, Angela Y. *Women, Race and Class*. New York: Vintage, 1983.

Dayan, Colin. *The Law Is a White Dog: How Legal Rituals Make and Unmake Persons*. Princeton, NJ: Princeton University Press, 2011.

DeLia, Demetria. "The Achilles Complex: Preoedipal Trauma, Rage, and Repetition." *Psychoanalytic Review* 91, no. 2 (2004): 179–99.

De Silva, Denise Ferreira. *Towards a Global Idea of Race*. Minneapolis: University of Minnesota Press, 2007.

De Silva, Denise Ferreira. "Toward a Black Feminist Poethics: The Quest(ion) of Blackness at the End of the World." *Black Scholar* 44, no. 2 (Summer 2014): 81–97.

Djudjic, Dunja. "This Photographer Helps Survivors of Domestic Violence to Love Themselves Again." *Photography*, May 6, 2018.

Donovan, Dolores A., and Stephanie Wildman. "Is the Reasonable Man Obsolete? A Critical Perspective on Self-Defense and Provocation." *Los Angeles Law Review* 14 (1981): 435–68.

Drewal, Margaret Thompson. "The Camp Trace in Corporate America: Liberace and the Rockettes at Radio City Music Hall." In *The Politics and Poetics of Camp*, edited by Moe Meyer, 149–81. New York: Routledge, 1994.

Dubrofsky, Rachel, and Shoshana Amielle Magnet, eds. *Feminist Surveillance Studies*. Durham, NC: Duke University Press, 2015.

Dyer, Richard. *White*. New York: Routledge, 2002.

Eckel, Julia, Bernd Leiendecker, Daniela Olek, and Christine Piepiorka, eds. *(Dis)Orienting Media and Narrative Mazes*. Bielefeld, Germany: Transcript, 2013.

Emberton, Carole. *Beyond Redemption: Race, Violence, and the American South after the Civil War*. Chicago: University of Chicago Press, 2013.

Emerling, Jae, and Ronna Gardner. "Architecture! (To Be Said Excitedly but with Real Frustration)." *Journal of Visual Culture* 15, no. 3 (2016): 295–300.

Faigman, David. "The Battered Woman Syndrome and Self-Defense: A Legal and Empirical Dissent." *Virginia Law Review* 72 (1986): 619–47.

Faigman, David L., and Amy J Wright, "The Battered Woman Syndrome in the Age of Science," *Arizona Law Review* 39 (Spring 1997): 68–115.

Fanon, Franz, and C. Geronimi. "Le T.A.T. chez les femmes musulumanes: Soci-
ologie de la perception et de l'imagination." *Congrès des Médecins Aliénistes et
Neurologistes de France*, 54th Session (1956): 364–68.

Farrand, Max, ed. *The Records of the Federal Convention of 1787*, vol. 3. New Haven,
CT: Yale University Press, 1911.

Feigenson, N., and C. Spiesel. *Law on Display: The Digital Transformation of Legal
Persuasion and Judgment*. New York: New York University Press, 2009.

Feigenson, Neil. "The Visual in Law: Some Problems for Legal Theory." *Law,
Culture and the Humanities* 10, no. 1 (2014): 13–23.

Finkelman, Paul. "Affirmative Action for the Master Class: The Creation of the
Proslavery Constitution." *Akron Law Review* 32, no. 3 (1999): 423–70.

Finn, Jonathan. *Capturing the Criminal Image: From Mug Shot to Surveillance Society*. Minneapolis: University of Minnesota Press, 2009.

Fleetwood, Nicole. *On Racial Icons: Blackness and the Public Imagination*. New
Brunswick, NJ: Rutgers University Press, 2015.

Fleetwood, Nicole. *Troubling Vision: Performance, Visuality and Blackness*. Chicago:
University of Chicago Press, 2011.

Foucault, Michel. *Discipline and Punish: The Birth of the Prison*. Translated by Alan
Sheridan. New York: Vintage Books, 1977.

Franklin, Seb. *Control: Digitality as Cultural Logic*. Cambridge, MA: MIT Press, 2015.

Gagné, Patricia. *Battered Women's Justice: The Movement for Clemency and the Politics
of Self-Defense*. New York: Twayne, 1998.

Gaines, Jane. "White Privilege in Looking Relations: Race and Gender in Feminist Film Theory." *Screen* 29, no. 4 (1988): 12–27.

Giddens, Anthony. *The Constitution of Society: Outline of the Theory of Structuration*.
Berkeley: University of California Press, 1984.

Gieser, Lon, and Morris I. Stein, eds. "An Overview of the Thematic Apperception
Test." In *Evocative Images: The Thematic Apperception Test and the Art of Projec-
tion*, edited by edited by L. Gieser and M. I. Stein, 3–12. Washington, DC:
American Psychological Association, 1999.

Gilje, Paul. *Rioting in America*. Bloomington: Indiana University Press, 1996.

Gillespie, Cynthia. *Justifiable Homicide: Battered Women, Self-Defense, and the Law*.
Columbus: Ohio State University Press, 1989.

Gilmore, Ruthie. *Golden Gulag: Prisons, Surplus, Crisis and Opposition in Globalizing
California*. Berkeley: University of California Press, 2007.

Gilroy, Paul. *The Black Atlantic: Modernity and Double Consciousness*. Cambridge,
MA: Harvard University Press, 1993.

Gitelman, Lisa. *Always Already New: Media, History and the Data of Culture*. Cambridge, MA: MIT Press, 2006.

Gitelman, Lisa. *Scripts, Grooves, and Writing Machines: Representing Technology in
the Edison Era*. Stanford, CA: Stanford University Press, 1999.

Green-Barteet, Miranda A. "The Loophole of Retreat: Interstitial Spaces in
Harriet Jacob's *Incidents in the Life of a Slave Girl*." *South Central Review* 30,
no. 2 (2013): 53–72.

Golan, Tal. *Laws of Men and Laws of Nature: The History of Scientific Expert Testimony in England and America*. Cambridge, MA: Harvard University Press, 2004.

Gonzalez Van Cleve, Nicole. *Crook County: Racism and Injustice in America's Largest Criminal Court*. Stanford, CA: Stanford University Press, 2015.

Goodrich, Peter. "Iconography of Nothing: Black Spaces in the Representation of Law in Edward VI and the Pope." In *Law and the Image: The Authority of Art and the Aesthetics of Law*, edited by Costas Douzinas and Lynda Nead, 89–116. Chicago: University of Chicago Press, 1999.

Gordon, Avery. *Ghostly Matters: Haunting and the Sociological Imagination*. Minneapolis: University of Minnesota Press, 2008.

Grier, William H., and Price M. Cobbs. *Black Rage*. New York: Basic Books, 1968.

Grossberg, Michael. *Governing the Hearth: Law and the Family in Nineteenth-Century America*. Chapel Hill: University of North Carolina Press, 1985.

Guth, Amber A., and H. Leon Pachter. "Domestic Violence and the Trauma Surgeon." *American Journal of Surgery* 179, no. 2 (2000): 134–40.

Gwaltney, John. *Drylongso: A Self-Portrait of Black America*. New York: New Press, 1980.

Haley, Sarah. *No Mercy Here: Gender, Punishment and the Making of Jim Crow Modernity*. Chapel Hill: University of North Carolina Press, 2016.

Halley, Janet. *Split Decisions: How and Why to Take A Break from Feminism*. Princeton, NJ: Princeton University Press, 2006.

Halley, Janet, Prabha Kotiswaran, Rachel Rebouché, and Hila Shamir, eds. *Governance Feminism: Notes from the Field*. Minneapolis: University of Minnesota Press, 2019.

Hammonds, Evelyn. "Black (W)holes and the Geometry of Black Female Sexuality." *differences: A Journal of Feminist Cultural Studies* 6, nos. 2–3 (Summer–Fall 1994): 127–45.

Han, Sora. *Letters of the Law: Race and the Fantasy of Colorblindness in American Law*. Stanford, Calif.: Stanford University Press, 2015.

Han, Sora. "Slavery as Contract: Betty's Case and the Question of Freedom." *Law and Literature* 27, no. 2 (2015): 395–416.

Hanson, Mark. *Bodies in Code: Interfaces with New Media*. London: Routledge, 2006.

Hardecker, David J. K., and Daniel B. M. Haun. "Approaching the Development of Hurt Feelings in Childhood." *New Ideas in Psychology* 59 (March 2020): 1–7.

Harris, Cheryl. "Whiteness as Property." *Harvard Law Review* 106, no. 8 (1993): 1707–91.

Hartman, Saidiya. *Scenes of Subjection: Terror, Slavery, and Self-Making in Nineteenth-Century America*. Oxford: Oxford University Press, 1997.

Hartman, Saidiya. "Venus in Two Acts." *Small Axe* 12, no. 2 (June 2008): 1–14.

Hartog, Hendrik. "Marital Exits and Marital Expectations in Nineteenth-Century America." *Georgetown Law Journal* 80 (October 1991): 95–130.

Hia, Rebecca. "Carrying That Weight: Domestic Abuse Awareness on Campus." *Yeshiva Observer*, November 13, 2014.

Hillewaert, Sarah. "Tactics and Tactility: A Sensory Semiotics of Handshakes in Coastal Kenya." *American Anthropologist* 118, no. 1 (2016): 49–66.

Hine, Darlene Clark. "Rape and the Inner Lives of Black Women in the Middle West." *Signs Journal of Women in Culture and Society* 14, no. 4 (1989): 912–20.

hooks, bell. *Ain't I a Woman? Black Women and Feminism*. Boston: South End Press, 1981.

hooks, bell. "Is Paris Burning?" In *Black Looks: Race and Representation*, 145–156. New York: Routledge, 2015.

Hugrass, L., J. Slavikova, M. Horvat, A. Al Musawi, and D. Crewther. "Temporal Brightness Illusion Changes Color Perception of 'The Dress.'" *Journal of Vision* 17, no. 5 (2017): 1–7.

Isachenka, Alina. "Domestic Violence: How Photos Are Helping Victims to Love Themselves Again." *BBC News*, April 10, 2018.

Isherwood, Christopher. *The World in the Evening*. London: Methuen, 1954.

Jackson, Sarah, Moya Bailey, and Brooke Foucault Welles. *Hashtag Activism: Networks of Race and Gender Justice*. Cambridge, MA: MIT Press, 2020.

Jackson, Zakiyyah Iman. *Becoming Human: Matter and Meaning in an Antiblack World*. New York: New York University Press, 2020.

Jackson, Zakiyyah Iman. "'Theorizing in a Void': Sublimity, Matter, and Physics in Black Feminist Poetics." *South Atlantic Quarterly* 117, no. 3 (2018): 617–48.

Jacobs, Harriet. *Incidents in the Life of a Slave Girl, as Written by Herself*. New York: Penguin Putnam, 2002 [1861].

James, Joy. "The Womb of Western Theory: Trauma Time Theft and the Captive Maternal." In *Challenging the Punitive Society: Carceral Notebooks*, edited by Perry Zurn and Andrew Dilts, 253–96. New York: Publishing Data Management, 2017.

Jasanoff, Sheila. *Science at the Bar: Law, Science, and Technology in America*. Cambridge, MA: Harvard University Press, 1995.

Johann, Sarah Lee, and Franklyn Mark Osanka, eds. *Representing Battered Women Who Kill*. Springfield, IL: Charles C. Thomas, 1989.

Johnson, E. Patrick. "Quare Studies, or (Almost) Everything I Know about Queer Studies I Learned from My Grandmother." *Text and Performance Quarterly* 21, no. 1 (2001): 1–25.

Johnson, Jessica M. *Wicked Flesh: Black Women, Intimacy and Freedom in the Atlantic World*. Philadelphia: University of Pennsylvania Press, 2020.

Johnson, Samuel. *Dictionary of the English Language*. London: J & P Knapton, 1755.

Jones-Rogers, Stephanie. *They Were Her Property: White Women as Slave Owners in the American South*. New Haven, CT: Yale University Press, 2019.

Kaplan, Sarah. "How a Mattress Became a Symbol for Student Activists against Sexual Assault." *Washington Post*, November 28, 2014.

Kapp, Ernst. *Elements of a Philosophy of Technology: On the Evolutionary History of Culture*, edited by Jeffrey West Kirkwood and Leif Weatherby, 3–250. Translated by Laura K. Wolfe. Minneapolis: University of Minnesota Press, 2018.

Keeling, Kara. *The Witch's Flight: The Cinematic, the Black Femme and the Image of Common Sense*. Durham, NC: Duke University Press, 2007.

Kelley, Lauren. "Who Bears Witness to a Hidden Epidemic?" *New York Times*, July 14, 2020.

Khanna, Ranjana. "The Lumpenproletariat, the Subaltern, the Mental Asylum." *South Atlantic Quarterly* 112, no. 1 (2013): 129–43.

King, Tiffany Lethabo. *The Black Shoals: Offshore Formations of Black and Native Studies.* Durham, NC: Duke University Press, 2019.

Kohler-Hausmann, Issa. "Managerial Justice and Mass Misdemeanors." *Stanford Law Review* 66 (March 2014): 611–94.

Kohler-Hausmann, Issa. *Misdemeanorland: Criminal Courts and Social Control in an Age of Broken Windows Policing.* Princeton, NJ: Princeton University Press, 2018.

Koss, Mary P., L. A. Goodman, A. Browne, L. F. Fitzgerald, G. P. Keita, and N. F. Russo. *No Safe Haven: Male Violence against Women at Home, Work and in the Community.* Washington, D.C.: American Psychological Association, 1994.

Krieger, Georgia. "Playing Dead: Harriet Jacobs's Survival Strategy in *Incidents in the Life of a Slave Girl.*" *African American Review* 42, no. 3 (2008): 607–21.

Labeau, Vicky. "Psycho-Politics: Frantz Fanon's *Black Skin, White Masks.*" In *Psycho-Politics and Cultural Desires,* edited by Jan Campbell and Janet Harbord, 107–17. London: University College London Press, 1998.

Lafer-Sousa, Rose, Katherine L. Herman, and Bevil R. Conway. "Striking Individual Differences in Color Perception Uncovered by 'The Dress' Photograph." *Current Biology* 25, no. 13 (2015): R545–46.

Larson, Jennifer. "Converting Passive Womanhood to Active Sisterhood: Agency, Power, and Subversion in Harriet Jacobs's *Incidents in the Life of a Slave Girl.*" *Women's Studies: An Interdisciplinary Journal* 35, no. 8 (2006): 739–56.

Latour, Bruno. *The Making of Law: An Ethnography of the Conseil d'Etat.* Cambridge: Polity Press, 2010.

Lemon, Nancy and Anne Perry. "Admissability of Hearsay Evidence under the Excited Utterance Exception in Abuse Prosecutions." *Family and Intimate Partner Violence Quarterly* 2, no. 3 (1997): 36–40.

Luhmann, Niklas. *Law as a Social System.* Oxford: Oxford University Press, 2004.

Lyon, David. *Surveillance Studies: An Overview.* Cambridge: Polity Press, 2007.

Maguigan, Holly. "Battered Women and Self-Defense: Myths and Misconceptions in Current Reform." *University of Pennsylvania Law Review* 140, no. 2 (1991): 379–486.

Mallinson, A. "Introduction to Visual–Vestibular Mismatch." PhD dissertation, Maastricht University, 2011.

Marcus, Sharon. "Fighting Bodies, Fighting Words: A Theory and Politics of Rape Prevention." In *Feminists Theorize the Political,* edited by Judith Butler and Joan Scott, 385–403. New York: Routledge, 1992.

Marriott, David. "Inventions of Existence: Sylvia Wynter, Frantz Fanon, and 'the Damned'" *New Centennial Review* 11, no. 3 (2011): 45–89.

Marriott, David. *Whither Fanon: Studies on the Blackness of Being.* Palo Alto, CA: Stanford University Press, 2018.

McMillan, Uri. *Embodied Avatars: Genealogies of Black Feminist Art and Performance.* New York: New York University Press, 2015.

Menkman, Rosa. "Glitch Studies Manifesto." In *Video Vortex Reader II: Moving Images beyond YouTube*, edited by Geert Lovink and Rachel Somers Miles, 336–47. Amsterdam: Institute of Network Cultures, 2011.

Merry, Sally Engle. "Governmentality and Gender Violence in Hawai'i in Historical Perspective." *Social and Legal Studies* 11, no. 1 (2002): 81–111.

Merry, Sally Engle. "Spatial Governmentality and the New Urban Social Order: Controlling Gender Violence through Law." *American Anthropologist* 103, no. 1 (2001): 16–29

Meyer, Moe, ed. *Archaeology of Posing: Essays on Camp, Drag and Sexuality*. Madison, WI: Macater Press, 2010.

Meyer, Moe, ed. *The Politics and Poetics of Camp*. New York and London: Routledge, 1994.

Mills, Charles W. *The Racial Contract*. Ithaca, NY: Cornell University Press, 1997.

Mirzoeff, Nicholas. *The Right to Look: A Counterhistory of Visuality*. Durham, NC: Duke University Press, 2011.

Mitchell, W. T. J. *What Do Pictures Want? The Lives and Loves of Images*. Chicago: University of Chicago Press, 2005.

Mnookin, Jennifer. "The Image of Truth: Photographic Evidence and the Power of Analogy." *Yale Journal of Law and the Humanities* 10, no. 1 (1998): 1–74.

Moore, Kelli. "The Digital Rape Complaint: Allegation Escrow Technology and the Social Dynamics of Rape Reporting, a Media Studies and Legal Theory Concern." *First Monday* special issue, "Video Evidence in Law and Policy," edited by Sandra Ristovska (forthcoming).

Moore, Kelli. "Held in the Light: Reading Rihanna's Abuse Photography." In *Feminist Surveillance Studies*, edited by Rachel E. Dubrofsky and Shoshana Amielle Magnet, 107–26. Durham, NC: Duke University Press, 2015.

Moore, Kelli. "Photographie Fèminine: Exile and Survival in the Photography of Ana Mendieta, Donna Ferrato and Nan Goldin." *Anglistica* 17, no. 1 (2013): 179–90.

Morgan, Jennifer. *Laboring Women: Reproduction and Gender in New World Slavery*. Philadelphia: University of Pennsylvania Press, 2004.

Morgan, Jennifer. "*Partus Sequitur Ventrem*: Law, Race, and Reproduction in Colonial Slavery." *Small Axe* 1, no. 55 (March 2018): 1–17.

Moten, Fred. *Stolen Life: Consent Not to Be a Single Being*. Durham, NC: Duke University Press, 2018.

Mulla, Sameena. *The Violence of Care: Rape Victims, Forensic Nurses and Sexual Assault Prevention*. New York: New York University Press, 2014.

Mulvey, Laura. "Visual Pleasure and Narrative Cinema." *Screen* 16, no. 1 (1975): 6–18.

Muñoz, José. *Cruising Utopia: The Then and There of Queer Futurity*. New York: New York University Press, 2009.

Muñoz, José. "Queerness as Horizon: Utopian Hermeneutics in the Face of Gay Pragmatism." In *A Companion to Lesbian, Gay, Bisexual, Transgender and Queer Studies*, edited by George E. Haggerty and Molly McGarry, 453–63. Oxford: Blackwell Publishing, 2007.

Murakawa, Naomi. *The First Civil Right: How Liberals Built Prison America.* Oxford; New York: Oxford University Press, 2014.

Musser, Amber Jamila. *Sensual Excess: Queer Femininity and Brown Jouissance.* New York, New York University Press, 2018.

Nash, Jennifer. *The Black Body in Ecstasy: Reading Race, Reading Pornography.* Durham, NC: Duke University Press, 2014.

Nash, Jennifer. *Black Feminism Reimagined: After Intersectionality.* Durham, NC: Duke University Press, 2019.

Neary, Janet. *Fugitive Testimony: On the Visual Logic of Slave Narratives.* New York: Fordham University Press, 2017.

Ngai, Sianne. *Our Aesthetic Categories: Zany, Cute, Interesting.* Cambridge, MA: Harvard University Press, 2012.

Ngai, Sianne. "Stuplimity: Shock and Boredom in Twentieth Century Aesthetics." *Postmodern Culture* 10, no. 2 (January 2000): 1–28.

Ngai, Sianne. *Ugly Feelings.* Cambridge, MA: Harvard University Press, 2005.

Nobles, Richard, and David Schiff. "Introduction." In *Law as a Social System.* Oxford: Oxford University Press, 2004.

O'Hear, Michael. "'Some of the Most Embarrassing Questions': Extraterritorial Divorces and the Problem of Jurisdiction before *Pennoyer* [1877]." *Yale Law Journal* 104 (March 1995): 1507–37.

Omolade, Barbara. *The Rising Song of African American Women.* New York: Routledge, 1994.

Parsons, Elaine Frantz. "Midnight Rangers: Costume and Performance in the Reconstruction Era Ku Klux Klan." *Journal of Southern History* 92, no. 3 (2005): 811–36.

Pateman, Carol. *The Sexual Contract.* Cambridge, MA: Polity Press, 1988.

Pateman, Carol, and Charles Mills. *Contract and Domination.* Cambridge: Malden, 2007.

Pelligrini, Ann. "After Sontag: Future Notes on Camp." In *A Companion to Lesbian Gay, Bisexual and Transgender and Queer Studies*, edited by George E. Haggerty and Molly McGarry, 168–93. Oxford: Blackwell, 2008.

Peterson, Christopher, Martin Seligman, and Steven Maier. *Learned Helplessness: A Theory for the Age of Personal Control.* New York: Oxford University Press, 1993.

Philips, Patricia C. "The Proportions of Paradox: The Work of Ellen Driscoll." *Sculpture* 19, no. 9 (2000): 30–37.

Pogrebin, Robin. "Madison Avenue Creates Stark Ad about Battering" *New York Times*, August 25, 1999.

Posch, Pamela. "The Negative Effects of Expert Testimony on the Battered Women's Syndrome." *Journal of Gender and the Law* 6, no. 2 (1998): 485–503.

Raley, Rita. *Tactical Media.* Minneapolis: University of Minnesota Press, 2009.

Randle, Gloria T. "Between the Rock and the Hard Place: Mediating Space in Harriet Jacobs's *Incidents in the Life of a Slave Girl*." *African American Review* 33, no. 1 (1999): 43–56.

Redfern, M. S., L. Yardley, and A. M. Bronstein. "Visual Influences on Balance." Special Contribution. *Journal of Anxiety Disorders* 15, nos. 1–2 (2001): 81–94.

Rentschler, Carrie. *Second Wounds: Victim's Rights and the Media in the U.S.* Durham, NC: Duke University Press, 2011.

Resnik, Judith, and Dennis E. Curtis. *Representing Justice: Intervention, Controversy, and Right in City-States and Democratic Courtrooms.* New Haven, CT: Yale University Press, 2011.

Richards, Leonard. *"Gentlemen of Property and Standing": Anti-Abolition Mobs in Jacksonian America.* New York: Oxford University Press, 1970.

Richardson, Allissa V. *Bearing Witness While Black: African Americans, Smartphones, and the New Protest #Journalism.* New York: Oxford University Press, 2020.

Roberts, Dorothy. "Criminal Justice and Black Families: The Collateral Damage of Over-Enforcement." *U.C. Davis Law Review* 34, no. 1005 (2001): 1006–1009.

Roberts, Dorothy. "The Social and Moral Cost of Mass Incarceration in African American Communities," *Stanford Law Review* 56 (2004): 1271–1305.

Roberts, Jenny. "Crashing the Misdemeanor System." *Washington and Lee Law Review* 70, no. 1089 (2013):1089–1131.

Robinson, Cedric. *Black Marxism: The Making of the Black Radical Tradition.* Chapel Hill: University of North Carolina Press, 1983.

Robles-Anderson, Erica. "The Crystal Cathedral: Architecture for Mediated Congregation." *Public Culture* 24 no. 3 (2012): 577–99.

Ronell, Avital. *The Telephone Book: Technology, Schizophrenia, Electronic Speech.* Lincoln: University of Nebraska Press, 1989.

Rosen, Hannah. *Terror in the Heart of Freedom: Citizenship, Sexual Violence and the Meaning of Race in Postemancipation South.* Chapel Hill: University of North Carolina Press, 2009.

Rosenzweig, Saul. "Pioneer Experiences in the Clinical Development of the Thematic Apperception Test." In *Evocative Images: The Thematic Apperception Test and the Art of Projection,* edited by Lon Gieser and Morris I. Stein, 39–50. Washington, DC: American Psychological Association, 1999.

Roth, Lorna. "Looking at Shirley, the Ultimate Norm: Colour Balance, Image Technologies, and Cognitive Equity. *Canadian Journal of Communication* 34, no. 1 (2009): 111–36.

Ryan, M. J. "Juries and the Criminal Constitution." *Alabama Law Review* 65, no. 4 (2014): 849–902.

"Scenes from Memphis, Tennessee—During the Riot—Shooting Down Negroes on the Morning of May 2, 1866." *Harper's Weekly,* May 26, 1866, 321.

Schaefer, Karine. "The Spectators as Witness? *Binlids* as Case Study." *Studies in Theater and Performance* 23, no. 1 (2003): 5–20.

Schlesinger, Martin. "Go Play Outside! Game Glitches." In *(Dis)orienting Media and Narrative Mazes,* edited by Julia Eckel, Bernd Leiendecker, Daniela Olek, and Christine Piepiorka, 93–110. Verlag: Bielefeld, 2013.

Schneider, Elizabeth. *Battered Women and Feminist Lawmaking.* New Haven, CT: Yale University Press, 2000.

Schuller, Regina A., and Neil Vidmar. "Battered Woman Syndrome Evidence in the Courtroom." *Law and Human Behavior* 16, no. 3 (1992): 273–91.

Schweninger, Loren. *Families in Crisis in the Old South: Divorce, Slavery and the Law.* Chapel Hill: University of North Carolina Press, 2012.

Sedgwick, Eve Kosofsky. *Epistemologies of the Closet.* Berkeley: University of California Press, 1990.

Sedgwick, Eve Kosofsky, and Adam Frank, eds. *Shame and Its Sisters: A Sylvan Tomkins Reader.* Durham, NC: Duke University Press, 1995.

Seligman, Martin E. P., and Steven F. Maier. *Learned Helplessness: A Theory for the Age of Personal Control.* New York; Oxford: Oxford University Press, 1993.

Selvaratnam, Tanya. "Where Can Domestic Violence Victims Turn during COVID-19?" *New York Times*, March 23, 2020.

Serres, Michel. *The Parasite.* Minneapolis: University of Minnesota Press, 2007.

Shabazz, Rashad. *Spatializing Blackness: Architectures of Confinement and Black Masculinity in Chicago.* Urbana: University of Illinois Press, 2015.

Shange, Savannah. "Black Girl Ordinary: Flesh, Carcerality and the Refusal of Ethnography." *Transforming Anthropology* 27, no. 1 (April 2019): 3–21.

Shange, Savannah. *Progressive Dystopia: Abolition, Anti-Blackness and Schooling in San Francisco.* Durham, NC: Duke University Press, 2019.

Sharpe, Christina. "The Weather." *New Inquiry*, January 19, 2017. https://thenewinquiry.com/the-weather/.

Shell, Hanna Rose. *Hide and Seek: Camouflage, Photography, and the Media of Reconnaissance.* New York, Zone Books, 2012.

Sherwin, Richard K. *Visualizing Law in the Age of the Digital Baroque: Arabesques and Entanglements.* Hoboken, NJ: Taylor & Francis, 2012.

Shim, Hyejin. "Roots of Survived & Punished." *No Perfect Victims Videos.* https://survivedandpunished.org/no-perfect-victims-videos/.

Silkenat, David. "'A Typical Negro': Gordon, Peter, Vincent Colyer, and the Story behind Slavery's Most Famous Photograph." *American Nineteenth-Century History* 15, no. 2 (2014): 169–86.

Silverman, Kaja. *The Miracle of Analogy: Or, The History of Photography, Part I.* Palo Alto, CA: Stanford University Press, 2015.

Simmons, R. "Re-Examining the Grand Jury: Is There Room for Democracy in the Criminal Justice System?" *Boston University Law Review* 82, no. 1 (2002): 1–76.

Simonson, Jocelyn. "The Criminal Court Audience in a Post-Trial World." *Harvard Law Review* 127, no. 8 (2014): 2174–2232.

Smith, Valerie. *Self-Discovery and Authority in Afro-American Narrative.* Cambridge, MA: Harvard University Press, 1991.

Snorton, C. Riley. *Black on Both Sides: A Racial History of Trans Identity.* Minneapolis: University of Minnesota Press, 2017.

Sokoloff, N., and Ida Dupont. "Domestic Violence at the Intersections of Race, Class, and Gender: Challenges and Contributions to Understanding Violence against Marginalized Women in Diverse Communities." *Violence against Women* 11, no.1 (January 2015): 38–64. https://doi.org/10.1177/1077801204271476.

Sontag, Susan. *Notes on Camp*. New York: Penguin Random House, 2018.

Soto, Isabel. "'The Spaces Left': Ambivalent Discourses in Harriet Jacobs and Frederick Douglass." In *Loopholes and Retreats: African American Writers and the Nineteenth Century*, edited by John Cullen Gruesser and Hannah Wallinger, 31–42. New Brunswick, NJ: Transaction Publishers, 2009.

Southall, Ashley. "Why a Drop in Domestic Violence Complaints Might Not Be a Good Sign." *New York Times*, April, 17, 2020. https://www.nytimes.com/2020/03/23/opinion/covid-domestic-violence.html?searchResultPosition=11.

Spillers, Hortense. *Black, White, and in Color: Essays on American Literature and Culture*. Chicago: University of Chicago Press, 2003.

Stein, Mark. "The Domestic Violence Clause in New Originalist Theory." *Hastings Constitutional Law Quarterly* 37, no. 1 (2009): 129–40.

Sterli, Martino. "Architecture and Visual Culture: Some Remarks on an Ongoing Debate." *Journal of Visual Culture* 15, no. 3 (2016): 311–16.

Sterne, Jonathan. *MP3: The Meaning of a Format*. Durham, NC: Duke University Press, 2012.

Stevenson, Brenda. "Distress and Discord in Virginia Slave Families, 1830–1860." In *In Joy and Sorrow: Women, Family, and Marriage in the Victorian South, 1830–1857*, edited by Carol Bleser, 103–24. New York: Oxford University Press, 1991.

Stockton, Kathryn Bond. *Beautiful Bottom, Beautiful Shame: Where "Black" Meets "Queer."* Durham, NC: Duke University Press, 2006.

Stoever, Jane. "Transforming Domestic Violence Representation." *Kentucky Law Journal* 101, no. 3, art. 3 (2013): 483–542.

Strick, Simon. *American Dolorologies: Pain, Sentimentalism, Biopolitics*. Albany: State University of New York Press, 2014.

Strings, Sabrina. *Fearing the Black Body: The Racial Origins of Fat Phobia*. New York: New York University Press, 2020.

Strings, Sabrina. "It's Not Obesity. It's Slavery." *New York Times*, May, 4, 2019.

Stubbs, Julie, and Julia Tolmie. "Race, Gender, and Battered Woman Syndrome." *Canadian Journal of Women and Law* 8 (1995): 122–58.

Taussig, Michael. *What Color Is the Sacred?* Chicago: University of Chicago Press, 2009.

Thompson, Debra. "An Exoneration of Black Rage." *South Atlantic Quarterly* 116, no. 3 (2017): 457–81.

Threadcraft, Shatema. *Intimate Justice: The Black Female Body and the Body Politic*. New York: Oxford University Press, 2016.

Threadcraft, Shatema. "North American Necropolitics and Gender: On #blacklivesmatter and Black Femicide." *South Atlantic Quarterly* 116, no. 3 (2017): 553–79.

Tomkins, Silvan. *Affect, Imagery, Consciousness: Volume 1*. New York: Springer, 2008.

Trinch, Shonna L. *Latinas' Narratives of Domestic Abuse: Discrepant Versions of Violence*. Philadelphia: John Benjamins Publishing, 2003.

"A Typical Negro." *Harper's Weekly*, July 4, 1863.

"Visit of the Ku-Klux." *Harper's Weekly*, February 24, 1872, 157.

Vismann, Cornelia. *Files: Law and Media Technology.* Palo Alto, CA: Stanford University Press, 2008.

Walker, Lenore E. *The Battered Woman Syndrome.* New York: Springer, 2009.

Wallace, Michele. *Black Macho and the Myth of the Superwoman.* London: Verso, 1999.

Wexler, Laura. *Tender Violence: Domestic Visions in an Age of US Imperialism.* Chapel Hill: University of North Carolina, 2000.

White, Deborah, and Janie DuMont, "Visualizing Sexual Assault: An Exploration in the Use of Optical Technologies in the Medico-Legal Context." *Social Science and Medicine* 68 (2009): 1–8.

Winston, Brian. *Technologies of Seeing: Photography, Cinematography, and Television.* London: British Film Institute Publishing, 1996.

Winston, Brian. "A Whole Technology of Dyeing: A Note on Ideology and the Apparatus of the Chromatic Moving Machine." *Daedalus* 11, no. 4 (1985): 105–23.

Witzel, Christoph, J., Kevin O'Regan, and Sabrina Hansmann-Roth. "The Dress and Individual Difference in the Perception of Surface Properties." *Vision Research* 141 (2017): 76–94.

Wood, Marcus. *Blind Memory: Visual Representations of Slavery in England and America, 1790–1865.* New York: Routledge, 2000.

INDEX

Note: Page numbers followed by *f* indicate figures.

Cartwright, Lisa, 81–82, 196nn42–43, 206n42

Cheng, Anne, 139–40

Chu, Andrea Long, 141, 143–44

citizenship, 54; Black, 33, 55–56; Black women and, 57, 95; performance of, 12, 105, 118

class, 2, 12, 76, 114, 157; intersectionality and, 77, 83, 152; social contract and, 161; white people as, 16; white women as, 182n35

clemency, 62, 77; Black women and, 182n42

Confrontation Clause, 5, 180n8

constitutional law, 3, 6–7, 11, 113, 149; abolitionist media and, 18–19; domestic violence and, 26–28; DV courtrooms and, 108, 152; courtroom architecture and, 119; Jacobs's slavery memoir and, 34; legal looking and, 101; slave law and, 51

Cooper, Brittney, 33, 157

corpsing, 107–108

cosmetics, 21, 123–24, 126–27, 133, 135, 144, 148, 206n38; color, 22, 134, 136–37, 140, 154

Cotton, Tom, 175–76

courtroom architecture, 3, 39, 94, 101–103, 119, 124, 164; DV images and, 98, 111, 118, 121, 160; testimony and, 86; witness anxiety and, 109

courtroom audiences, 2, 12, 73–74, 93–95, 101–103, 107, 119, 127; vestibular imbalance and, 116; visual evidence and, 7–8, 194n23; witness testimony and, 98

COVID-19, 173–74, 210n2

Crary, Jonathan, 40–41, 57

Crawford v. Washington, 5–7, 60, 108, 146, 156, 159–60, 170, 180n8

Crenshaw, Kimberlé, 150, 160, 171

cybernetic logic, 130–34, 152, 154

cybernetics, 17, 20–21, 64, 71, 73, 75–76, 90, 165–66

Cycle of Violence, 20–21, 63, 65, 68–69, 71–76, 84–86, 88–90, 124, 131–32, 149

daguerreotypes, 31, 33; slave, 19, 42, 49, 51, 158–59, 177, 189n49. See also "The Scourged Back"

Daubert v. Merrill Dow Pharmaceuticals, 78–83, 195n35, 196n50

domestic abuse, 17, 21, 66, 81, 92, 96, 100, 104, 138, 186n22; adjudication of, 95; claims, 180n6; hotlines, 128–29; injuries, 153; intersectionality and, 77; investigations, 42; legal camp and, 137, 206n50; photography of, 2–3, 13, 93, 116, 120, 124–28, 136, 144, 154; Power and Control Wheel and, 90; PTSD and, 83; survivors, 146; trials, 76, 94, 118, 120, 198n1, 206n50; victims of, 2, 8–9, 11, 29, 122, 130; Violence Against Women Act (VAWA) and, 5, 7; visual evidence of, 49, 64, 115, 127–28; white femininity and, 140. See also Crawford v. Washington

domestic Violence (dV), 1, 3–4, 28–31, 35–36, 55, 59, 152, 154, 164, 210n5; DV photography and, 12; enslaved women and, 16

Domestic Violence Clause of the US Constitution, 1, 3, 12, 28, 34, 41, 61, 156, 170; Black women's testimony about white violence and, 36; drafting history of, 47–48, 59, 165–66; evidence and, 32, 177; spousal abuse and, 186n23

Drewal, Margaret, 125, 133

Driscoll, Ellen, 36, 41; The Loophole of Retreat, 31, 32f, 38–42

Du Bois, W. E. B., 3, 182n42

DV courtroom, 10–12, 20, 49, 84, 149–50, 166; architecture of, 160; color cards and, 115; corpsing and, 108; cybernetic theory and, 63–64; documentary realism of, 157; loophole of retreat and, 19; minor affects and, 97–98; "One Photo a Day" and, 139; participation in, 95; racial looking and, 154; spatialization of, 167–68; testimony, 118, 120; visual culture of, 64–65; visual/photographic evidence and, 30, 44, 60, 99, 103

Pelligrini, Ann, 143–44

police images, 116, 150; legally camped, 147, 203n7

police photography, 114, 116, 120, 126, 131–32, 139, 159; customs, 137; of DV victims, 8; of battered women, 124, 168, 172

post-traumatic stress disorder (PTSD), 82–83, 149

Power and Control Wheel, 20–21, 61, 63, 65, 68–74, 84–90, 124, 132, 149, 161

protection orders, 1, 111, 125

queer aesthetics, 124, 128, 203n6

race, 2, 4, 9, 11–12, 76–77, 83, 95, 114, 157; flesh and, 10; historical reality of, 207n50; ideologies of, 30; nation and, 151; pseudoscience of, 42, 115–16, 120; riots, 175; violence, 33

Raley, Rita, 127, 137

rape, 2, 21, 163–64, 172; black women and, 54–55, 57–58, 95; date, 186n22; dissemblance and, 185n8; forensic exams and, 13; *Mattress Performance (Carry That Weight)* (Sulkowicz), 141, 143–44; *No Perfect Victims* and, 152; Reconstruction-era, 191n3; victims, 116

Reconstruction, 29–30; Black women's rape claims during, 95, 191n3; Black women's testimony and, 150; Second, 20; white violence against Black women and, 33, 54–55, 185n8

repeating bodies, 12, 22, 31–32, 42, 51, 186n11, 188n42

representation, 9, 11, 125–26, 130; of anxiety, 99, 106; Black feminist concerns with, 22, 84, 167; of domestic violence, 155; of inner life of the enslaved, 38; *Loophole of Retreat* (Driscoll) and, 39; of suffering, 94; technologies of, 3, 26, 49, 90, 185n9; visual, 8

Rosen, Hannah, 34, 53–54, 56–58, 95, 150

San Diego Family Justice Center, 100, 111, 113, 115

Schweninger, Loren, 13–14, 17, 182n35

"The Scourged Back," 18, 42–45, 48–49, 51, 59, 189n49. *See also* torture

Sedgwick, Eve Kosofsky, 64, 192n4, 193n12

self-defense strategy, 78–80, 195n32. *See also Crawford v. Washington; Ibn-Tamas v. United States*

Seligman, Martin, 19–20, 63, 66–68, 85, 87, 90, 132, 165, 192–93n8, 194n22. *See also* learned helplessness

sentimentalism, 44, 49, 184n1; white, 18

settler colonialism, 73–74, 169

sexual assault, 2, 13, 83, 113, 170, 185n8

sexuality, 2, 4, 12, 67, 76, 83, 185n8

Shange, Savannah, 27, 201n50

Shell, Hanna Rose, 128, 139

Shim, Hyejin, 149–50, 151f

Silkenat, David, 44, 48, 190n55

skin color, 115–16, 133, 137, 154

slave economy, 34, 45–46

slave law, 28, 32, 34, 38, 51, 58, 184n8, 198n7

slave memoirs, 30, 34, 39, 61

slave narratives, 19–20, 26, 29–30, 33–34, 39, 50, 159, 165; authorial power of, 187n35; visual cultures of, 55. *See also* Jacobs, Harriet

slave relations, 29, 32–34, 57, 164; violence of, 55

Snorton, C. Riley, 50, 125–26, 171

social media, 2, 94, 125, 135, 138, 163–64, 177–78; activism, 156; and/as contract, 161; as loophole of retreat, 169; #MeToo and, 170

Spillers, Hortense, 10, 15, 94, 97–98, 100, 103, 117. *See also* flesh-body distinction; vestibule

Stein, Mark, 35, 186n23, 187n27

strategies of the flesh, 10, 21–22, 164, 168–69, 174, 189n49, 209n16; abolitionist, 44. *See also* legal camp

subjectivity, 117, 119, 207n50; battered women's, 20; Black, 19, 33, 63, 89; future, 44; passive, 68; white, 41, 169

suffering, 27, 36, 49, 65, 94, 111, 133, 174; Black, 11–12, 154; of domestic abuse, 104; images of, 12, 26; slave's, 38

sulking, 18, 26–27, 50–51, 60–61, 165, 184n3
Sulkowicz, Emma, 141–44, 146–47, 150
sulks, the, 18–19, 26, 50–51, 60–62, 165, 184n3
Supreme Court, 5–7, 60, 78–79, 156, 159, 180n8
surveillance, 6, 14, 114, 116, 181n11; of Black women's insurrection, 51; racialized, 181n28; state, 5, 129
Survived and Punished (S&P), 77, 148; *No Perfect Victims*, 148–52, 153f
suspended agency, 27, 97–99, 108–110, 118, 142, 160; forensic time and, 114; garret as space of, 165; legal camp and, 154; minor affects and, 117, 159; *No Perfect Victims* and, 152; ugly feelings and, 170
swamp, 19, 43, 47, 50–51, 60, 165, 177

tactical media, 21, 121, 127, 133–34, 136–37, 139–40, 148; activism, 126, 154, 160, 170; artivists, 153; white feminist, 168
technology, 194n23; allegation escrow, 172; of DV awareness campaigns, 124; critical theories of, 129; foren- sic, 96; information, 206n50; Kapp's philosophy of, 192n3; of media of reconnaissance, 128; narrative and visual, 18; philosophy of, 183n43; pho- tographic image as, 185n9; polygraph, 78; PowerPoint, 92, 102; projection, 108; smartphone, 183n44; spatialization of, 20; studies, 100
Thain, Alastair, 122, 130–31, 133, 154
theatrical(ity), 9, 39, 103, 122, 130
Thematic Apperception Test (TAT), 63, 86–88, 132
theory of control, 76, 84–85, 88–90, 124, 152
thrown projection, 93–94, 99, 105–106
Tomkins, Sylvan, 19–20, 62–63, 71–72, 74–75, 85, 90, 165, 193–94nn12–13, 194n22. *See also* affective scripts
torture, 43, 66–67, 83, 177, 192n8
trauma, 66, 129, 144, 146, 192n8; bystander, 174–75; skin, 116; theory, 75–76
"A Typical Negro," 42–43, 45–49, 51

ugly feelings, 21, 97, 161, 183n45, 191–92n3, 201n50; suspended agency and, 170. *See also* minor affects; sulks, the
US Constitution, 47, 60, 116, 119, 154, 158, 160, 167; black slave fugitivity and, 156, 165; domestic Violence (dV) and, 3–4, 12, 28–29, 35–36, 59, 152; First Amendment to, 12, 101, 206n42; moral spectatorship and, 206n42; Sixth Amendment to, 5, 12, 101, 180n8, 206n42. *See also* Domestic Violence Clause of the US Constitution
vertigo, 18, 40–41, 49, 97, 109, 118, 187n35, 189n47
vestibular imbalance, 18, 40–41, 49, 98, 118, 142–43; testimony and, 86, 93–94, 107–109, 116
vestibule, 39–40, 98, 103, 118
victimization, 55, 149, 170, 172; Black women's claims to, 26, 28, 56
violence, 10, 12–13, 20, 35, 41, 59, 61–62, 64–65, 88, 104, 116, 119, 140; against Black women, 9; against women, 4–5, 29; battered woman syndrome (BWS) and, 89; Black queer victims of, 124; carceral, 27–28; colonial, 22; criminal justice, 148; cycle of, 66, 75–76, 80, 95; dating, 29, 186n22; decolonial, 177–78; discourses on, 151; disciplinary, 113; domestic sphere and, 192n3; gender, 121, 149–50; gun, 85; Jim Crow, 185n8; male, 129; of photographic objectifi- cation, 189n49; police, 9; Power and Control Wheel and, 68–69, 73–74, 86; race, 33; racial, 29, 85, 133; of rape, 143, 163; sexual, 83–84, 95, 170; slaves and, 15–16, 45, 51, 182n35; structural, 141; technologies, of, 117; theory of, 26; visualizing, 155; white, 33–34, 36, 53–58, 63, 67. *See also* intimate partner violence
Violence Against Women Act (VAWA), 5–9, 68, 95, 108, 111, 127, 132, 147, 156, 159, 170, 179n6
violent intimacies, 2, 25, 49, 56, 127, 160; domestic Violence (dV) and, 4, 29, 59

www.ingramcontent.com/pod-product-compliance
Lightning Source LLC
Chambersburg PA
CBHW071738270326
41928CB00013B/2720